How Power Shapes Energy Transitions in Southeast Asia

An understanding of the role of energy-related governance systems and the conditions required for a shift towards renewables in developing countries is urgently needed in order to tap into the global potential of low-carbon development. Although renewable energy sources have become technically feasible and economically viable, social and political factors persist as the most critical obstacles to their dissemination.

How Power Shapes Energy Transitions in Southeast Asia conceptualizes power for the field of sustainable energy governance. Based on empirical findings from the Philippines and Indonesia, the book develops an analytical approach that incorporates power theory into a multi-level governance framework. The book begins with an in-depth background overview of renewable energy development around the world and presents major trends in development cooperation. A power-based multi-level governance approach is introduced, that is rooted in development thinking. Examining how coordination and power relations shape the development and dissemination of renewable energy technologies, the book also shows how decentralization affects low-carbon development in emerging economies.

Sparking debate on the ways in which energy transitions can be triggered and sustained in developing countries, this book will be of great interest to students and scholars of renewable energy development and environmental politics and governance as well as practitioners in development cooperation.

Jens Marquardt is a post-doctoral researcher and lecturer at the University of Halle-Wittenberg, Germany and associated with the Environmental Policy Research Centre in Berlin. His main research interests include the links between social sciences and environmental technologies, the role of power and coordination in complex governance arrangements, development theory and sustainability transitions.

Routledge Studies in Energy Transitions

Considerable interest exists today in energy transitions. There is a need for deci-sion-making and action on low carbon pathways, as well as for new strategies to improve energy access, resilience and security.

Routledge Studies in Energy Transitions will deepen understanding of the complex theme of energy systems change. Old paradigms will be revisited with new knowledge. Novel paradigms will also be explored by connecting distinct lines of inquiry from planning and policy, engineering and the natural sciences, inter-national development, history of science and technology, STS, and manage-ment. The series aims to provide primary references which could function like a set of international, technical meetings in oneís library. Single and co-authored monographs will be welcomed, as well as edited volumes relating to themes such as decarbonisation, safety, security and access, and resilience.

Series Editor: Dr. Kathleen Araújo, Stony Brook University, USA

Titles in this series include:

How Power Shapes Energy Transitions in Southeast Asia
A complex governance challenge
Jens Marquardt

How Power Shapes Energy Transitions in Southeast Asia

A complex governance challenge

Jens Marquardt

LONDON AND NEW YORK

First published 2017
by Routledge

2 Park Square, Milton Park, Abingdon, Oxfordshire OX14 4RN
711 Third Avenue, New York, NY 10017

Routledge is an imprint of the Taylor & Francis Group, an informa business

First issued in paperback 2018

British Library Cataloguing in Publication Data
A catalogue record for this book is available from the British Library

Library of Congress Cataloging in Publication Data
Names: Marquardt, Jens, author.
Title: How power shapes energy transitions in Southeast Asia : a complex
governance challenge / Jens Marquardt.
Description: Abingdon, Oxon ; New York, NY : Routledge, 2017. |
Series: Routledge studies in energy transitions
Identifiers: LCCN 2016027958| ISBN 9781138677906 (hb) |
ISBN 9781315559261 (ebook)
Subjects: LCSH: Energy policy–Environmental aspects–Southeast Asia. |
Energy development–Southeast Asia. | Renewable energy sources–
Southeast Asia.
Classification: LCC HD9502.A7852 M37 2017 | DDC 333.790959–dc23
LC record available at https://lccn.loc.gov/2016027958

ISBN: 978-1-138-67790-6 (hbk)
ISBN: 978-1-138-39347-9 (pbk)

Typeset in Goudy
by Wearset Ltd, Boldon, Tyne and Wear

Contents

Figures

Tables

Acknowledgments

This book is dedicated to the inspiring people of the Philippines and Indonesia whom I met during my time in Southeast Asia. Their knowledge and practical experiences, together with an overwhelming hospitality, are the main contributions to this work. I am grateful for the support of so many people. Be it in Batangas, Palawan or Cebu in the Philippines or in Yogyakarta, Bali or Central Kalimantan in Indonesia – professionals and ordinary people alike always helped me whenever possible.

I cannot thank all the interview partners enough for their patience, for sharing their knowledge and for arranging field trips to renewable energy project sites. I very much appreciate the support of extraordinary people like Mario Marasigan, Bert Dalusong, Anna Abad, Fort Sibayan, Pedro Maniego, Juderico Figeues, Roslyn Arayata, Gia Ibay, Edmar Rieta, Olegario Serafica and Laurie Navarro in the Philippines. To name just a few of the wonderful people I met in Indonesia, let me thank Ganis Ramadhani, Juhani Härkönen, Eriell Salim, Hendro Saputro, Indira Nurtanti, Raymond Bona, Philip Hewitt, Hindun Mulaika, Arif Fuadi Nasution, Sundar Bajgain, Djoko Tri, Yani Witjaksono and Dewa Weda. I would like to thank Jalton Garces Taguibao, Clarita Carlos, Kendra Gotangco, Bobby Julian, Fitrian Ardiansyah, Rachmawan Budiarto, Andi Hamdani, Soeharwinto and Jon Respati for their academic expertise and critical comments.

Special thanks go to the Deutsche Gesellschaft für Internationale Zusammenarbeit (GIZ) and its counterparts. I am particularly thankful to Hendrik Meller, Dr. Bernd-Markus Liss, Ferdinand Larona, Dr. Rudolf Rauch, Arne Schweinfurth and Robert Schultz with his EnDev-team for their support during my time in Southeast Asia. This book would not have been possible without them!

I wish to express my gratitude to Prof. Dr. Miranda Schreurs for her patience and constant motivation for this book. I am also thankful to Prof. Dr. Aurel Croissant for his valuable feedback. A big thank you goes to Chunhung, Hamed, Karo, Nhlanhla, Olivia, Sascha, Weila and other colleagues at the Environmental Policy Research Centre in Berlin for bringing this project forward. Finally, it was my friends and family who supported and encouraged me most throughout the years to get this done!

Last but not least, I would like to thank the scholarship program of the Deutsche Bundesstiftung Umwelt (German Federal Environmental Foundation, DBU). Without their financial support, this research would not have been possible.

Jens Marquardt

Abbreviations

ADB	Asian Development Bank
AMORE	Alliance for Mindanao Off-Grid Renewable Energy
ASEAN	Association of Southeast Asian Nations
AusAID	Australian Agency for International Development
BAPPEDA	*Badan Perencanaan Pembangunan Daerah* (Indonesia)
BAPPENAS	*Badan Perencanaan Pembangunan Nasional* (Indonesia)
BIRU	*Program Biogas Rumah* (Indonesia)
BMU	German Federal Ministry for the Environment, Nature Conservation and Nuclear Safety
BMWi	German Federal Ministry for the Economy and Technology
BMZ	German Federal Ministry for Economic Cooperation and Development
BRECDA	*Barangay* Renewable Energy and Community Development Association
CBRED	Capacity Building to Remove Barriers to Renewable Energy Development
CDM	Clean Development Mechanism
CEnergy	Climate Change and Clean Energy
CO_2	carbon dioxide
DENA	German Energy Agency
DILG	Department of the Interior and Local Government (Philippines)
DOE	Department of Energy (Philippines)
EBTKE	Directorate General for New and Renewable Energy and Energy Conservation (Indonesia)
EC	electric cooperative
EEP	Finnish Energy and Environment Partnership
EIA	United States Energy Information Administration
EnDev	Energising Development
EPIMB	Electric Power Industry Management Bureau (Philippines)
EPIRA	Electric Power Industry Reform Act (Philippines)
ERC	Energy Regulatory Commission (Philippines)
EREC	European Energy Council

ESDM	Ministry for Energy and Mineral Resources (Indonesia)
EU	European Union
FiT	feed-in tariff
GDP	gross domestic product
GEF	Global Environment Facility
GIZ	Deutsche Gesellschaft für Internationale Zusammenarbeit
Gt	gigaton
GTZ	German Technical Cooperation
HDI	Human Development Index
HIVOS	Humanist Institute for Cooperation
ICED	Indonesian Clean Energy Development
IEA	International Energy Agency
IMF	International Monetary Fund
IPP	independent power producer
IRENA	International Renewable Energy Agency
JICA	Japan International Cooperation Agency
KW/h	kilowatt per hour
LCOE	levelized costs of energy
LCORE	Promotion of Least Cost Renewables in Indonesia
LEAP	Long-range Energy Alternatives Planning
LGU	Local Government Unit (Philippines)
MSIP	Municipal Solar Infrastructure Project
MTOE	million tons of oil equivalent
MW	megawatt
MW/h	megawatt per hour
NEA	National Electrification Administration (Philippines)
NEDA	National Economic Development Authority (Philippines)
NGO	non-governmental organization
NPC	National Power Corporation (Philippines)
NPC SPUG	National Power Corporation Small Power Utilities Group (Philippines)
NREB	National Renewable Energy Board (Philippines)
NREP	National Renewable Energy Program (Philippines)
ODA	Official Development Assistance
OECD	Organisation for Economic Co-operation and Development
PLN	*Perusahaan Listrik Negara* (Indonesia)
PLTS	*Pembangkit listrik tenaga Surya* (Indonesia)
PNOC	Philippine National Oil Company
PNRELSP	Palawan New and Renewable Energy and Livelihood Support Project
PPA	power purchase agreement
PV	photovoltaic
RAD-GRK	*Rencana Aksi Daerah penurunan emisi Gas Rumah Kaca* (Indonesia)
RAN-GRK	*Rencana Aksi Nasional penurunan emisi Gas Rumah Kaca* (Indonesia)

RE Act	Renewable Energy Act (Philippines)
REMB	Renewable Energy Management Bureau (Philippines)
REN21	Renewable Energy Policy Network for the 21st Century
RPS	Renewable Portfolio Standard
RUED	*Rencana Umum Energi Daerah* (Indonesia)
SAP	Structural Adjustment Program
SDG	Sustainable Development Goal
SE4ALL	Sustainable Energy for All Initiative (United Nations)
SEP	German-Philippine Special Energy Program
SNV	Stichting Nederlandse Vrijwilligers (Foundation of Netherlands Volunteers)
Support CCC	Support to the Philippine Climate Change Commission with the implementation of the National Climate Change Strategy and the National Climate Change Action Plan
TPED	Total Primary Energy Demand
TW/h	terawatt per hour
UNCED	United Nations Commission for Environment and Development
UNDP	United Nations Development Programme
UNFCCC	United Nations Framework Convention on Climate Change
UNIDO	United Nations Industrial Development Organization
USAID	United States Assistance for International Development
WBGU	German Advisory Council on Global Change

Part I

Introduction

1   The politics of energy and development

Introduction

Sustainable energy has become a major topic on the international agenda. The United Nations (2012) initiative Sustainable Energy for All and the inclusion of energy in the post-2015 Sustainable Development Goals (SDGs) underline the increasing importance of this policy field. Providing sustainable energy to developing countries has also become a core element of a global commitment against global warming as outlined in the 2015 Paris Agreement under the United Nations Framework Convention on Climate Change (UNFCCC). With increasing climate change impacts, growing energy demand, aging infrastructure and energy security concerns linked to rising fuel prices, new and alternative models for energy paths are urgently needed. While some developing countries hope to leapfrog into the low-carbon era, others are trapped in fossil-intensive lock-ins relying on coal and oil. Although growth of renewable energy capacities and investments in recent years has been strongest in countries outside the Organisation for Economic Co-operation and Development (OECD), research related to energy transitions in developing regions is still scarce. Understanding the role of energy-related governance systems and the conditions required for a shift towards renewables in the developing world is urgently needed to tap the full potential of low-carbon energy supply around the world.

Southeast Asia is one of the most vibrant and fastest-growing developing regions in the world. Economic progress is mainly driven by fossil fuels, leading to environmental degradation, negative health impacts and a massive increase in greenhouse gas emissions. Energy transitions in Southeast Asia could significantly reduce worldwide emissions and thus effectively combat climate change. Yet, these transitions are a challenging endeavor in a region with substantial coal and oil resources and ever-increasing energy demand. Energy systems are dominated by fossil fuels, incentives for renewables are rare, and skepticism towards modern renewables is high. Above all, the political systems are anything but consolidated; changes in power structures, societal transformations and political developments are almost impossible to predict. A better understanding of the complex governance systems and power relations will thus make an important contribution to the quest for energy transitions in Southeast Asia.

Taking a multi-level governance approach combined with insights from power theory, this book illuminates how multiple jurisdictional levels affect energy transitions in Southeast Asian countries in general, and donor-driven renewable energy projects specifically. The book reveals how governance structures, power resources and capacities influence the promotion of renewables in Indonesia and the Philippines. Both countries went through a process of radical decentralization, leading to substantial local autonomy. Both archipelagos have ambitious renewable energy targets, but struggle to fully implement supportive policies. Rapid economic growth makes them increasingly relevant for global energy demand and greenhouse gas emissions.

A power-based multi-level governance approach is presented here that helps to shed light on the politics of an energy transition in a developing country context. The framework sheds light on the distribution of resources and the capacities needed to mobilize these resources within complex governance arrangements. Project developers are encouraged to use it as an assessment tool for donor-driven renewable energy activities. Most of the development projects presented here struggle to scale up results due to the complex multi-level governance frameworks in which they operate.

Linking energy to development

Renewable energy development and technology transfer play an increasingly important role in the developing world. International development programs aiming to promote sustainable energy systems have diversified over the decades – from technology-specific small-scale demonstration projects towards more and more advisory activities for supportive market structures, industrial development and regulatory frameworks. This shift towards social and political-institutional aspects underlines that renewable energy technologies are becoming market-ready and economically feasible even in non-OECD countries.

Between 1980 and 2015, donors implemented almost 12,000 projects around the world promoting renewables in the electricity sector alone (AidData 2016). These activities offered US$118 billion of international funding. Being one of the most active donors in the field, Germany's grants, loans and technical assistance targeted at promoting access to sustainable energy amounted to EUR 1.86 billion in 2011 and to over EUR 6 billion during the period between 2004 and 2011 (BMZ, 2014, p. 9), making energy-related expenses the single largest share of Germany's aid budget. Despite these large financial flows and a long history of donor-driven support, the relation between isolated donor interventions and more structural effects towards an energy transition remains underexplored. Better understanding the links between development cooperation and an aid-receiving country's political system will increase the chances of triggering energy system change through international cooperation.

Southeast Asia represents an excellent region for investigating that link. Strong economic development, rapid increase in energy demand, high natural potentials for renewables and an extraordinary active donor community are just a few of the most obvious justifications, which are accompanied by the development of incentive schemes for renewables, environmental degradation due to fossil fuels, and massive climate change impacts. Donors have tried to push green and sustainable energy supply through the promotion of renewable energy projects for more than 50 years. Most activities were designed for local contexts and off-grid electrification to demonstrate the feasibility of specific renewable energy technologies. Today, bi- and multilateral donors also provide policy advice for national governments, acknowledging the multi-level complexity of the political system they are operating in. Despite long-term support from various donors and numerous projects being framed as success stories, no significant shift towards renewables in the electricity sector of Southeast Asian countries can be observed. The International Energy Agency (IEA 2013) even predicts a decreasing share of renewables in the region's electricity mix.

Contribution of this book

In times of global ecological crises such as climate change, cooperation in efforts to achieve a sustainable future is needed more than ever before. Global collaboration, learning from other experiences, and knowledge exchange in the field of energy systems can contribute to energy transitions and thus a reduction in greenhouse gas emissions all over the world. Supporting emerging countries in reducing the use and development of fossil fuels today can prevent a lock-in into a fossil fuel-based energy system that is just being established today, but would last for decades.

Renewable energy technologies have the potential to tackle climate change and ensure an environmentally friendly energy supply without putting economic development at risk. In Southeast Asia, the share held by renewables in the energy mix is low, and in some cases even decreasing. Understanding the divide between international ambitions for renewables and the persistent domination of fossil fuels in most countries makes research in this field highly relevant. Studies about the political dimension of renewable energy development focus heavily on industrialized countries. Qualitative data from the developing world and research on the impact of cooperation between OECD and non-OECD countries on the issue of sustainable energy has been rare so far. Framing it as a major area for further research in social sciences, Sovacool (2014, p. 22) even asks whether "best practices exist for communities wishing to transition to alternative energy sources in the developing world?" This book provides answers to whether and how development assistance can deliver or promote these kinds of best practices.

Over the last six decades, development assistance has changed enormously and has experienced a variety of shifting paradigms (Rauch 2009). In terms of its effectiveness, results have been disheartening (Doucouliagos and Paldam 2009; McGillivray et al. 2006). Organizations such as the OECD (2011) and the World Bank (1999) draw a rather positive picture, but have also identified shortcomings. While no one expects development cooperation to transform societies, there is an expectation, or at least a hope, that the impact of a project will extend beyond the immediate location where it is carried out to contribute to the fulfillment of overarching (sustainable development) goals. This book contributes to broader discussions about the meaning of development cooperation, its impact on sustainable development and its future.

Going beyond mainstream paradigms in development cooperation, this book critically takes into consideration decades of failure and frustration. This reflects a time when unlimited growth and modernization are being questioned and sustainability has become the leading paradigm for both developed and developing countries. Since the term *sustainability* alone remains fuzzy and highly contested, new ideas and alternative concepts are needed to make international cooperation work so that it can promote broader transitions towards sustainability, not only in the energy sector. Understanding the complex multi-level governance structures in countries like the Philippines or Indonesia is a prerequisite for effective donor-driven clean energy assistance. Making that link needs to incorporate issues of power and coordination. This leads to a power-based multi-level governance approach that helps us not only to better understand energy transitions in developing countries, but also to critically investigate the effectiveness of development cooperation.

This book speaks to practitioners and an academic audience interested in energy transitions in a developing context, in the role of foreign aid in energy policy-making, and in the diffusion of policies and general conditions for renewables. Discussing the meaning of governance structures, power resources and capacities in emerging economies, this contribution aims to spark debate around ways in which sustainable energy transitions can be triggered and sustained where economic pressure for additional energy demand and the potential for leapfrogging are highest. According to the Asian Development Bank (ADB 2013), electricity demand in Southeast Asia is expected to increase by 5 percent annually between 2005 and 2030, tripling the region's 2005 electricity generation by 2030.

Practitioners promoting renewables in developing countries can benefit from empirical insights from the Philippines and Indonesia, two archipelagos with complex governance structures and fragmented power relations that are struggling to foster the development of renewables despite supportive natural, economic and political conditions. A power-based multi-level governance framework for analyzing the link between development projects and governance structures is developed to shed light on the role of power resources, capacities and structures for energy transitions. The book critically assesses the possibility of triggering structural effects in the electricity system via development cooperation promoting renewables. Finally, promising approaches to support renewables within complex governance structures of developing countries are identified.

Taking a multi-level governance perspective

Sustainable development has become a major paradigm for development cooperation. It was in the aftermath of Our Common Future (Brundtland Report, WCED 1987) and the agreement to the Rio Declaration on Environment and Development (UNEP 1992) that sustainability became a key objective and expectation for development projects. Since then, projects, which are often small-scale, local and temporary, and dependent on external resources, have struggled to fulfill these expectations and provide sustainable impact in aid-receiving countries. Not surprisingly, development cooperation has been criticized for contributing too little to its own sustainable development agenda (Doucouliagos and Paldam 2009; Hansen and Tarp 2000; OECD 2008).

Articulating broad and ambitious goals in declarations like the SDGs, development cooperation aims to achieve structural effects or systemic change in developing countries. In contrast, most projects in the field address very site-specific problems at the local level, with limited effects on overarching, mainly national structures (Stockmann 1997). This gap explains the difficulties that small-scale donor-driven activities face in achieving upscaling, diffusion, spill-over and learning effects. This well-known "micro-macro paradox" (Mosley 1987) also represents a serious challenge for environmental development cooperation and renewable energy projects (Wilkins 2002).

Donors aim to overcome the micro-macro paradox with the help of a multi-level approach that reflects the importance of different jurisdictional levels (Neumann-Silkow 2010). In practice, these projects often fall short of addressing challenges arising from the multi-level governance systems' complexity. This is especially important for the field of sustainable energy systems, where coordination between stakeholders at different jurisdictional levels is crucial (Ohlhorst and Tews 2013). Taking a multi-level governance perspective means acknowledging the complex political systems that shape energy transitions and donor-driven interventions in developing countries. The framework enables discussion of coordination efforts among the different levels of government in highly complex energy-related governance arrangements in emerging economies. With its focus on the national, provincial and municipal levels of decision-making, this book provides insights into the multi-level character of an energy transition and shows the tremendous challenge for donors to promote renewables in such a context. Multi-level governance, combined with insights from power theory, also provides a useful framework for modeling and understanding energy transitions towards renewables outside the OECD world.

Outline

Following the introductory chapters (Part I) that introduce the role of power and governance frameworks for renewables and present the underlying research design, this book is structured into five main parts.

Development cooperation for sustainable energy (Part II). Promoting sustainable energy has become a major field in development cooperation (United Nations, 2012). A more and more fragmented donor landscape (Acharya et al. 2006), an expansion of development activities related to environmental issues (Hicks et al. 2008) and the consideration of a multi-level perspective (Neumann-Silkow 2010) are major trends in development cooperation that also affect sustainable energy development. Part II describes these overarching trends, outlines key challenges and drivers for renewables in developing countries, and presents the status and perspectives of energy transitions in Southeast Asia.

Setting the scene: theory and analytical framework (Part III). Developing the theoretical framework for this book, Part III lays the ground for the subsequent analysis. Shifting paradigms have largely influenced development theory and practice (Hermes and Lensink 2001), but the actual impact and effectiveness of development cooperation are highly contested. In the light of the limits of development thinking, grounded theory (Charmaz 2006) helps to develop a promising analytical framework for donor-driven interventions. The approach combines a multi-level governance framework with insights from pluralist power theory (Bacharach and Lawler 1980; Lukes 1995; Rhodes 1999). Different juris-dictional levels, coordination, and the distribution of soft and hard power resources and capacities clearly shape renewable energy governance and the effectiveness of donor-driven interventions. This book delineates how to expli-citly conceptualize power in multi-level governance frameworks and suggests a qualitative approach for investigating the case studies.

The Philippines (Part IV). The Philippines has successfully developed renew-able energy technologies since the 1980s and 1990s, but the country is strug-gling to implement its comprehensive 2008 Renewable Energy Act. The empowerment of subnational authorities after the regime of former president Ferdinand Marcos was abolished led to new institutional arrangements and responsibilities. New power constellations as well as coordination gaps that affect the implementation of renewable energy projects and policies emerged with the liberalization of the electricity market in 2001. Current national energy planning overlooks or neglects local conditions, while local authorities are either not capable or not willing to fully support clean energy initiatives driven by the national government or external donors. Part IV illustrates how power resources and capacities are fragmented and unequally distributed across national and subnational levels, and how development cooperation struggles to address issues related to power and coordination.

Indonesia (Part V). Indonesia reveals how radical decentralization can be a burden for renewable energy development. Key barriers include a complex system of corruption, insufficient coordination between the central government and local authorities, and failure of local inclusion. Critical links between decentralized political structures and effective environmental governance hamper donor-driven interventions. Taking a multi-level governance per-spective, Part V shows that most donor activities focus on a specific level of intervention, but fail to include other jurisdictional levels that are vital for sustaining or upscaling results beyond a project's narrow context. Integrating theories about power in central–local relations reveals further critical obstacles for project developers, such as conflicting rules and regulations, a lack of coherent energy planning, or seriously deficient capacities at the local level. A large number of veto players, both vertically and horizontally, block or seriously delay sustainable energy policies and projects.

Conclusions (Part VI). The final part of this book recapitulates the volume and provides a cross-country comparison that also reflects experiences from other developing countries. A summary wraps up empirical insights from the Philippines and Indonesia. Both countries teach us how complex issues of coordination and the distribution of power resources and capacities in multi-level governance systems affect societal transformation processes, such as energy transition, and thus issues of sustainable development. Practical as well as theoretical implications are derived. In particular, development theorists and sustainability transitions researchers and practitioners should benefit from the approach that is applied here. Empirical results are linked to broader debates about the role of political factors that determine environmental governance in emerging economies. A better understanding of these links is a prerequisite for effective clean energy projects.

References

Acharya, A., de Lima, A.T.F., and Moore, M., 2006. Proliferation and fragmentation: Transactions costs and the value of aid. *Journal of Development Studies*, 42(1), pp. 1–21.

ADB, 2013. *Energy outlook for Asia and the Pacific*, Manila: Asian Development Bank.

AidData, 2016. AidData 3.0. Open Data for International Development. Available at: http://aiddata.org/ [accessed March 30, 2016]

Bacharach, S.B. and Lawler, E.J., 1980. *Power and politics in organizations*, London: Jossey-Bass.

BMZ, 2014. *Nachhaltige Energie für Entwicklung: Die Deutsche Entwicklungszusammenarbeit im Energiesektor*, Bonn: Bundesministerium für wirtschaftliche Zusammenarbeit und Entwicklung.

Charmaz, K., 2006. *Constructing grounded theory. A practical guide through qualitative analysis*, Thousand Oaks: Sage.

Doucouliagos, H. and Paldam, M., 2009. The aid effectiveness literature: The sad results of 40 years of research. *Journal of Economic Surveys*, 23(3), pp. 433–461.

Hansen, H. and Tarp, F., 2000. Aid effectiveness disputed. *Journal of International Development*, 12(3), pp. 375–398.

Hermes, N. and Lensink, R., 2001. Changing the conditions for development aid: A new paradigm? *Journal of Development Studies*, 37(6), pp. 1–16.

Hicks, R.L., Parks, B.C., Roberts, J.T. and Tierney, M.J., 2008. *Greening aid? Understanding the environmental impact of development assistance*, Oxford: Oxford University Press.

IEA, 2013. *Southeast Asia energy outlook. World energy outlook special report*, Paris: International Energy Agency.

Lukes, S., 1995. *Power: A radical view*, London: Longman.

McGillivray, M., Feeny, S., Hermes, N. and Lensink, R., 2006. Controversies over the impact of development aid: It works; it doesn't; it can, but that depends …. *Journal of International Development*, 18(7), pp. 1031–1050.

Mosley, P., 1987. *Overseas development aid: Its defence and reform*, Brighton: University Press of Kentucky.

Neumann-Silkow, F., 2010. *Scaling up in development cooperation. Practical guidelines*, Eschborn: Gesellschaft für Technische Zusammenarbeit.

OECD, 2008. *The Paris Declaration on Aid Effectiveness and the Accra Agenda for Action*, Paris: Organisation for Economic Co-operation and Development.

OECD, 2011. *The Busan partnership for effective development co-operation*, Paris: Organisation for Economic Co-operation and Development.

Ohlhorst, D. and Tews, K., 2013. Energiewende als Herausforderung der Koordination im Mehrebenensystem. *Technikfolgenabschätzung – Theorie und Praxis*, 22(2), pp. 48–55.

Rauch, T., 2009. *Entwicklungspolitik. Theorien, Strategien, Instrumente*, Braunschweig: Westermann.

Rhodes, R.A.W., 1999. *Control and power in central-local relations*, 2nd ed., Aldershot: Ashgate.

Sovacool, B.K., 2014. What are we doing here? Analyzing fifteen years of energy scholarship and proposing a social science research agenda. *Energy Research and Social Science*, 1, pp. 1–29.

Stockmann, R., 1997. The sustainability of development projects: An impact assessment of German vocational-training projects in Latin America. *World Development*, 25(11), pp. 1767–1784.

UNEP, 1992. *Rio Declaration on Environment and Development*, Nairobi: United Nations Environment Programme.

United Nations, 2012. *Sustainable energy for all. A global action agenda. Pathways for concerted action towards sustainable energy for all*, New York: United Nations.

WCED. 1987. *Our common future*, New York: World Commission on Environment and Development.

Wilkins, G., 2002. *Technology transfer for renewable energy: Overcoming barriers in developing countries* (Sustainable Development Programme (Royal Institute of International Affairs) Ed.), London: The Royal Institute of International Affairs.

World Bank, 1999. *Entering the 21st century – World Development Report 1999/2000*, Washington, DC: World Bank.

2 Power and governance frameworks for sustainable energy

Introduction

Renewables represent an environmentally friendly and socially valuable solution for decentralized energy production. A large number of pilot projects in off-grid areas all over the world have demonstrated their technological feasibility. Critical factors for transferring these experiences to the national level have been identified (Wilkins 2002), but a clear research gap exists with regard to the impact of local projects on national policies and their potential to be replicated or transferred to other project sites. Comprehensive impact evaluations that monitor the projects' sustainability far beyond their official termination by the donor are rare, so it remains unclear what actually works under which conditions (Caspari and Barbu 2008).

By taking a multi-level governance perspective, this book contributes to that debate. Intergovernmental relations are crucial for development cooperation, because donor-driven projects ideally aim to scale up or diffuse results beyond their direct project level of intervention. Institutionalizing long-term structural change, including in relation to renewable energy development, depends on decisions not only at the national level, but also at subnational jurisdictions.

Going beyond technical and economic aspects

Due to technological improvements over the last 30 years, renewable energy sources such as wind, solar or biomass have become more and more competitive with fossil fuels. Considering their levelized cost of energy (LCOE), renewables are already economically feasible under current conditions or are likely to become competitive with fossil fuels in the near future (Kost et al. 2013; NREL 2013). LCOE takes into account the construction and operational costs of a power plant over its assumed life cycle. Real energy prices are difficult to compare, because they depend on factors, such as political conditions, technical expertise or subsidies, that go beyond pure fuel costs.

According to the International Energy Agency (IEA 2015), global fossil fuel consumption subsidies amounted to US$548 billion in 2013. Kost et al. (2013) argue that increasing costs for imports and a price for CO_2 emissions will most likely increase costs for conventional power plants. At the same time, technological costs for renewables, such as for photovoltaic (PV) (Hernández-Moro and Martínez-Duart 2013) or wind power (IPCC 2012), are expected to decrease due to expanding experiences and learning curves. Bazilian et al. (2013) have calculated that residential PV module prices went down by 75 percent between 2010 and 2012, bringing retail prices to a competitive level not only in countries such as Denmark, Spain and Germany, but also in Turkey and Brazil. The potential for residential PV is highest in developing regions such as North India, South China and Indonesia.

Although debates about technical aspects (Isoard and Soria 2001; Popp et al. 2011; Wilkins 2002) and economic issues (Frondel et al. 2010; Hvelplund 2006; Menanteau et al. 2003; Short et al. 1995) dominate the debate about renewable energy development, these factors are becoming less relevant over the years. To investigate the barriers to and potential of an energy transition, political issues such as support mechanisms, policy frameworks, institutional aspects, coordination and governance need to be considered (Langniß 2003; Michalena and Hills 2014; Sovacool 2011; Spreng et al. 2012).

Most studies about governance structures for renewables limit their focus to policy designs and market mechanisms. They reduce the role of governments to regulators that need to provide an enabling environment for renewables (Jordan-Korte 2011; Langniß 2003). At the same time, scholars from a variety of social science disciplines deal with perceptions (van der Horst 2007), social acceptance (Wüstenhagen et al. 2007) or institutional frameworks (Jacobsson and Lauber 2006) to enrich our understanding of how renewables can be implemented successfully into a complex sociopolitical context.

Governance frameworks for renewables

Social sciences have been widely neglected in the field of renewable energy research. Compared with technoeconomic studies, they "are presumed to be irrelevant or useless in the energy field" (Goldblatt et al. 2012, p. 3). Not surprisingly, energy-related debates are described as "unreasonably narrow" (Mitcham and Rolston 2013, p. 313) and limited to numbers and technical terms. Governance-related energy research goes beyond its "instrumentalised functions of acceptance research and market introduction" (Minsch et al. 2012, p. 23). Placing it "on an equal footing with engineering and natural sciences" (Spreng et al. 2012, p. v) is a challenging endeavor.

> The fields of history, sociology, philosophy, political science, and psychology – with their insight into how consumers and politicians behave and practices of consumption become routine – have been treated as secondary and peripheral to the "hard" or "objective" disciplines of economics, statistics, mathematics, physics, and engineering. Affiliations with industry or government, interdisciplinary training, and comparative case studies were uncommon.
>
> (Sovacool 2014, p. 25)

Sovacool (2014, p. 25) argues that energy research could benefit a lot from qualitative research methods such as interviews or case studies and a stronger focus on the developing world. Taking these arguments seriously, this book presents a qualitative study about two rapidly developing countries that are currently building up their energy systems. Global energy outlooks predict an excessive increase in energy demand and energy-related emissions until 2030, especially in the developing world (ASEAN 2011; EIA 2013; IEA 2012). This book sheds light on renewable energy governance in emerging economies that will significantly influence the global energy landscape of the future.

Despite its diversity, most research related to energy transitions still focuses on legal and economic aspects, especially in industrialized countries. Major volumes include Jacobs' (2012) study about policy instruments in the European Union (EU), Leal-Arcas et al.'s (2015) analysis of legal issues related to renewable energy governance, and Michalena and Hills' (2014) compendium on the complexity of renewable energy governance. The last volume discusses the question of how to transform an existing, highly developed electricity system towards renewables. An OECD-centric perspective becomes obvious when it identifies climate change and environmental concerns as the main drivers behind renewable energy development. This does not necessarily need to be the case in emerging economies, where security of supply with domestic energy sources, lack of energy access and high costs for transmission lines can be the key drivers for renewables (REN21 2015).

Looking at renewable energy governance means investigating institutional arrangements and macrostructural elements, political mechanisms, informal patterns and formalized policies as well as levels of decision-making and issues of coordination that shape energy transitions (Langniß 2003; Michalena and Hills 2014; Smith 2007). Whereas earlier research focused on the effects and effectiveness of regulations and support mechanisms for renewables (Langniß 2003; Menanteau et al. 2003; Sijm 2002), recent studies discuss a broader spectrum of sociopolitical aspects, such as institutional factors (Koster and Anderies 2013), bureaucracies (Fokaides et al. 2013) or environmental communication (Skanavis et al. 2013), to cover the complexity of renewable energy governance. Despite some exceptions (Marquardt 2014; Mwangi et al. 2013; Nakhooda 2011), most research related to renewable energy governance is still focused on OECD countries and pays little attention to the developing world.

Supportive national policy frameworks and incentives for renewables exist all over the world. In parallel, subnational activities and bottom-up processes push renewable energy development in cities and communities (Community Energy Association 2008; Schönberger 2013). Not only do national governments and subnational jurisdictions affect renewable development. As global environmental concerns such as climate change become more and more relevant, international environmental regimes and commitments such as the Paris Agreement also affect sustainable energy development (Busch 2005; Hirschl and Petschow 2005; Podobnik 1999). At the same time, global environmental governance is highly ineffective and fragmented (Zelli and van Asselt 2013). Organizations such as the International Renewable Energy Agency (IRENA) and the Renewable Energy Policy Network for the 21st Century (REN21) were established to reduce fragmentation, collect and distribute information, and strengthen the role of renewables internationally (Van de Graaf 2013).

Power in central–local relations

Multi-level governance provides a useful approach for analyzing and understanding decision-making in complex political systems. In contrast to similar concepts such as federalism, state–local relations or intergovernmental relations, the approach has already been widely used as a conceptual framework for investigating environmental and sociotechnical innovations (Barbosa and Brusca 2015; Bisaro et al. 2010; Daniell et al. 2014), particularly in the context of renewables (Klagge and Asbach 2013; Ohlhorst and Tews 2013; Smith 2007). At the same time, it remains a rather descriptive concept that needs to incorporate insights from other political science theories. Because issues of power and capacity are dominant political factors influencing energy transitions not only in OECD countries, but also in emerging economies, this book integrates aspects from power theory into the multi-level governance framework to widen the perspective on the role of power in central–local relations when it comes to energy transitions and donor-driven support.

Power theory as such is a highly contested field. Concepts follow different and often conflicting interpretations (Haugaard 2002; Morris 2002; Parsons 2002). Following a rather pluralist view on power, and inspired by the policy arrangement approach (Arts and van Tatenhove 2000, 2004), this work identifies three important layers of power that influence decision-making processes: the availability of soft and hard power resources, the capacity to mobilize these resources, and overarching structural elements in which the decision-making processes are embedded. Such a perspective reflects the asymmetric distribution of resources in a society, the ability of actors to mobilize these resources in order to achieve certain outcomes in social relations, and the overarching structures and institutions that determine societal interactions and decision-making. These structures can be identified and described with the help of the multi-level governance framework, which reflects on the role of central–local relations in decentralized political systems like the ones presented here.

In many developing countries, the relations between central governments and local authorities have significantly changed over the last decades. Decentralization has been enforced in development cooperation due to its positive connotation in relation to good governance, democratization and effectiveness (Manor 1999). This book reveals that decentralized political structures can also severely hamper energy transitions in general, and donor-driven interventions for renewables in particular.

References

Arts, B. and Tatenhove, J. van, 2000. Environmental policy arrangements: A new concept. In H. Goverde, ed. *Global and European polity? Organizations, policies, contexts,* Aldershot: Ashgate, pp. 223–237.

Arts, B. and Tatenhove, J. van, 2004. Policy and power: A conceptual framework between the "old" and "new" policy idioms. *Policy Sciences,* 37(3–4), pp. 339–356.

ASEAN, 2011. *The 3rd ASEAN Energy Outlook,* Institute of Energy Economics Japan, ASEAN Centre for Energy, National ESSPA Project Teams.

Barbosa, A. and Brusca, I., 2015. Governance structures and their impact on tariff levels of Brazilian water and sanitation corporations. *Utilities Policy,* 34, pp. 94–105.

Bazilian, M., Onyeji, I., Liebreich, M., MacGill, I., Chase, J., Shah, J., Gielen, D., Arent, D., Landfear, D. and Zhengrong, S., 2013. Re-considering the economics of photovoltaic power. *Renewable Energy,* 53, pp. 329–338.

Bisaro, A., Hinkel, J. and Kranz, N., 2010. Multi-level water, biodiversity and climate adaptation governance: Evaluating adaptive management in Lesotho. *Environmental Science and Policy,* 13(7), pp. 637–647.

Busch, P.-O., 2005. The global diffusion of regulatory instruments: The making of a new international environmental regime. *The ANNALS of the American Academy of Political and Social Science,* 598(1), pp. 146–167.

Caspari, A. and Barbu, R., 2008. *Wirkungsevaluierungen: Zum Stand der internationalen Diskussion und dessen Relevanz für Evaluierungen der deutschen Entwicklungszusammenarbeit,* Bonn: Bundesministerium für wirtschaftliche Zusammenarbeit und Entwicklung.

Community Energy Association, 2008. *Policy and Governance Tools: A module of the Renewable Energy Guide for Local Governments in British Columbia,* Vancouver: Community Energy Association.

Daniell, K.A., Coombes, P.J. and White, I., 2014. Politics of innovation in multi-level water governance systems. *Journal of Hydrology,* 519, pp. 2415–2435.

EIA, 2013. *International Energy Outlook 2013,* Washington, DC: US Energy Information Administration.

Fokaides, P.A., Poullikkas, A. and Christofides, C., 2013. Lost in the national labyrinths of bureaucracy: The case of renewable energy governance in Cyprus. In J.M. Hills and E. Michalena, eds. *Renewable energy governance,* Dordrecht: Springer, pp. 169–181.

Frondel, M., Ritter, N., Schmidt, C.M. and Vance, C., 2010. Economic impacts from the promotion of renewable energy technologies: The German experience. *Energy Policy,* 38(8), pp. 4048–4056.

Goldblatt, D.L., Minsch, J., Flüeler, T. and Spreng, D., 2012. Introduction. In D. Spreng et al., eds. *Tackling long-term global energy problems. The contribution of social science,* Dordrecht: Springer, pp. 3–10.

Haugaard, M., 2002. *Power: A reader,* Manchester: Manchester University Press.

Hernández-Moro, J. and Martínez-Duart, J.M., 2013. Analytical model for solar PV and CSP electricity costs: Present LCOE values and their future evolution. *Renewable and Sustainable Energy Reviews,* 20, pp. 119–132.

Hirschl, B. and Petschow, U., 2005. Building a global renewable energy regime – What can be learned from other (environmental) regimes? Paper presented at the Conference on the Human Dimensions of Global Environmental Change, Berlin, December 2–3.

Hvelplund, F., 2006. Renewable energy and the need for local energy markets. *Energy,* 31, pp. 1957–1966.

IEA, 2012. *World energy outlook 2012*, Paris: International Energy Agency.

IEA, 2015. Energy subsidies. *World energy outlook.* Available at: www.worldenergy outlook.org/resources/energysubsidies/ [accessed April 15, 2015].

IPCC, 2012. *Renewable energy sources and climate change mitigation*, Geneva: Intergovernmental Panel on Climate Change.

Isoard, S. and Soria, A., 2001. Technical change dynamics: Evidence from the emerging renewable energy technologies. *Energy Economics*, 23, pp. 619–636.

Jacobs, D., 2012. *Renewable energy policy convergence in the EU: The evolution of feed-in tariffs in Germany, Spain and France*, Farnham: Ashgate.

Jacobsson, S. and Lauber, V., 2006. The politics and policy of energy system transformation – explaining the German diffusion of renewable energy technology. *Energy Policy*, 34, pp. 256–276.

Jordan-Korte, K., 2011. *Government promotion of renewable energy technologies: Policy approaches and market development in Germany, the United States, and Japan*, Wiesbaden: Gabler Research.

Klagge, B. and Asbach, C., eds., 2013. *Governance-Prozesse für erneuerbare Energien*, Hannover: Akademie für Raumforschung und Landesplanung.

Kost, C., Mayer, J.N., Thomsen, J., Hartmann, N., Senkpiel, C., Philipps, S., Nold, S., Lude, S., Saad, N. and Schlegel, T., 2013. *Levelized cost of electricity renewable energy technologies*, Freiburg: Fraunhofer Institut für Solare Energiesysteme.

Koster, A.M. and Anderies, J.M., 2013. Institutional factors that determine energy transitions: A comparative case study approach. In J.M. Hills and E. Michalena, eds. *Renewable energy governance*, Dordrecht: Springer, pp. 33–61.

Langniß, O., 2003. *Governance structures for promoting renewable energy sources*, dissertation, Lund University.

Leal-Arcas, R., Filis, A. and Gosh, E.S.A., 2015. *International energy governance: Selected legal issues*, Northampton: Edward Elgar.

Manor, J., 1999. *The political economy of democratic decentralization*, Washington, DC: World Bank.

Marquardt, J., 2014. A struggle of multi-level governance: Promoting renewable energy in Indonesia. *Energy Procedia*, 58, pp. 87–94.

Menanteau, P., Finon, D. and Lamy, M.L., 2003. Prices versus quantities: Choosing policies for promoting the development of renewable energy. *Energy Policy*, 31(2003), pp. 799–812.

Michalena, E. and Hills, J.M., eds., 2014. *Renewable energy governance: Complexities and challenges*, Dordrecht: Springer.

Minsch, J., Goldblatt, D.L., Flüeler, T. and Spreng, D., 2012. The indispensable role of social science in energy research. In D. Spreng et al., eds. *Tackling long-term global energy problems. The contribution of social science*, Dordrecht: Springer, pp. 23–43.

Mitcham, C. and Rolston, J.S., 2013. Energy constraints. *Science and Engineering Ethics*, 19, pp. 313–319.

Morriss, P., 2002. Power: A philosophical analysis. In M. Haugaard, ed. *Power: A reader*. Manchester: Manchester University Press, pp. 274–303.

Mwangi, J., Kimani, N. and Muniafu, M., 2013. Renewable energy governance in Kenya: Plugging into the grid "plugging into progress." In J.M. Hills and E. Michalena, eds. *Renewable energy governance*, Dordrecht: Springer, pp. 119–135.

Nakhooda, S., 2011. Asia, the multilateral development banks and energy governance. *Global Policy*, 2, pp. 120–132.

NREL, 2013. Simple levelized cost of energy (LCOE) calculator documentation. *National Renewable Energy Laboratory*. Available at: www.nrel.gov/analysis/tech_lcoe.html [accessed May 29, 2015].

Ohlhorst, D. and Tews, K., 2013. Energiewende als Herausforderung der Koordination im Mehrebenensystem. *Technikfolgenabschätzung – Theorie und Praxis*, 22(2), pp. 48–55.

Parsons, T., 2002. On the concept of political power. Sociological theory and modern society. In M. Haugaard, ed. *Power: A reader*, Manchester: Manchester University Press.

Podobnik, B., 1999. Toward a sustainable energy regime: A long-wave interpretation of global energy shifts. *Technological Forecasting and Social Change*, 62(3), pp. 155–172.

Popp, D., Hascic, I. and Medhi, N., 2011. Technology and the diffusion of renewable energy. *Energy Economics*, 33(4), pp. 648–662.

REN21, 2015. *Renewables 2015: Global status report*, Paris: Renewable Energy Policy Network for the 21st Century.

Schönberger, P., 2013. *Municipalities as key actors of German renewable energy governance. An analysis of opportunities, obstacles, and multi-level influence*, Wuppertal: Wuppertal Institut für Klima, Umwelt, Energie.

Short, W., Packey, D.J. and Holt, T., 1995. A manual for the economic evaluation of energy efficiency and renewable energy technologies, *NREL Technical Report*, (March), pp. 1–120.

Sijm, J.P.M., 2002. *The performance of feed-in tariffs to promote renewable electricity in European countries*, Amsterdam: Energy Research Centre of the Netherlands.

Skanavis, C., Giannoulis, C. and Skanavis, V., 2013. The significance of the environmental communication for the renewable energy governance scenario: Who decides for whom? In J.M. Hills and E. Michalena, eds. *Renewable energy governance*, Dordrecht: Springer, pp. 351–362.

Smith, A., 2007. Emerging in between: The multi-level governance of renewable energy in the English regions. *Energy Policy*, 35(12), pp. 6266–6280.

Sovacool, B.K., 2011. An international comparison of four polycentric approaches to climate and energy governance. *Energy Policy*, 39(6), pp. 3832–3844.

Sovacool, B.K., 2014. What are we doing here? Analyzing fifteen years of energy scholarship and proposing a social science research agenda. *Energy Research and Social Science*, 1, pp. 1–29.

Spreng, D., Flüeler, T., Goldblatt, D.L. and Minsch, J., 2012. *Tackling long-term global energy problems. The contribution of social science*, Dordrecht: Springer.

Van de Graaf, T., 2013. Fragmentation in global energy governance: explaining the creation of IRENA. *Global Environmental Politics*, 13(3), pp. 14–33.

van der Horst, D., 2007. NIMBY or not? Exploring the relevance of location and the politics of voiced opinions in renewable energy siting controversies. *Energy Policy*, 35, pp. 2705–2714.

Wilkins, G., 2002. *Technology transfer for renewable energy: Overcoming barriers in developing countries*, London: Earthscan.

Wüstenhagen, R., Wolsink, M. and Bürer, M.J., 2007. Social acceptance of renewable energy innovation: An introduction to the concept. *Energy Policy*, 35, pp. 2683–2691.

Zelli, F. and van Asselt, H., 2013. Introduction: The institutional fragmentation of global environmental governance: Causes, consequences, and responses. *Global Environmental Politics*, 13(3), pp. 1–13.

3 Research design, methods and case selection

Aim of the book

Successful energy transitions can be a key determinant for developing countries to achieve economic and environmental goals at the same time. Although development projects in Southeast Asia and other parts of the world have shown the feasibility of renewables even in the remotest areas, they have done little to scale up results or lead to broader renewable energy deployment and acceptance in developing countries. Looking at two decentralized Southeast Asian countries, this book argues that understanding the complexity of political systems is a prerequisite for successful donor interventions. It raises two fundamental questions:

> How do the complex governance structures, especially in the developing country's electricity sector, affect renewable energy development and donor-driven interventions?

> How does development cooperation address the complexity of energy-related governance structures in developing countries?

Structural effects towards an energy transition are the dependent variable in this book. These depend on a large number of factors. Going beyond technical and economic arguments and concentrating on the role of governance structures, this book looks at the inclusion of multiple jurisdictional levels, the actual project level of intervention, centralization of governance and fragmentation of power as the four main independent variables. The success of donor-driven renewable energy projects thus depends not only on their project designs, but also on the political frameworks and macrosocietal governance structures they are confronted with in emerging economies. Four hypotheses formulate the expected relation between complex governance arrangements and structural effects through development cooperation.

Hypothesis 1. Interactions between various jurisdictional levels shape renewable energy projects – and determine their success. Local demonstration projects are more likely to influence the electricity system if national government authorities are involved. National advisory activities can better promote legislation for renewables if they can be linked to specific project experiences and best practices on the local level that demonstrate the positive effects of renewables. The more jurisdictional levels are actively involved during implementation, the more likely it is that there will be structural effects beyond the project's level of intervention.

Hypothesis 2. Aiming at broader impacts on the electricity system of an aid-receiving country, development cooperation has shifted its focus from local demonstration projects towards national activities. National advisory projects target broader framework conditions for renewables in developing countries. If successful, they are more likely to achieve structural effects for renewables in the recipient countries' electricity systems than local demonstration projects or technology-specific experiments.

Hypothesis 3. Vertical and horizontal coordination between multiple authorities at different jurisdictional levels shapes the decision-making process for renewables. A powerful central coordinating body can spread the use of renewable energy technologies. Such an authority can foster the institutionalization of results, ensure knowledge management and support the replication of best practices. The more centralized governance structures are in the electricity sector, the more likely it is that structural changes will result from donor-driven renewable energy projects.

Hypothesis 4. Power resources and the ability or capacity to make use of these resources can be unevenly distributed or fragmented across jurisdictional levels. Donors struggle to identify all national, provincial and municipal authorities that are relevant for scaling up results and include them during project implementation. If a donor organization's direct counterpart is a powerful actor, development projects are more likely to affect the electricity system. The more fragmented power resources, and capacities to mobilize these resources for promoting renewable energy, are across jurisdictional levels, the harder it is for development cooperation to achieve structural effects through modes of upscaling, learning or diffusion.

Energy transitions depend on a complex multi-level governance framework that involves a variety of authorities at different jurisdictional levels (Corfee-Morlot et al. 2009; Long and Hernandez 2012; Reddy and Painuly 2004; Smith 2007). This book shows how central–state–local relations affect renewable energy development in emerging economies. The analytical framework developed here incorporates power-related aspects into a multi-level governance perspective.

Using grounded theory

Grounded theory helps researchers (especially in social sciences) to develop a theoretical approach inductively from a rather open collection of data and information. Based on experiences from the field or "grounded" in data, it leads to theoretical approaches to understanding social behavior, processes or relations and can offer comprehensible explanations for the field of study (Glaser and Strauss 1967). Discovering a theory "from data systematically obtained from social research" rather than generating theory "by logical deduction from a priori assumptions" (Glaser and Strauss 1967, pp. 2–3) is a key principle behind grounded theory.

Theoretical implications about renewable energy governance were inductively derived from interviews and field trips. As it turned out that political factors massively shape renewable energy development, further field trips, observations and interviews helped to specify this first preliminary result. Due to the observed relevance of coordination and power, the analytical framework of multi-level governance was extended with insights from power theory in central–local relations. Figure 3.1 visualizes the research process that led to the identification of relevant political factors and the development of an appropriate theoretical framework.

Instead of testing and verifying already existing theories, this book aims to generate new ones. Such an approach provides a useful starting point for qualitative and explorative research in a field that is characterized by a high level of complexity and a vast number of possibly relevant and influential factors.

Qualitative and exploratory research

Research about development cooperation as well as sustainability transitions is far from having a consistent epistemological approach. Both fields are characterized by a constant, conflict-laden struggle between positivism and constructivism. This book claims that a better understanding of multi-level governance systems and their underlying power structures helps development cooperations to identify potential barriers to renewable energy support and discover shortcomings of their project activities. Because the complexity of political factors, limited access to information and a lack of data make any kind of quantitative analysis difficult, this research follows an interpretative, exploratory and qualitative research design (Lewins et al. 2005).

Acknowledging the "complexity paradigm" (Morin 1992), governance structures are too complex to be reduced to a number of controllable variables that development cooperation simply needs to take into account to be successful. Promoting renewables involves a variety of different actors with diverse narratives, perceptions and attitudes towards sustainable energy. The field of investigation is highly reflexive and socially constructed (Berger and Luckmann 1967). Putting it into predetermined categories or quantifiable numbers or statistics would leave out important parts of the story. Power, in the light of the complexity paradigm, is not simply a stable resource that can be bargained with in a certain system, but, rather, dynamic and the result of intersystemic conflicts, cooperation and coordination.

Development projects have fundamentally changed over the decades. Whereas technology-specific local demonstration projects had a clear (and measurable) focus on a relatively narrow local project environment, more and more national advisory projects are confronted with factors they cannot easily

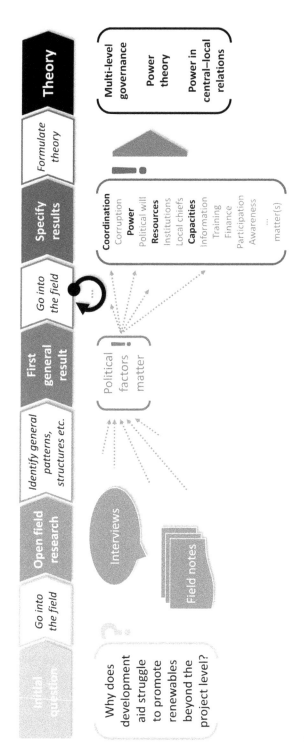

Figure 3.1 From grounded theory to a theoretical framework.
Source: illustration by the author.

influence or control. If a project promotes a feed-in tariff for renewables and thereafter a country adopts such a support mechanism, it does not necessarily mean that the project was the cause for that decision. Such kinds of causal relations need to be questioned. Taking into account and acknowledging the complexity of the issue area, a qualitative analysis judges the likelihood of these relations based on expert interviews, discourses and other interpretive methods.

Using a qualitative approach also needs to be seen in the light of a typical problem in development cooperation evaluation practice – the so-called "attribution gap" (Annecke 2008, p. 2842). Instead of analyzing quantifiable indicators used for monitoring and evaluating donor interventions (money spent, households electrified, jobs created etc.), this research aims, rather, to trace structural outcomes. These include unquantifiable processes of coordination between different levels of decision-making, learning, diffusion and upscaling of results or forms of institutionalization. These factors cannot be simply linked to a donor's activity performance. Scholars like Stockmann (1992; 1997) specify the fundamental problem of measuring outcomes and impact for projects promoting sustainability.

Exploratory research allows us to remain flexible and open to aspects that might not be covered by conventional theoretical approaches. At the same time, demonstrating validity and reliability remains a challenging task. Any conclusions and generalizations about causal relations need to be drawn with caution. Recommendations beyond the cases presented here need to carefully reflect experiences from other empirical studies.

Case selection

Following a case study approach (Gerring 2009; Thomas 2011; Yin 2009), Indonesia and the Philippines serve as the country-level case studies for investigating how governance structures affect energy transitions and donor-driven support. Fourteen selected development activities act as project cases to highlight and specify with empirical evidence what has been outlined for the broader country-level environment. Identifying and analyzing these case studies has been a "linear, but iterative process" (Yin 2009). This allows an in-depth analysis of complex societal phenomena and can lead to a "better understanding of the whole by focusing on a key part" (Gerring 2009, p. 1).

Southeast Asia is considered to be a "boom region" for renewable energy development (Franz 2010), which is driven by stable economic growth and increasing energy demand (ADB 2013). The German Energy Agency (DENA) identified high potential for renewables particularly in the Philippines and Indonesia (Franz 2010). For both archipelagos, renewables can have positive effects, especially for electrifying remote off-grid areas. With their complex, decentralized political systems and strong local authorities, the Philippines and Indonesia also represent two promising countries for investigating the link between governance systems and donor-driven renewable energy support. National governments have provided incentives for renewables, and donors have actively promoted sustainable energy projects for decades, but despite high natural and technical potential as well as political support, developing renewables faces severe obstacles in both countries.

Data collection and analysis

This book follows a narrative case study approach, as undertaken by other scholars in the field (Sovacool 2013), to discuss and evaluate renewable energy development in multi-level governance systems. As narratives, biased perceptions and personal perspectives are considered here, triangulation of different methods for data collection is essential to encompass "multiple sources of evidence" (Yin 2009, p. 97). Data from semi-structured interviews with experts from the energy sector and field research in Indonesia and the Philippines were the main sources of information. Legal documents and citable material such as consultancy reports, newspaper articles, evaluations and project design documents were also reviewed to substantiate and critically reflect findings from interviews and field trips. Participant observation from different events related to renewables and the field trips to selected case studies added information to the overall picture.

More than 100 semi-structured expert interviews with relevant stakeholders of the electricity sector were conducted in the Philippines and Indonesia. The interview partners covered most, but not all, of the main institutions involved in energy planning, regulation and implementation, as well as most major donor organizations that are actively promoting renewables. Interviews were carried out between 2013 (Philippines) and 2014 (Indonesia). Appendix II provides a list of the interview partners (partly anonymous). Figure 3.2 divides them into six main stakeholder groups.

The expert interviews shed light on the political environment related to an energy transition and the relevant actors' perceptions, perspectives and narratives. These insights were substantiated with empirical data from documents and field trips.

This research also takes into account experiences from participant observation (Hammersley and Atkinson 1983; Spradley 2008). Extensive field research allowed the author to participate in several workshops and training sessions related to renewable energy development. It was possible to establish a closer relationship with potential interview partners and gain further insights into ongoing debates. Based on Hammersley and Atkinson's (1983, p. 93) differentiation between different roles of the researcher in participant observation, the author can be described as an "observer as participant," being transparent about his actual status as a researcher, but taking part in and giving personal insights during field trips, workshops and other events. Participant observation helped to identify patterns of argumentation, interpretation, motives and interactions, as well as the stakeholders' inner perspectives related to renewables and development cooperation in supporting renewables.

Following an interpretive research philosophy, qualitative data analysis was used to extract "some form of explanation, understanding or interpretation"

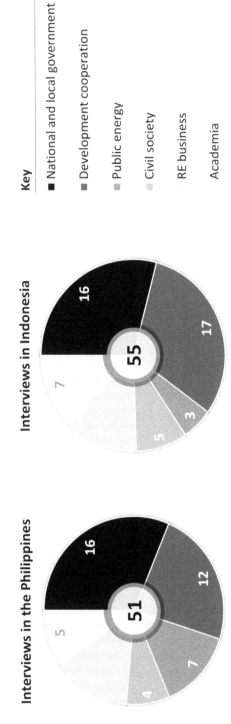

Interviews in the Philippines

Interviews in Indonesia

Key
- National and local government
- Development cooperation
- Public energy
- Civil society
- RE business
- Academia

Figure 3.2 Interview partners in the Philippines and Indonesia.
Source: illustration by the author.

(Lewins et al. 2005) from the data collected. Interview transcripts, notes from participant observations and reports from field trips provided the main text material. Doing qualitative data analysis is iterative and reflexive; it is often referred to as a process of progressive focusing (Parlett and Hamilton 1972). Despite the iterative character, the collection of information needs to consider multiple sources of evidence, develop a case study database and maintain a chain of evidence to pursue particular arguments (Yin 2009, p. 97). To identify patterns and arguments, the transcripts as well as the notes from the field were coded into themes (Basit 2003) with the help of computer-assisted qualitative data analysis (using MaxQDA). Eventually, these arguments were interpreted and discussed within their broader context.

Figure 3.3 summarizes the research process, which started with a theoretical discussion about the role of development cooperation and a selection of potential country cases. Preliminary interviews were conducted before broad categories were used for grounded theory-based research in the Philippines. These categories were then narrowed down to political factors and further specified to issues in central–local relations. Power was integrated into the multi-level governance framework before empirical research was undertaken in Indonesia.

Putting energy transitions and donor-driven renewable energy projects into the context of this book, findings from additional developing countries are discussed in the light of the results presented here.

Limitations

Qualitative research is often criticized for being less replicable by other researchers than quantitative measurements and statistics. Yet, the qualitative methods presented above are most appropriate to identify and discuss issues related to power or governance arrangements that cannot be quantified. Dealing with the role of complex governance structures involves a high number of variables that cannot be covered here in full. Making the methodological approach as transparent and comprehensible as possible should increase this study's reliability and potential replicability.

Generalizing results from a qualitative, exploratory and interpretive study might be considered as the biggest weakness of this approach compared with natural science experiments or quasi-experimental designs, but it reflects the vagueness and complexity of perceptions, preferences and personal perspectives that shape an energy transition. A support mechanism for renewables does not only depend on market structures or an institutional framework, but also on the decision-makers' attitude towards renewables or the power of supporters for this mechanism. These kinds of variables are influenced by a large number of factors that cannot be controlled. It is unlikely to be possible to predict a certain policy's or project's success in a given environment, but this book shows how power and capacities affect renewable energy development in emerging economies.

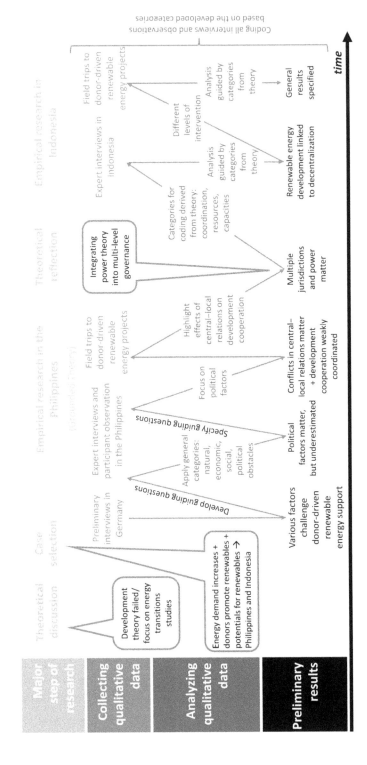

Figure 3.3 Collecting and analyzing qualitative data.

Source: illustration by the author.

References

ADB, 2013. *Energy outlook for Asia and the Pacific*, Manila: Asian Development Bank.

Annecke, W., 2008. Monitoring and evaluation of energy for development: The good, the bad and the questionable in M&E practice. *Energy Policy*, 36, pp. 2829–2835.

Basit, T., 2003. Manual or electronic? The role of coding in qualitative data analysis. *Educational Research*, 45(2), pp. 143–154.

Berger, P.L. and Luckmann, T., 1967. *The social construction of reality: A treatise in the sociology of knowledge*, London: Penguin Books.

Corfee-Morlot, J., Kamal-Chaoui, L., Donovan, M.G., Cochran, I., Robert, A. and Teasdale, P.-J., 2009. *Cities, climate change and multilevel governance*, Franz, S., 2010. Renewable Energy Opportunities in South East Asia.

Franz, S., 2010. *Renewable energy opportunities in South East Asia*, Berlin: Deutsche Energie-Agentur.

Gerring, J., 2009. *Case study research. Principles and practices*, Cambridge: Cambridge University Press.

Glaser, B.G. and Strauss, A.L., 1967. *The discovery of grounded theory: Strategies for qualitative research*, New Brunswick: Aldine Transaction.

Hammersley, M. and Atkinson, P., 1983. *Ethnography. Principles in practice*, London: Routledge.

Lewins, A., Taylor, C. and Gibbs, G.R., 2005. What is Qualitative Data Analysis (QDA)? *Online QDA*. Available at: http://onlineqda.hud.ac.uk/Intro_QDA/what_is_qda.php [accessed August 16, 2016].

Long, W. and Hernandez, J.A., 2012. Transition to renewable energy in developing countries: Promoting energy policy and innovation. *Lecture Notes in Information Technology*, 13, pp. 479–486.

Morin, E., 1992. From the concept of system to the paradigm of complexity. *Journal of Social and Evolutionary Systems*, 15(4), pp. 371–385.

Parlett, M. and Hamilton, D., 1972. *Evaluation as illumination: A new approach to the study of innovatory programs*, Edinburgh.

Reddy, S. and Painuly, J.P., 2004. Diffusion of renewable energy technologies: Barriers and stakeholders' perspectives. *Renewable Energy*, 29(9), pp. 1431–1447.

Smith, A., 2007. Emerging in between: The multi-level governance of renewable energy in the English regions. *Energy Policy*, 35(12), pp. 6266–6280.

Sovacool, B.K., 2013. A qualitative factor analysis of renewable energy and sustainable energy for all (SE4ALL) in the Asia-Pacific. *Energy Policy*, 59, pp. 393–403.

Spradley, J.P., 2008. *Participant observation*, New York: Holt, Rinehart and Winston.

Stockmann, R., 1992. *Die Nachhaltigkeit von Entwicklungsprojekten. Eine Methode zur Evaluierung am Beispiel von Berufsbildungsprojekten*, 2nd ed., Opladen: Westdeutscher Verlag.

Stockmann, R., 1997. The sustainability of development projects: An impact assessment of German vocational-training projects in Latin America. *World Development*, 25(11), pp. 1767–1784.

Thomas, G., 2011. *How to do your case study. A guide for students and researchers*, London: Sage.

Yin, R.K., 2009. *Case study research. Design and methods*, Los Angeles: Sage.

Part II

Development cooperation for sustainable energy

4   Promoting sustainable energy

Introduction

Investigating energy transitions in Southeast Asia, this book brings together two main fields of research: renewable energy development in emerging economies and the role of development cooperation. Renewable energy projects, as well as support mechanisms and incentives for renewables, have encountered a rapid growth in terms of numbers and countries involved – especially in the developing world. In recent years, developing and emerging economies have even been the driving force for supportive policy expansion, accounting for more than 100 of the 145 countries with incentive structures for renewables (REN21 2015a, p. 14).

Climate change and environmental concerns might be the main driver for debates on energy transitions in industrialized countries. In the developing world, renewables are much more related to aspects such as energy security, rural electrification or additional energy demand. According to the World Economic Forum (WEF 2013, p. 2), it is not only climate change, but also "the worry that the current energy mix will not prove adequate to meet the rapidly growing energy needs of emerging market nations," that is a major driving force for renewable energy development around the world.

Development cooperation is assumed to have the potential for fostering, or at least supporting, this development through modes of technology transfer, demonstration projects and policy advice. In practice, such an ambition is hard to fulfill. Donor-driven interventions are diverse, complex and controversial, not only in the field of renewables. These projects are shaped by overarching trends in development cooperation, such as fragmentation or diversification of aid. However, projects related to environmental concerns or sustainable development – including renewable energy activities – have also seen an increasing relevance over the last decades.

Taking a global perspective

There is no doubt that energy transitions are extraordinary complex societal phenomena and cover a broad range of research topics – even if we only narrowly define an energy transition as the compensation of fossil fuels and nuclear energy with renewable and environmentally friendly energy sources. These highly complex societal transformation processes cover economic (technologies, markets, costs), environmental (climate change mitigation, emissions reduction, nature conservation), social (ownership, democratization, social justice) and political (decision-making, interests, power coalitions) aspects, and are expected to take decades (Smil 2010). Research on the historical dimension of energy transitions (Solomon and Krishna 2011), pathways towards sustainable energy in the future (Riahi 2012) or political incentives (Jaccard 2012) is abundant. Having mainly emerged in the Netherlands, the field of sustainability transitions research has led to a substantial amount of knowledge about the role of and interaction between overarching landscape developments, regime structures and niche experiments for an energy transition (Geels 2005; Loorbach 2010; van den Bergh et al. 2011). Empirical insights from developing countries remain a rare exception (Marquardt et al. 2015).

Future energy demand is heavily increasing in developing countries, whereas the demand in the OECD is predicted to remain almost stable until 2030 (OECD and IEA 2012). The picture looks similar for global renewable energy investments, which are expected to decline in OECD countries, but will increase in emerging economies (McCrone et al. 2014). According to the Renewable Energy Network for the 21st Century (REN21 2015a), developing countries already show the highest numbers in terms of renewable energy investments and additional installed capacity. At the same time, most English-based research on energy transitions and renewable energy focuses on industrialized countries, whereas literature on renewable energy support in developing countries narrowly emphasizes the role of small-scale projects for rural electrification. Considering its global relevance, the role of broader frameworks for renewables as well as social and political factors in non-OECD countries remains an extraordinarily underresearched field.

Looking at renewables from a global perspective leads to mixed results regarding their success. On the one hand, global data shows a significant increase in renewable energy research, investments, installed capacity and even supportive political frameworks. In 2013, renewables provided an estimated 19.1 percent (including 9 percent from traditional biomass) of global final energy consumption (REN21 2015a, p. 6). By the end of 2014, 22.8 percent of global electricity supply was covered by renewables, with 16.4 percent coming from hydropower. Global annual investments reached their peak with US$279 billion in 2011 (McCrone et al. 2014). Renewable energy targets are in place in at least 164 countries, and support policies exist in 145 countries (REN21 2015a, p. 7). International bodies such as the International Renewable Energy Agency (IRENA) and REN21 further promote renewable energy development around the world.

On the other hand, global energy demand has more than doubled since the 1970s, with renewables covering additional demand, but not substantially substituting for fossil fuels (IEA 2012). Energy outlooks from the International Energy Agency (IEA 2013) and the US Energy Information Administration

(EIA) predict an increasing importance of renewables, making them the "world's fastest-growing source of electric power" (EIA 2013, p. 12) until 2040. At the same time, their share of total electricity generation will increase only marginally, from 21 percent to 25 percent, due to increasing overall demand. Although investments and installed capacity, particularly in modern renewables such as wind and solar photovoltaic (PV), have massively increased since 2004, the overall global energy mix changed little between 1973 and 2015.

Exploring renewables from a more country-specific or subnational perspective makes the picture look even more complex – with experiences from around the world. Not only do research activities cover national ambitions and policies for an energy transition in countries such as Germany (SRU 2011), the Netherlands (Verbong and Geels 2007) and Denmark (Meyer and Koefoed 2003), but also local municipalities (Schönberger 2013) and city networks (Morlet and Keirstead 2013), as well as network-like initiatives (Johansson et al. 2012), are becoming more and more important for promoting renewables. Harder to find are studies that tackle the political dimension of an energy transition in developing countries – despite a variety of market studies (BMWi 2013), energy outlooks (Ölz and Beerepoot 2010) and project reports (UN Economic Commission for Africa 2006).

The political dimension of renewable energy support

Even with technologies and financing available, implementing renewable energy technologies is not an easy task. They depend on positive enabling conditions such as incentive structures, political support and institutional capacity. Despite the availability of country-specific renewable energy potential analyses and economic feasibility studies, a comprehensive overview of the political dimension beyond support schemes, but including relevant governance structures for promoting renewables in developing countries, is still missing (REN21 2015b). Political aspects are highly relevant to renewable energy development, but are too often neglected or underestimated by policy-makers and project developers.

Incentive structures and support schemes for renewables represent the most widely discussed political aspects related to energy transitions. Policies include fiscal mechanisms such as tax exemptions or cash revenues, but especially nonfiscal mechanisms such as a renewable portfolio standard, feed-in tariffs or a priority dispatch for renewables. Scholars such as Komor (2004) and Hirschl (2008) provide overviews on possible policy interventions to promote renewables. Thiam (2011) investigates how tariff policies could push renewable energy development. These and other regulatory interventions mobilize and facilitate private investment and finance. They aim to provide some structural advantage for renewables in their competition with fossil fuels (UNEP Finance Initiative 2012, p. 9).

Beyond these classical government-led instruments, promoting renewables can be linked to more fundamental governance issues such as participation, democratization and decentralization in the energy sector (O'Riordan 1996). A decentralized electricity system based on small-scale renewables can lead to people's involvement and even ownership of the system. Participation and ownership are also key aspects in development cooperation when aiming for self-sustained projects. At the same time, the national government needs to set priorities for renewables. The German Advisory Council on Global Change (WBGU 2011, p. 1) calls for a "proactive state [...] that actively sets priorities for the transformation, at the same time increasing the number of ways in which its citizens can participate to support a transition towards sustainability."

Energy transitions can be initiated not only at the national, but also at the local level. Renewable energy development can be investigated as a bottom-up process with people and local authorities pushing for change, but also from a top-down perspective, with a central government being in charge of national energy planning, energy security etc. (Geels 2011; Jørgensen 2012; Weischer et al. 2011). In both cases, coordinating renewable energy development strategies within multi-level governance frameworks is a key challenge due to the involvement of different (planning and implementing) actors with diffuse interests at various levels of decision-making. Competencies, conflicts, capacities, power structures and issues of coordination play an important role in understanding the potential of and barriers to an energy transition. Additional aspects such as corruption, nepotism or patronage can be dominant factors, especially in the developing world.

For developing countries, renewables are often seen as a possible solution for their energy dilemma – a tension between the need for energy security in the light of growing demand and the need to reduce environmental degradation and check the rise of air pollutants and greenhouse gas emissions tied to climate change at the same time (e.g. Bradshaw 2014; Hallding et al. 2009; Sovacool 2008). Regulating this area of tension requires political decisions in favor of or against a certain path of energy system development.

Development cooperation, multi-level governance and power

This research brings in empirical insights from energy transitions in Southeast Asia to contribute to the debate about the role of governance structures in developing countries, as well as the meaning and success of donor-driven interventions in the field. Investigating 14 renewable energy projects that were implemented at various jurisdictional levels adds further detail to the arguments outlined here. Local solar and biomass power projects as well as advisory activities for provincial and national governments are taken into account.

A multi-level governance approach is developed and applied to enhance our knowledge about the barriers to and potential of energy transitions in developing countries in general, and for donor-driven renewable energy projects in particular. The approach examines how various jurisdictional levels shape the decision-making process for renewables. National, provincial and municipal governmental authorities all play a role when it comes to renewable energy development. Which jurisdictional levels are driving forces? Where are potential veto players? Which actors are crucial? How do they interact or coordinate with each other? Taking a multi-level governance perspective helps to discuss these and other questions related to the governance framework for renewables. Linking research about environmental development cooperation to insights from multi-level governance research can be beneficiary for both research fields, because it helps development cooperation practitioners and researchers alike to better understand the relation between often very site-specific donor-driven interventions and the complex political system of the recipient country.

Not only do governance structures and issues of coordination across jurisdictional levels shape energy transitions, but also power relations, fragmentation and the distribution of power among various jurisdictional levels determine renewable energy development. Taking a closer look at power, this book argues that not only are power resources such as political power, regulatory power or the power to frame a topic unevenly distributed across jurisdictional levels, but also the different jurisdictions' capacities or abilities to make use of these resources to achieve certain policy outcomes can vary greatly across these levels. Capacities include manpower, know-how and finance. Arguments from power theory (e.g. Lukes 1995) and power in central–local relations (e.g. Rhodes 1986) are therefore integrated into the multi-level governance approach. Until now, not much has been written about the role of these factors in developing countries when it comes to societal transitions towards sustainability.

Despite the vast number of donor-driven interventions promoting renewable energy for decades, "surprisingly little empirical evidence exists on their achievement or non-achievement of sustainability after the initial project activity was completed" (Terrapon-Pfaff et al. 2014, p. 813). Investigating the role of political factors should enhance our understanding of the success and failure of renewable energy interventions and their sustainability. Especially small-scale demonstration projects with new technologies such as solar PV turned out to be problematic for rural electrification. Beneficiaries were not able to sustain the projects or even expand them without funding from foreign donors due to a lack of manpower, know-how and financial capacity at the local level, weak coordination with provincial and national authorities, and a lack of clear rules and regulations (Marquardt 2014).

References

BMWi, 2013. Die Exportinitiative Erneuerbare Energien. *Bundesministerium für Wirtschaft*. Available at: www.export-erneuerbare.de/EEE/Navigation/DE/Home/home. html [accessed May 27, 2015].

Bradshaw, M., 2014. *Global energy dilemmas*, Cambridge: Polity.

EIA, 2013. *International energy outlook 2013*, Washington, DC: US Energy Information Administration.

Geels, F.W., 2005. The dynamics of transitions in socio-technical systems: A multi-level analysis of the transition pathway from horse-drawn carriages to automobiles (1860–1930). *Technology Analysis & Strategic Management*, 17(4), pp. 445–476.

Geels, F.W., 2011. The multi-level perspective on sustainability transitions: Responses to seven criticisms. *Environmental Innovation and Societal Transitions*, 1(1), pp. 24–40.

Hallding, K., Han, G. and Olsson, M., 2009. China's climate- and energy-security dilemma: Shaping a new path of economic growth. *Journal of Current Chinese Affairs*, 38(3), pp. 119–134.

Hirschl, B., 2008. *Erneuerbare Energien-Politik: Eine Multi-Level Policy-Analyse mit Fokus auf den deutschen Strommarkt*, Wiesbaden: VS Verlag für Sozialwissenschaften.

IEA, 2012. *World energy outlook 2012*, Paris: International Energy Agency.

IEA, 2013. *Southeast Asia energy outlook. World energy outlook special report*, Paris.

Jaccard, M., 2012. Policies for energy system transformations: Objectives and instruments. In International Institute for Applied Systems Analysis, ed. *Global energy assessment: Towards a sustainable future*, Cambridge: Cambridge University Press, pp. 1551–1602.

Johansson, T.B., Nakicenovic, N., Patwardhan, A. and Gomez-Echeverri, L., 2012. *Global energy assessment: Towards a sustainable future*, International Institute for Applied Systems Analysis, ed., Cambridge: Cambridge University Press.

Jørgensen, U., 2012. Mapping and navigating transitions – The multi-level perspective compared with arenas of development. *Research Policy*, 41(6), pp. 996–1010.

Komor, P., 2004. *Renewable energy policy*, Lincoln: The Diebold Institute for Public Policy Studies.

Loorbach, D., 2010. Transition management for sustainable development: A prescriptive, complexity-based governance framework. *Governance*, 23(1), pp. 161–183.

Lukes, S., 1995. *Power: A radical view*, London: Longman.

Marquardt, J., 2014. How sustainable are donor-driven solar power projects in remote areas? *Journal of International Development*, 26(6), pp. 915–922.

Marquardt, J., Steinbacher, K. and Schreurs, M., 2016. Driving force or forced transition? The role of development cooperation in promoting energy transitions in the Philippines and Morocco. *Journal of Cleaner Production*, 128, pp. 22–33.

McCrone, A., Usher, E., Sonntag-O'Brien, V., Moslener, U. and Grüning, C., 2014. *Global trends in renewable energy investment 2014*, Frankfurt am Main: Frankfurt School of Finance & Management.

Meyer, N.I. and Koefoed, A.L., 2003. Danish energy reform: Policy implications for renewables. *Energy Policy*, 31(7), pp. 597–607.

Morlet, C. and Keirstead, J., 2013. A comparative analysis of urban energy governance in four European cities. *Energy Policy*, 61, pp. 852–863.

O'Riordan, T., 1996. Democracy and the sustainability transition. In W. Lafferty and J. Meadowcroft, eds. *Democracy and the environment. Problems and prospects*, Northampton: Edward Elgar, pp. 140–156.

OECD and IEA, 2012. *World energy outlook 2012. Executive summary*. Paris: International Energy Agency.

Ölz, S. and Beerepoot, M., 2010. *Deploying renewables in Southeast Asia. Trends and potentials*, Paris: International Energy Agency.

REN21, 2015a. *Renewables 2015: Global status report*, Paris: Renewable Energy Policy Network for the 21st Century.

REN21, 2015b. Renewables international map. *Renewable Energy Policy Network for the 21st Century*. Available at: http://map.ren21.net [accessed May 29, 2015].

Rhodes, R.A.W., 1986. *Control and power in central-local government relations*, Aldershot: Gower.

Riahi, K., 2012. Energy pathways for sustainable development. In International Institute for Applied Systems Analysis, ed. *Global energy assessment: Towards a sustainable future.* Cambridge: Cambridge University Press.

Schönberger, P., 2013. *Municipalities as key actors of German renewable energy governance. An analysis of opportunities, obstacles, and multi-level influence*, Wuppertal: Wuppertal Institut für Klima, Umwelt, Energie.

Smil, V., 2010. *Energy transitions: History, requirements, prospects*, Santa Barbara: Praeger.

Solomon, B.D. and Krishna, K., 2011. The coming sustainable energy transition: History, strategies, and outlook. *Energy Policy*, 39(11), pp. 7422–7431.

Sovacool, B.K., 2008. *The dirty energy dilemma: What's blocking clean power in the United States*, Westport: Praeger.

SRU, 2011. *Pathways towards a 100% renewable electricity system*, Berlin: German Advisory Council on the Environment (SRU).

Terrapon-Pfaff, J., Dienst, C., König, J. and Ortiz, W., 2014. How effective are small-scale energy interventions in developing countries? Results from a post-evaluation on project-level. *Applied Energy*, 135, pp. 809–814.

Thiam, D.R., 2011. An energy pricing scheme for the diffusion of decentralized renewable technology investment in developing countries. *Energy Policy*, 39(7), pp. 4284–4297.

UN Economic Commission for Africa, 2006. *Report on "Energy for Sustainable Development,"* Addis Ababa: United Nations Economic Commission for Africa.

UNEP Finance Initiative, 2012. *Financing renewable energy in developing countries: Drivers and barriers for private finance in sub-Saharan Africa*, Nairobi: United Nations Environment Programme.

van den Bergh, J.C.J.M., Truffer, B. and Kallis, G., 2011. Environmental innovation and societal transitions: Introduction and overview. *Environmental Innovation and Societal Transitions*, 1(1), pp. 1–23.

Verbong, G. and Geels, F.W., 2007. The ongoing energy transition: Lessons from a socio-technical, multi-level analysis of the Dutch electricity system (1960–2004). *Energy Policy*, 35(2), pp. 1025–1037.

WBGU, 2011. *World in transition: A social contract for sustainability (summary for policymakers)*, Berlin: German Advisory Council on Global Change (WBGU).

WEF, 2013. *Energy vision 2013. Energy transitions: Past and future*, Geneva: World Economic Forum.

Weischer, L., Wood, D., Ballesteros, A. and Fu-bertaux, X., 2011. *Grounding green power. Bottom-up perspectives on smart renewable energy policy in developing countries*, Washington, DC: The German Marshall Fund of the United States.

5 Key challenges and drivers in developing countries

The benefits of renewables

Energy is crucial for development. Fossil fuels as well as renewables are the basis not only for industrialization and economic growth, but also for all sorts of human development. At the same time, producing and consuming energy have severe impacts on health and the environment. International organizations and donors therefore advocate renewables in developing countries. They stress the strong nexus between modern renewable energy sources and sustainable, environmentally friendly development (e.g. BMZ 2008; IEA 2012; OECD and IEA 2010; United Nations 2010). Renewable energy technologies could meet future demand with fewer negative side effects than fossil fuels.

> As with industrialized countries, renewable energy technologies can contribute to greater energy security and diversity, foreign exchange savings on fossil fuel imports, reduction of local air pollution and greenhouse gas emissions, as well as employment and industrial development.
>
> (Boyle et al. 2006, p. 9)

In addition to this, off-grid solutions such as micro hydro installations or solar mini grids also hold the potential to facilitate the provision of basic services such as electricity, pumped drinking water and cooking (Boyle et al. 2006, p. 9). In developing countries, renewables contribute to energy security (Jacob et al. 2013), access to energy, environmental protection, rural development (Byrne et al. 1998), poverty alleviation (Biswas et al. 2001) and local empowerment. Also, electrification through renewable energy not only "improves education and the study environment for school children, enables small businesses and provides greater security, but also brings entertainment and information through the use of television" (IEG 2008, p. xv).

Developing countries hold huge technical potential for electricity production from solar, wind, biomass or hydro (BMU 2012; REN21 2015b), which could be used to save costs by avoiding importing oil and coal from other countries, thus enhancing energy security. Even solar PV systems can be economically feasible and competitive, especially for off-grid electrification, as an alternative to diesel electricity generation. Data from the International Renewable Energy Agency (IRENA 2012) indicates that even grid-connected PV in Africa has become competitive with diesel-generated electricity, making it a viable option for electricity generation in developing countries (Bazilian et al. 2013; Pearson 2012).

Renewables provide decentralized small-scale energy supply, especially in remote off-grid areas and on islands with little access to other forms of energy apart from traditional biomass. With 1.3 billion people without access to electricity, and more than 2.6 billion people depending on traditional biomass (REN21 2015a, p. 17), small-scale renewable energy facilities such as mini hydro grids or household photovoltaic (PV) installations are often considered for basic access to electricity and rural electrification, but not for mainstream electricity supply (Elias and Victor 2005, p. 21). Getting connected to the national grid is associated with more stable, reliable and cost-efficient forms of conventional energy. The United Nations (2012) Sustainable Energy for All initiative aims to combine both targets (access to electricity and sustainability) and achieve universal access to modern energy by 2030. Similarly, the Organisation for Economic Co-operation and Development and the International Energy Agency (OECD and IEA 2010) discuss how to end energy poverty by 2030 with the help of renewables.

An increase in energy consumption is often "in direct proportion" (Boyle et al. 2006, p. 10) to local air pollution. Renewables could reverse this trend. Conventional pollutants such as nitrogen monoxide, carbon monoxide, sulfur dioxide and acid rain can be reduced to minimize or avoid serious health and environmental threats. In terms of total global emissions, developing countries have already overtaken the OECD. Substituting fossil fuels with renewables also slows the increase in global greenhouse gas emissions.

Positive expectations associated with renewable energy investments include "industrial development, job creation and increased exports for developing countries" (Boyle et al. 2006, p. 10). Compared with large-scale fossil fuel power stations, small-scale decentralized forms of renewable energy supply generate significantly more local added-value and jobs per installed capacity in megawatts (Greenpeace 2012). With the help of market mechanisms or microcredit schemes, renewables "may improve the quality of life of rural people and provide income-generating opportunities" (Biswas et al. 2001, p. 342). Instead of environmental effects, Jaramillo-Nieves and del Río (2010) identify poverty alleviation and security of supply as the two main drivers for renewables in developing countries. In practice, little if any attention is paid to either of these particularities in the developing world.

In most non-OECD countries, the majority of the population still lives in rural areas. Electrification with grid-connected solutions remains "very expensive and unaffordable to the rural poor" (Kaundinya et al. 2009, p. 2042). Small-scale decentralized electricity supply can help to overcome this challenge and empower local communities by promoting their development. Not surprisingly, renewables are often positively associated with human development, because they serve basic human needs such as water supply, education and health (Yu et al. 1997, p. 167). Compared with diesel generators, they create fewer negative side effects such as noise or pollution (Solano-Peralta et al. 2009, p. 2290). The United Nations (2012, p. 4) even formulates the claim that "sustainable development is not possible without sustainable energy."

Donors and international organizations raise additional political benefits. They stress the need for participation, civil society actors and bottom-up processes for developing and implementing renewables and democratizing the energy system. In practice, energy transitions often follow a top-down approach with central planning, project development and policy implementation undertaken by the national government, due in part to a lack of local capacity for or awareness of renewables.

Despite the widely acknowledged benefits of renewables for developing countries, the International Evaluation Group of the World Bank admits that "the evidence base remains weak for many of the claimed benefits" (IEG 2008, p. xvii). Developing countries, especially in Asia, are currently building up their energy infrastructures, but mainly invest in fossil fuels (IEA 2014, p. 84). Since the potential to leapfrog fossil fuel technologies and avoid coal-based electricity systems is highest in emerging economies (Sharif 1989; Tukker 2005), a larger portion should be diverted towards renewable energy infrastructure as the basis for future investments.

Key challenges

Annual electricity demand in developing countries is increasing rapidly due to economic progress, changing patterns of consumption and population growth. Although more than 80 percent of the world's population live in less developed countries, they consume only about 54 percent of global commercial energy. Until 2040, non-OECD countries are expected to account for 65 percent of global energy consumption (EIA 2014). Promoting renewables in these countries is therefore less about substituting already existing capacities, and more about meeting additional demand and building up complementary energy production capacities. Emerging economies like China and Brazil, as well as developing nations like the Philippines and Indonesia, have ambitious targets and extensive programs for renewable energy development. In 2013, a total amount of US$93 billion was invested into renewables in developing countries (REN21 2015a, p. 67). At the same time, renewables are still perceived as a costly alternative to conventional sources of energy.

Over the past decades, various attempts were made to promote renewables in developing countries with the help of technology transfer (IPCC 2000; Martinot and McDoom 2000; Wilkins 2002) through various channels such as official development assistance (ODA) or the Clean Development Mechanism under the Kyoto Protocol (van der Gaast et al. 2009). Their overall success was limited and hampered by economic and political barriers. Transferring small-scale renewable energy technologies such as biogas cooking stoves or solar heaters failed not only due to high costs, but also because of political factors such as "instability, corruption, lack of institutional support, lack of planning for energy or land use, low technical capacity of domestic firms" (Boyle et al. 2006, p. 10).

Research related to energy transitions needs to consider developing countries more seriously due to their current, but especially due to their future, relevance for the global climate and environment. Action in these countries could prevent non-OECD countries from taking a similar emissions-intensive path of economic growth and development as the industrialized world (Ahlborg and Hammar 2012; DIE 2004; Pachauri and Jiang 2008). Combatting climate change requires radical and challenging societal shifts. Over the next two decades, less developed countries "are expected to add around 80 percent of all new electric generation capacity worldwide" (Weischer et al. 2011, p. 1), but most of these countries "still lack the capacity and technology to shift to more sustainable and affordable supplies of energy without external assistance" (Halff et al. 2014, p. 21) provided by development cooperation. At the same time, current donor-driven activities are ineffective and often fail, because they neglect the sociopolitical complexity of renewable energy development.

> Program managers need not only focus on making high quality, standardized technology that works well, they must also get the price signals and financing right, mold cultural values and expectations, spread awareness, align political regulations, and build institutional capacity.
>
> (Sovacool 2012, p. 280)

Such a perception stands in sharp contrast to most development cooperation reports and other rather optimistic studies about the potential of renewable energy technology transfer for rural electrification (e.g. Böhnke 1992). For a developing country like Nepal, Rai (2004, p. 50) stresses the potential of solar PV systems, which can be "an effective way to stimulate quick and effective rural development," and Gurung et al. (2011, p. 3209) highlight the success of mini hydro schemes "in improving the socio-economic status of [their] consumers."

Drivers for successful development

Over the last decade, bi- and multilateral donors have not only implemented technology-specific pilot projects, but also fostered broader programs for rural electrification and provided policy advice for renewable energy development. Reflecting these trends, most academic literature about renewable energy support in developing countries is related to three main topics: technology transfer and international cooperation, incentive schemes and supportive governance frameworks, and the broad field of rural electrification. Research projects are closely linked to practical experiences and specific (donor-driven) projects or programs (Sovacool 2013).

In order to foster private investments for renewable energy projects, the United Nations Secretary-General's High-Level Group on Sustainable Energy

for All (United Nations 2012) has formulated three fundamental recommendations or factors of success for renewable energy development in non-OECD
countries:

1   Supportive institutional arrangements are needed not only at the national,
    but especially at the local level. A national authority should bundle
    responsibilities for renewables. Local capacity with trained personnel as
    well as awareness of renewables is crucial for supporting project develop-
    ments, providing licenses and monitoring project implementation (Islam
    et al. 2006).
2   Transparent standards and predictable processes for project developers facil-
    itate private investments. A clear procedure for renewable energy project
    developers is a prerequisite for calculating administrative and transaction
    costs. Technical standards need to be coherent (Ahmad et al. 2011).
3   Innovative financing mechanisms are needed to lower the relatively high up-
    front costs for renewables for businesses and consumers alike. Microcredits,
    community funding and low interest rates are tools that can facilitate small-
    scale renewable energy development in remote areas (Liming 2009).

These rather general remarks are underlined by various empirical studies.
Based on more than 400 interviews and 90 site visits to renewable energy projects, Sovacool (2013) elaborates in one of the most extensive studies on the
factors for success and failure of renewable energy access programs. According to
Sovacool (2013, p. 394), success correlates with ten main factors:

1   Appropriate technologies need to be identified through feasibility studies
    and surveys.
2   Renewable energy activities need to be coupled with other income-
    generating activities.
3   Access to (micro)finance needs to be facilitated to cover high up-front
    costs.
4   National and local policies need to be aligned.
5   Investments in local institutional capacity are needed.
6   Donors need to be flexible and adapt to changing circumstances.
7   Projects need to be accompanied by outreach and marketing campaigns.
8   Active participation of communities is essential.
9   Communities also need to share costs.
10 Technical standards need to be enforced.

Sovacool and Drupady (2012) draw 12 similar lessons from rural electrification programs in Asia for governing small-scale renewable energy activities –
including technological appropriateness, community commitment and
awareness-raising.

Solar PV programs can increase their effectiveness by shifting their primary
focus from input (pure amount of investments) to output indicators and by

concentrating on the development of necessary infrastructure (information for project developers, maintenance for solar facilities, transparent procedures) and the establishment of local technical capacity (e.g. training for microfinance and credit monitoring or regular funding for technicians) that help to sustain the projects (Palit 2013). Evaluating donor-driven small-scale interventions promoting renewables in developing countries leads to the conclusion that sustainable project implementation does "not only depend on the reliability of the technological innovation alone, but the embedding of the technology in the socio-cultural, political and ecological context" (Terrapon-Pfaff et al. 2014, p. 813). Non-technical factors such as the creation of ownership or the availability of human capacities, as well as sociocultural aspects such as beliefs and perceptions, influence a project's sustainability. As one example, Zomers (2003) emphasizes the critical role of the utility organization that needs to be integrated into rural electrification programs.

Supportive policy frameworks, investment schemes and market conditions are much broader success factors for renewable energy development. Studies about emerging economies like China (Wang et al. 2010; Cherni and Kentish 2007), India (Shrimali and Tirumalachetty 2013) or Brazil (Geller et al. 2004; Pereira et al. 2012) describe financial obstacles for renewables and assess market potential in order to explore how public policies can overcome market barriers. The government's role is often reduced "to develop[ing] regulatory measures and laws" (Krause et al. 2003, p. 18) for electricity supply with renewables. Broader sociopolitical conditions, including the political system, civil society actors or decision-making processes are rarely investigated, although scholars such as Krause et al. (2003, p. 42) highlight that "fragmentation between agents at different administrative levels" can negatively affect renewable energy development.

Realizing energy transitions depends not only on technical and financial factors, but also on institutions, culture and social behavior. Painuly's (2001) list of barriers for renewables in developing countries includes uncertain government policies, a weak regulatory framework, a lack of involvement of relevant decision-makers and little consumer acceptance for renewables. Empirical studies from Mexico (Mallett 2007) and China (Yuan et al. 2011) argue that renewable energy technologies also struggle to gain social acceptance in these countries. Apart from that, there are almost no studies that examine the meaning of sociopolitical conditions such as decentralization, local protest movements or social acceptance for energy transitions in a developing country context.

Sociopolitical aspects and governance issues are playing an increasingly important role in energy-related research with a focus on developing countries, but the field is still dominated by discussions about market designs and political incentives. Most studies investigate technology-specific rural electrification programs (local demonstration projects), but rarely discuss donor-driven interventions at the national level (e.g. policy advice, academic support, institution-building). Academic debates often follow a rather positivistic, market-based and management approach that is seldom criticized or scrutinized. Insights from constructivist approaches are rare. English-based literature shows a bias towards OECD countries, whereas arguments from inside developing countries are not commonly represented, either in the academic discourse or among practitioners.

References

Ahlborg, H. and Hammar, L., 2012. Drivers and barriers to rural electrification in Tanzania and Mozambique: Grid-extension, off-grid, and renewable energy technologies. *Renewable Energy*, 61, pp. 117–124.

Ahmad, S., Kadir, M.Z.A.A. and Shafie, S., 2011. Current perspective of the renewable energy development in Malaysia. *Renewable and Sustainable Energy Reviews*, 15(2), pp. 897–904.

Bazilian, M., Onyeji, I., Liebreich, M., MacGill, I., Chase, J., Shah, J., Gielen, D., Arent, D., Landfear, D. and Zhengrong, S., 2013. Re-considering the economics of photovoltaic power. *Renewable Energy*, 53, pp. 329–338.

Biswas, W.K., Bryce, P. and Diesendorf, M., 2001. Model for empowering rural poor through renewable energy technologies in Bangladesh. *Environmental Science and Policy*, 4(6), pp. 333–344.

BMU, 2012. *Erneuerbare Energien in Zahlen. Nationale und internationale Entwicklung*, Berlin: Bundesministerium für Umwelt, Naturschutz und Reaktorsicherheit.

BMZ, 2008. *Entwicklung braucht nachhaltige Energie*, Bonn: Bundesministerium für wirtschaftliche Zusammenarbeit und Entwicklung.

Böhnke, H.-W., 1992. *Opening the PV market: The development of a rural photovoltaic electrification model in the Philippines*, Eschborn: Deutsche Gesellschaft für Technische Zusammenarbeit.

Boyle, G., Deepchand, K., Hua, L. and La Rovere, E.L., 2006. *Renewable energy technologies in developing countries. Lessons from Mauritius, China and Brazil*, Yokohama: United Nations University Institute for Advanced Studies.

Byrne, J., Shen, B. and Wallace, W., 1998. The economics of sustainable energy for rural development: A study of renewable energy in rural China. *Energy Policy*, 26(1), pp. 45–54.

Cherni, J.A. and Kentish, J., 2007. Renewable energy policy and electricity market reforms in China. *Energy Policy*, 35(7), pp. 3616–3629.

DIE, 2004. *Klimaschutz und Energiepolitik in der Entwicklungszusammenarbeit – der Beitrag der erneuerbaren Energien*, Bonn: Deutsches Institut für Entwicklungspolitik.

EIA, 2014. *International energy outlook 2014*, Washington: US Energy Information Administration.

Elias, R.J. and Victor, D.G., 2005. *Energy transitions in developing countries: A review of concepts and literature*, Stanford: Stanford University.

Geller, H., Schaeffer, R., Szklo, A. and Tolmasquim, M., 2004. Policies for advancing energy efficiency and renewable energy use in Brazil. *Energy Policy*, 32(12), pp. 1437–1450.

Greenpeace, 2012. *Green is gold: How renewable energy can save us money and generate jobs*, Quezon City: Greenpeace International.

Gurung, A., Gurung, O.P. and Oh, S.E., 2011. The potential of a renewable energy technology for rural electrification in Nepal: A case study from Tangting. *Renewable Energy*, 36(11), pp. 3203–3210.

Halff, A., Sovacool, B.K. and Rozhon, J. eds., 2014. *Energy poverty: Global challenges and local solutions*, Oxford: Oxford University Press.

IEA, 2012. The world energy outlook in the energy and development debate. *International Energy Agency*. Available at: www.iea.org/publications/worldenergyoutlook/ resources/energydevelopment [accessed May 20, 2014].

IEA, 2014. *World energy investment outlook*, Paris: International Energy Agency.

IEG, 2008. *The welfare impact of rural electrification: A reassessment of the costs and benefits*, Washington, DC: World Bank Independent Evaluation Group.

IPCC, 2000. *Methodological and technological issues in technology transfer*, Cambridge: Intergovernmental Panel on Climate Change.

IRENA, 2012. *Renewable power generation costs*, Abu Dhabi: International Renewable Energy Agency.

Islam, A.K.M.S., Islam, M. and Rahman, T., 2006. Effective renewable energy activities in Bangladesh. *Renewable Energy*, 31, pp. 677–688.

Jacob, K., Kauppert, P. and Quitzow, R., 2013. *Green growth strategies in Asia. Drivers and political entry points*, Berlin: Friedrich Ebert Stiftung.

Jaramillo-Nieves, L. and del Río, P., 2010. Contribution of renewable energy sources to the sustainable development of islands: An overview of the literature and a research agenda. *Sustainability*, 2(3), pp. 783–811.

Kaundinya, D.P., Balachandra, P. and Ravindranath, N.H., 2009. Grid-connected versus stand-alone energy systems for decentralized power: A review of literature. *Renewable and Sustainable Energy Reviews*, 13(8), pp. 2041–2050.

Krause, M., Jansen, S., Jung, S., Paschke, S. and Rösch, M., 2003. *Sustainable provision of renewable energy technologies for rural electrification in Brazil: An assessment of the photovoltaic option*, Bonn: German Development Institute.

Liming, H., 2009. Financing rural renewable energy: A comparison between China and India. *Renewable and Sustainable Energy Reviews*, 13, pp. 1096–1103.

Mallett, A., 2007. Social acceptance of renewable energy innovations: The role of technology cooperation in urban Mexico. *Energy Policy*, 35(5), pp. 2790–2798.

Martinot, E. and McDoom, O., 2000. *Promoting energy efficiency and renewable energy: GEF climate change projects and impacts*, Washington, DC: Global Environmental Facility.

OECD and IEA, 2010. *Energy poverty. How to make modern energy access universal?* Washington, DC: International Energy Agency; United Nations Development Programme; United Nations Industrial Development Organization.

Pachauri, S. and Jiang, L., 2008. The household energy transition in India and China. *Energy Policy*, 36(11), pp. 4022–4035.

Painuly, J.P., 2001. Barriers to renewable energy penetration: A framework for analysis. *Renewable Energy*, 24(1), pp. 73–89.

Palit, D., 2013. Solar energy programs for rural electrification: Experiences and lessons from South Asia. *Energy for Sustainable Development*, 17(3), pp. 270–279.

Pearson, N.O., 2012. Solar cheaper than diesel making India's Mittal believer. *Bloomberg*. Available at: www.bloomberg.com/news/articles/2012-01-25/solar-cheaper-than-diesel-making-india-s-mittal-believer-energy [accessed December 10, 2012].

Pereira, M.G., Camacho, C.F., Freitas, M.A.V. and Da Silva, N.F., 2012. The renewable energy market in Brazil: Current status and potential. *Renewable and Sustainable Energy Reviews*, 16(6), pp. 3786–3802.

Rai, S., 2004. Sustainable dissemination of solar home systems for rural development: Experiences in Nepal. *Energy for Sustainable Development*, 8(2), pp. 47–50.

REN21, 2015a. *Renewables 2015: Global status report*, Paris: Renewable Energy Policy Network for the 21st Century.

REN21, 2015b. Renewables international map. *Renewable Energy Policy Network for the 21st Century.* Available at: http://map.ren21.net [accessed May 29, 2015].

Sharif, M.N., 1989. Technological leapfrogging: Implications for developing countries. *Technological Forecasting and Social Change*, 36, pp. 201–208.

Shrimali, G. and Tirumalachetty, S., 2013. Renewable energy certificate markets in India: A review. *Renewable and Sustainable Energy Reviews*, 26, pp. 702–716.

Solano-Peralta, M., Moner-Girona, M., van Sark, W.G.J.H.M. and Vallvè, X., 2009. "Tropicalisation" of feed-in tariffs: A custom-made support scheme for hybrid PV/diesel systems in isolated regions. *Renewable and Sustainable Energy Reviews*, 13(9), pp. 2279–2294.

Sovacool, B.K., 2012. The political economy of energy poverty: A review of key challenges. *Energy for Sustainable Development*, 16, pp. 272–282.

Sovacool, B.K., 2013. A qualitative factor analysis of renewable energy and sustainable energy for all (SE4ALL) in the Asia-Pacific. *Energy Policy*, 59, pp. 393–403.

Sovacool, B.K. and Drupady, I.M., 2012. *Energy access, poverty, and development. The governance of small-scale renewable energy in developing Asia*, Farnham: Ashgate.

Terrapon-Pfaff, J., Dienst, C., König, J. and Ortiz, W., 2014. How effective are small-scale energy interventions in developing countries? Results from a post-evaluation on project-level. *Applied Energy*, 135, pp. 809–814.

Tukker, A., 2005. Leapfrogging into the future: Developing for sustainability. *International Journal of Innovation and Sustainable Development*, 1(1/2), p. 65.

United Nations, 2010. *Energy for a sustainable future. The Secretary-General's Advisory Group on Energy and Climate Change (AGECC)*, New York: United Nations.

United Nations, 2012. *Sustainable energy for all. A global action agenda. Pathways for concerted action towards sustainable energy for all*, New York: United Nations.

van der Gaast, W., Begg, K. and Flamos, A., 2009. Promoting sustainable energy technology transfers to developing countries through the CDM. *Applied Energy*, 86(2), pp. 230–236.

Wang, F., Yin, H. and Li, S., 2010. China's renewable energy policy: Commitments and challenges. *Energy Policy*, 38(4), pp. 1872–1878.

Weischer, L., Wood, D., Ballesteros, A., Fu-bertaux, X. 2011. *Grounding green power. Bottom-up perspectives on smart renewable energy policy in developing countries*, Washington, DC: The German Marshall Fund of the United States.

Wilkins, G., 2002. *Technology transfer for renewable energy: Overcoming barriers in developing countries*. Sustainable Development Programme (Royal Institute of International Affairs), ed., London: The Royal Institute of International Affairs.

Yu, X., Taplin, R. and Gilmour, A., 1997. Overseas market development: A strategy for Australian renewable energy industries. *Australian Geographer*, 28(2), pp. 159–171.

Yuan, X., Zuo, J. and Ma, C., 2011. Social acceptance of solar energy technologies in China: End users' perspective. *Energy Policy*, 39(3), pp. 1031–1036.

Zomers, A., 2003. The challenge of rural electrification. *Energy for Sustainable Development*, 7(1), pp. 69–76.

6 Trends in development cooperation

Introduction

Post-World War II development cooperation is complex and controversial. Since its evolvement in the 1960s, it has changed enormously. Debates about effectiveness, fragmentation or diversification accompany the development of the field. Following the emerging paradigm of sustainable development, donor-driven support has greened over the last decades. Promoting sustainable energy has become a major field of official development assistance (ODA) activities. Talking about donor-driven renewable energy support needs to reflect these major trends.

Diversification in development cooperation

Initially, only a handful of donors provided grants to a few aid-receiving countries. Today, the donor landscape has diversified, and development cooperation can be described as fragmented (Klingebiel et al. 2016). Over the decades, "new donors emerged, and developed countries created increasing numbers of aid partnerships" (Santiso and Frot 2013). The average number of donors per country has nearly tripled over the last 50 years, rising from about 12 in the 1960s to about 33 between 2001 and 2005 (Sindzingre 2012). In the 1960s, donors disbursed aid to fewer than 50 countries. At that time, every developing country received ODA from about two donors on average. In 2006, the number of recipient countries had more than doubled; each country was receiving aid from 28 donors on average (Santiso and Frot 2013). In 2009, 64 developing countries received aid from 25 donors per country; 16 to 24 donors were active in each of another 46 countries (OECD 2011, p. 5).

This general proliferation of donors is thought to have severe negative effects on the effectiveness of development projects (OECD 2005), project efficiency (Djankov et al. 2009) and the recipient countries' institutions (Knack and Rahman 2007) due to a higher chance for project duplication and corruption. The World Bank and the International Monetary Fund (IMF) warn that "when aid comes in too many small slices from too many donors, transaction costs go up and recipient countries have difficulty managing their own development agenda" (World Bank and IMF 2010, p. 131). The Organisation for Economic Co-operation and Development (OECD 2011, p. 3) adds that "a large number of donors with different and often uncoordinated management practices [...] places a heavy burden on the administrative capacity" of the partner countries, which are confronted with multiple donors' requirements and administrative procedures. According to Easterly (2007), donor agencies are not only unable to learn from their own previous experiences, but also fail in building up a strong knowledge management system that helps them to exchange experiences among each other. The lack of selectivity in a fragmented development cooperation landscape can be described as "the permanence of the status quo and repetition of past mistakes" (Sindzingre 2012, p. 34).

In response to rising criticism, the OECD donor community adopted the Paris Declaration on Aid Effectiveness in 2005, proclaiming the need for harmonization and coordination of development activities in order to improve their effectiveness (Annen and Moers 2012). The declaration calls for "a pragmatic approach to the division of labor and burden sharing [to increase] complementarity and [...] reduce transaction costs" (OECD 2005, p. 6). The Accra Agenda for Action underlines the commitment and urges donors to use "existing channels for aid delivery [...] before creating separate new channels that risk further fragmentation and complicate co-ordination at country level" (OECD 2008, p. 18).

Coordination and regular communication between donors are prerequisites to avoid unnecessary project duplication. Specialization, or *lead donorship*, can help to streamline efforts in a particular sector and/or a certain country (Steinwand 2015). This means that a particular donor is responsible for coordinating activities in a sector such as renewable energy development. Coordinating activities in line with the aid-receiving country's own efforts is also essential to respond to the recipient country's actual demand. This requires a strong authority in the developing country that is powerful enough to steer the donor organizations' activities. Learning and knowledge exchange, as well as monitoring and ex-post evaluations, are also crucial to avoid similar or even the same mistakes in later projects (implemented by the same or other donors). Fragmentation negatively affects sustainable learning from past experiences and mistakes (Easterly 2007; Sindzingre 2012; Steinwand 2015). Division of labor is another crucial factor to avoid ineffective aid. In practice, this means a certain degree of specialization among donors that matches donor country-specific competencies with the recipient country's demand. Despite these calls for better coordination, empirical studies reveal that donors largely fail to achieve their target to reduce aid fragmentation (Aldasoro et al. 2009; Nunnenkamp et al. 2011).

Negative effects of fragmentation occur "when there are too many donors giving too little aid to too many countries" (OECD 2014). This makes donor agencies less accountable to their intended beneficiaries (Easterly and Pfutze 2008). Smaller projects increase their administrative (overhead) costs, aid flows become non-transparent, and channels for ODA are ineffective in a more diversified donor landscape – with potentially less impact on economic growth or human development (Djankov et al. 2009; Kimura et al. 2012). Fragmentation can erode bureaucratic quality, overburden the institutional capacity and increase corruption (Knack 2006; Knack and Rahman 2007) due to the manpower and capacity needed for a large number of relatively small-scale project activities. Multiple donors' requirements and administrative procedures can be challenging for a recipient country with limited implementation capacities. Fragmented ODA makes it difficult for recipient countries to pursue their individual development agenda (World Bank and IMF 2010, p. 131). For the donor organizations, fragmentation leads to increasing transaction costs. At the same time, it leads to tied aid with positive effects only for the donor country (Knack and Smets 2013). Anderson (2012) estimates that bilateral donors could reduce their transaction costs by US$2.5 billion annually through greater specialization.

Positive effects of aid diversification are less pronounced, but are also part of the debate and are often referred to using the terms *pluralism* and *competition*. A certain degree of diversification is required to avoid monopolistic donor structures, when only one or a small number of donors control and monopolize a field of activity such as sustainable energy. Diversifying the donor landscape could avoid donors dictating which contractors are to be used and reduce issues of tying aid. More pluralistic development assistance can foster competition among donors and increase the recipient country's bargaining power – also to implement its own development agenda (Frot and Santiso 2009; Rogerson 2005). New non-Western donors such as China or India also hold the potential to increase competition among donors and provide alternative development concepts and strategies (O'Keefe 2009, p. 11).

Despite a vibrant debate on the general effects of aid diversification and global calculations about fragmentation, there is a lack of sector-specific case studies to provide empirical contributions to that rather abstract discussion. Empirical studies, especially in the environmental sector or with regard to renewable energy, are therefore desperately needed.

The importance of a multi-level approach

Critical debates about aid effectiveness are closely related to discussions about the challenges for upscaling results, project replication and the need for a so-called *multi-level approach* (Neumann-Silkow 2010). Such an approach acknowledges that modern development cooperation addresses development problems at multiple jurisdictional levels. Bi- and multilateral donors not only implement technology-specific demonstration projects at the local level, but also provide advisory activities to national or regional governments and related authorities. Programs and projects should lead to effects at different levels in the recipient country. Acknowledging the interplay between various levels of decision-making, local pilot projects need to be connected to national ministries to be successful and allow upscaling effects. According to Ohno and Ohno (2013, p. 156), German development cooperation differentiates between macro-level measures (e.g. regulatory frameworks or competitive environments), meso-level measures (e.g. institutional environment) and micro-level measures (e.g. inter-firm linkages and industrial human resources). The complex environment of development cooperation requires a conceptual framework for multi-level assessments in order to evaluate impact, trace structural effects or target the poor (Fritzen and Brassard 2007).

Concerning donor-driven renewable energy interventions, the United Nations Industrial Development Organization (UNIDO 2009) formulates a number of recommendations for their replication and potential for upscaling or diffusing results beyond the project's direct context. These include structural elements such as a supportive institutional and policy environment, market-oriented research and development, regional integration, networking with different stakeholder groups and capacity building, especially at the local level. The Dutch Ministry of Foreign Affairs (MOFAN 2013) outlines similar challenges for upscaling small-scale solar PV or biogas facilities within complex multi-level governance arrangements. Despite these rhetorical reflections and a general awareness of governance-related issues, donors do extraordinarily little to implement a multi-level approach in practice.

Greening development cooperation

Over the decades, sustainable development has replaced the aims of catch-up development and industrialization as the primary paradigm behind development cooperation. At least since the 1990s, the goal of development assistance has shifted from its narrow focus on economic growth towards the more holistic principle of – environmental, social and economic – sustainability. The United Nations Conference on the Human Environment in 1972 in Stockholm as well as the establishment of the United Nations Commission for Environment and Development in 1983 brought the topic of environmental development cooperation onto the international agenda. With the Rio Earth Summit in 1992 and its vision for an integrated global effort for environment and development, sustainable development became an integral part of development cooperation and a guiding principle (Bethge et al. 2011, p. 38) that emphasizes the nexus between poverty eradication and environmental protection.

The increase in international environmental regimes and commitments (Keohane and Levy 1996; Miles 2002; Victor 1998) has brought sustainability issues also to development cooperation, leading not only to more projects, but also to a critical debate on the role of development cooperation as such. "The issue of how foreign aid can damage or protect the global environment has been the source of protests, legislative debate, and reform efforts at development agencies around the world" (Hicks et al. 2008, p. v). The European Commission (2001, p. 4) developed extensive strategies to integrate environmental issues into its development assistance programs in order to better "respond to the environmental challenges" in developing countries. As one example, Japan has become a "global power in environmental aid" (Dauvergne 1998, p. 1) with about one-quarter of its ODA loans committed to environmental issues.

In their extensive volume *Greening Aid*, Hicks et al. (2008) evaluate the environmental impact of development cooperation around the world. Making the distinction between "green aid" and "dirty aid," they conclude that investments for environmental ODA more than tripled (from US$3 billion to about US$10 billion per year) between 1980 and 1999. At the same time, conventional development assistance remained relatively unchanged at about US$30 billion per year (Hicks et al. 2008, p. 247). Climate change and biodiversity activities were "increasing substantially" only at the end of the twentieth century, whereas desertification and land degradation were "largely neglected throughout the two decades" (Hicks et al. 2008, p. 247). Total commitments for annual environmental development assistance increased from approximately US$10 billion in 2000 to US$15 billion in 2008 (Buntaine and Parks 2013, p. 65). OECD statistical data reveals an average annual value of environmental ODA of US$25.4 billion between 2009 and 2010 (OECD-DAC 2012).

Despite these significant numbers, little is known about the actual impact of environmental ODA. "Indeed, available evidence suggests that externally funded projects focused on environmental protection are generally less successful than traditional development projects" (Buntaine and Parks 2013, p. 66) due to higher social and political demands for sustaining the projects. To be successful, environmental activities need sufficient governance capacity in the recipient countries and effective public sector institutions (Buntaine and Parks 2013; Ostrom et al. 2001). Evaluating the sustainability of donor-driven renewable energy projects, Terrapon-Pfaff et al. (2014) find positive outcomes at the local level, but also demand further research "if replication and dissemination are to be achieved" (Terrapon-Pfaff et al. 2014, p. 9).

The environmental projects' poor performance can also be related to the conceptual vagueness of sustainability. Post-development thinkers even go beyond this neutral interpretation and argue that sustainable development only justifies a further growth-oriented model of development by combining economic growth and the environment without acknowledging the development countries' contexts and demands (Escobar 2011). This stands in sharp contrast to the idea of a paradigm shift in development cooperation.

Promoting renewable energy

Promoting renewables has become a core topic in environmental ODA. Donors link their renewable energy activities to human development, or even frame them as a necessity for development as such (BMZ 2007, 2008; OECD 2012). For the United Nations (2010, p. 7), "clean, efficient, affordable and reliable energy services are indispensable for global prosperity." Donor-driven activities are either local activities such as solar mini grids or micro hydro projects related to rural development and household electrification (Ahlborg and Hammar 2012; Bambawale et al. 2011; Palit 2013; Palit and Chaurey 2011; Rai 2004; Schmidt et al. 2013; Zomers 2003) or advisory projects related to the energy sector, such as power sector reforms, capacity building or incentive structures for renewables (Niles and Lloyd 2013; Sihag et al. 2004; Welle-Strand et al. 2012; Williams 2001). Although development cooperation for renewables has expanded extraordinarily over the last years, little is known about its effectiveness and actual impact in developing countries. Robust evidence for the success of donor-driven renewable energy projects is scarce (MOFAN 2013, p. 14).

Sovacool (2013) differentiates between three consecutive paradigms of development cooperation for renewables: the "donor gift paradigm" (1970s–1990s) with technical demonstration projects, the "market creation paradigm" (1990s–2000s) demonstrating business models, and the "sustainable program paradigm" (mid-2000s till present) as a more holistic economic, social and institutional approach. Martinot et al. (2002) had already framed this development 10 years earlier as a shift from "donor aid" (for small-scale technologies such as biogas, wind turbines or solar heaters) to "sustainable markets" – with devastating results in its early phase. By the late 1980s, "donors had become disillusioned, and aid recipients had come to view renewables as second-class technologies that industrialized countries were unwilling to adopt themselves" (Martinot et al. 2002, p. 313). A lack of the donor projects' sustainability or replicability led to a stronger orientation towards the market. But even with increasing funding from multilateral donors such as the Global Environment Facility (GEF), the World Bank or the United Nations Development Programme (UNDP) for promoting the diffusion of renewable energy technologies and appropriate market designs "by removing key barriers related to skills, financing, institutional and business models, and policies" (Martinot et al. 2002, p. 314), the success of these efforts was limited and could not be replicated beyond the donors' activities. "Many projects were considered failures because of poor technical performance, and poor suitability to user needs and local conditions" (Martinot et al. 2002, p. 313).

Since social factors and human behavior seem to be more influential on the use of energy than technological design features, donor organizations are focusing more and more on economic and institutional conditions for renewables as well as the creation of enabling policy and regulatory frameworks (Weischer et al. 2011) rather than following a technology-based project-by-project approach. At the same time, donors still contribute with technology-specific pilot projects to programs such as the United Nations' Sustainable Energy for All (SE4ALL) initiative. The initiative aims to achieve universal access to modern energy sources, double the global rate of energy efficiency improvement and double the global share of renewables by 2030.

Donors are critical for financing the implementation of renewable energy projects, but they often struggle or fail to sustain these activities (Marquardt 2014). Success factors for donor activities are diverse and often context specific. Extensive empirical investigations identify aspects such as political will at various levels of decision-making, multi-stakeholder engagement, or access to training and finance as crucial success factors for specific renewable energy activities (Sovacool and Drupady 2012). As development projects cannot easily

tackle these structural elements, renewable energy solutions need to be established from within the developing country.

> Do not rely predominately on western consultants, foreign manufacturers,
> or expertise and knowledge from "outside" of a country. Instead, start by
> communicating directly with these that intend to use a particular energy
> service or technology from the "inside."
>
> (Sovacool and Drupady 2012, p. 297)

Electricity production enables growth and the development of other economic
sectors. Development cooperation related to energy sector reforms should therefore "contribute more effectively to positive development outcomes when combined with appropriate investments in other infrastructures and related services"
(Welle-Strand et al. 2012, p. 33). Donors should avoid individual technical demonstration projects and evaluating their success too narrowly by a certain number
of installed systems. By project completion, the amount of hardware installed is
much less significant than whether the business, delivery and credit models are
viable, sustainable and being replicated (Martinot et al. 2002, pp. 339–340).

References

Ahlborg, H. and Hammar, L., 2012. Drivers and barriers to rural electrification in Tanza-
nia and Mozambique: Grid-extension, off-grid, and renewable energy technologies.
Renewable Energy, pp. 1–8.
Aldasoro, I., Nunnenkamp, P. and Thiele, R., 2009. *Less aid proliferation and more donor
coordination? The wide gap between words and deeds*, Kiel: Kiel Institute for the World
Economy.
Anderson, E., 2012. Aid fragmentation and donor transaction costs. *Economics Letters*,
117(3), pp. 799–802.
Annen, K. and Moers, L., 2012. *Donor competition for aid impact, and aid fragmentation*,
Washington, DC: International Monetary Fund.
Bambawale, M.J., D'Agostino, A.L. and Sovacool, B.K., 2011. Realizing rural electrifica-
tion in Southeast Asia: Lessons from Laos. *Energy for Sustainable Development*, 15(1),
pp. 41–48.
Bethge, J.P., Steurer, N. and Tscherner, M., 2011. Nachhaltigkeit. Begriff und Bedeu-
tung in der Entwicklungszusammenarbeit. In J. König and J. Thema, eds. *Nachhaltigkeit
in der Entwicklungszusammenarbeit*. Wiesbaden: VS Verlag für Sozialwissenschaften,
pp. 15–40.
BMZ, 2007. *Sektorkonzept Nachhaltige Energie für Entwicklung. Strategiepapier des BMZ*,
Bonn: Bundesministerium für wirtschaftliche Zusammenarbeit und Entwicklung.
BMZ, 2008. *Entwicklung braucht nachhaltige Energie*, Bonn: Bundesministerium für wirtschaftliche Zusammenarbeit und Entwicklung.
Buntaine, M.T. and Parks, B.C., 2013. When do environmentally focused assistance pro-
jects achieve their objectives? Evidence from World Bank post-project evaluations.
Global Environmental Politics, 13(2), pp. 65–88.
Dauvergne, P., 1998. *The rise of an environmental superpower? Evaluating Japanese environ-
mental aid to Southeast Asia*, Canberra: Australian National University.

Djankov, S., Montalvo, J.G. and Reynal-Querol, M., 2009. Aid with multiple personalities. *Journal of Comparative Economics*, 37(2), pp. 217–229.

Easterly, W., 2007. Are aid agencies improving? *Economic Policy*, 22(52), pp. 633–678.

Easterly, W. and Pfutze, T., 2008. Where does the money go? Best and worst practices in foreign aid. *Journal of Economic Perspectives*, 22(2), p. 59.

Escobar, A., 2011. *Encountering development: The making and unmaking of the Third World*, Princeton: Princeton University Press.

European Commission, 2001. *Integrating the environment into EC economic and development co-operation*, Brussels: Commission of the European Communities.

Fritzen, S.A. and Brassard, C., 2007. Multi-level assessments for better targeting of the poor: A conceptual framework. *Progress in Development Studies*, 7(2), pp. 99–113.

Frot, E. and Santiso, J., 2009. *Crushed aid: Fragmentation in sectoral aid*, Stockholm: Stockholm School of Economics.

Hicks, R.L., Parks, B.C., Roberts, J.T. and Tierney, M.J., 2008. *Greening aid? Understanding the environmental impact of development assistance*, Oxford: Oxford University Press.

Keohane, R.O. and Levy, M.A., 1996. *Institutions for environmental aid: Pitfalls and promises*, Cambridge: MIT Press.

Kimura, H., Mori, Y. and Sawada, Y., 2012. Aid proliferation and economic growth: A cross-country analysis. *World Development*, 40(1), pp. 1–10.

Klingebiel, S., Mahn, T. and Negre, M., eds., 2016. *The fragmentation of aid: Concepts, measurements and implications for development cooperation*, London: Palgrave Macmillan.

Knack, S., 2006. *Donor fragmentation and aid effectiveness. Aid is more effectively delivered by fewer donors*, Washington, DC: World Bank.

Knack, S. and Rahman, A., 2007. Donor fragmentation and bureaucratic quality in aid recipients. *Journal of Development Economics*, 83(1), pp. 176–197.

Knack, S. and Smets, L., 2013. Aid tying and donor fragmentation. *World Development*, 44(January), pp. 63–76.

Marquardt, J., 2014. How sustainable are donor-driven solar power projects in remote areas? *Journal of International Development*, 26(6), pp. 915–922.

Martinot, E., Chaurey, A., Lew, D., Moreira, J.R. and Wamukonya, N., 2002. Renewable energy markets in developing countries. *Annual Review of Energy and the Environment*, 27(1), pp. 309–348.

Miles, E.L., 2002. *Environmental regime effectiveness: Confronting theory with evidence*, Cambridge: MIT Press.

MOFAN, 2013. *Renewable energy: Access and impact. A systematic literature review of the impact on livelihoods of interventions providing access to renewable energy in developing countries*, Den Haag: Ministry of Foreign Affairs of the Netherlands.

Neumann-Silkow, F., 2010. *Scaling up in development cooperation. Practical guidelines*, Eschborn: Gesellschaft für Technische Zusammenarbeit.

Niles, K. and Lloyd, B., 2013. Small island developing states (SIDS) and energy aid: Impacts on the energy sector in the Caribbean and Pacific. *Energy for Sustainable Development*, 17(5), pp. 521–530.

Nunnenkamp, P., Öhler, H. and Thiele, R., 2011. *Donor coordination and specialization: Did the Paris declaration make a difference?* Kiel: Kiel Institute for the World Economy.

O'Keefe, J., 2009. Aid: From consensus to competition. In L. Brainard and D. Chollet, eds. *Global development 2.0. Can philanthropists, the public, and the poor make poverty history?* Washington, D.C.: Brookings Institution Press.

OECD, 2005. *The Paris declaration on aid effectiveness*, Paris: Organisation for Economic Co-operation and Development.

OECD, 2008. *Accra agenda for action*, Paris: Organisation for Economic Co-operation and Development.

OECD, 2011. *2011 OECD report on division of labour: Addressing cross-country fragmentation of aid*, Paris: Organisation for Economic Co-operation and Development.

OECD, 2012. *Linking renewable energy to rural development*, Paris: Organisation for Economic Co-operation and Development.

OECD, 2014. Aid fragmentation and aid orphans. *Aid Architecture*. Available at: www.oecd.org/dac/aid-architecture/fragmentation-orphans.htm [accessed May 29, 2015].

OECD-DAC, 2012. *Aid in support of environment: Statistics based on DAC members' reporting on the environment policy marker, 2009–2010*, Paris: Organisation for Economic Co-operation and Development.

Ohno, K. and Ohno, I. eds., 2013. *Eastern and western ideas for African growth: Diversity and complementarity in development aid*, London: Routledge.

Ostrom, E., Gibson, C., Shivakumar, S. and Andersson, K., 2001. *Aid, incentives, and sustainability. An institutional analysis of development cooperation*, Stockholm: Swedish International Development Cooperation Agency.

Palit, D., 2013. Solar energy programs for rural electrification: Experiences and lessons from South Asia. *Energy for Sustainable Development*, 17(3), pp. 270–279.

Palit, D. and Chaurey, A., 2011. Off-grid rural electrification experiences from South Asia: Status and best practices. *Energy for Sustainable Development*, 15(3), pp. 266–276.

Rai, S., 2004. Sustainable dissemination of solar home systems for rural development: Experiences in Nepal. *Energy for Sustainable Development*, 8(2), pp. 47–50.

Rogerson, A., 2005. Aid harmonisation and alignment: Bridging the gaps between reality and the Paris reform agenda. *Development Policy Review*, 23(5), pp. 531–552.

Santiso, J. and Frot, E., 2013. Crushed aid: Why is fragmentation a problem for international aid? *VoxEU.org*. Available at: www.voxeu.org/article/crushed-aid-why-fragmentation-problem-international-aid [accessed March 30, 2015].

Schmidt, T.S., Blum, N.U. and Sryantoro Wakeling, R., 2013. Attracting private investments into rural electrification: A case study on renewable energy based village grids in Indonesia. *Energy for Sustainable Development*, 17(6), pp. 581–595.

Sihag, A.R., Misra, N. and Sharma, V., 2004. Impact of power sector reform on the poor: Case-studies of South and South-East Asia. *Energy for Sustainable Development*, 8(4), pp. 54–73.

Sindzingre, A., 2012. *Theoretical criticism and policy optimism: Assessing the debate on foreign aid*, Vienna: Institute of Development Studies, University of Vienna.

Sovacool, B.K., 2013. A qualitative factor analysis of renewable energy and sustainable energy for all (SE4ALL) in the Asia-Pacific. *Energy Policy*, 59, pp. 393–403.

Sovacool, B.K. and Drupady, I.M., 2012. *Energy access, poverty, and development. The governance of small-scale renewable energy in developing Asia*, Farnham: Ashgate.

Steinwand, M.C., 2015. Compete or coordinate? Aid fragmentation and lead donorship. *International Organization*, 69(2), pp. 443–472.

Terrapon-Pfaff, J., Dienst, C., König, J. and Ortiz, W., 2014. A cross-sectional review: Impacts and sustainability of small-scale renewable energy projects in developing countries. *Renewable and Sustainable Energy Reviews*, 40, pp. 1–10.

UNIDO, 2009. *Scaling up renewable energy in Africa*, Vienna: United Nations Industrial Development Organization.

United Nations, 2010. *Energy for a sustainable future. The Secretary-General's Advisory Group on Energy and Climate Change (AGECC)*, New York: United Nations.

Victor, D.G., 1998. *The implementation and effectiveness of international environmental commitments: Theory and practice*, Cambridge: MIT Press.

Weischer, L., Wood, D., Ballesteros, A. and Fu-bertaux, X., 2011. *Grounding green power. Bottom-up perspectives on smart renewable energy policy in developing countries*, Washington, DC: The German Marshall Fund of the United States.

Welle-Strand, A., Ball, G., Hval, M.V. and Vlaicu, M., 2012. Electrifying solutions: Can power sector aid boost economic growth and development? *Energy for Sustainable Development*, 16(1), pp. 26–34.

Williams, R.H., 2001. Addressing challenges to sustainable development with innovative energy technologies in a competitive electric industry. *Energy for Sustainable Development*, 5(2), pp. 48–73.

World Bank and IMF, 2010. *Global monitoring report: The MDGs after the crisis*, Washington, DC: World Bank.

Zomers, A., 2003. The challenge of rural electrification. *Energy for Sustainable Development*, 7(1), pp. 69–76.

7 Energy transitions in Southeast Asia

Introduction

Brunei, Cambodia, Laos, Malaysia, Myanmar, Indonesia, the Philippines, Singapore, Thailand, Timor-Leste and Vietnam are far from being a set of similar or even homogeneous countries. Together they constitute Southeast Asia, a fascinating and ever-changing region that does not only attract attention from political scientists. Cultural diversity, political transformation processes and economic development, together with environmental threats and social conflicts, enable a broad range of studies for social scientists.

Governance challenges with an impact on energy transitions arise from rapid political change, power shifts and uncertainties combined with decentralization and democratization processes – especially in not yet fully consolidated political systems. Energy demand is increasing rapidly due to economic progress and impressive development success. Together with China and India, Southeast Asian countries are "shifting the centre of gravity of the global energy system to Asia" due to "a near tripling of the region's economy" (IEA 2013, p. 11), but not without massive environmental threats. Because most additional energy is predicted to come from coal, CO_2 emissions are expected to almost double by 2035, reaching 2.3 Gt. Donors have long promoted environmental protection and renewable energy project in the region, but with limited structural success so far. Exploration of the reasons for this needs to take into account the complexity of governance arrangements and political systems. When talking about energy transitions, it is necessary to consider sociopolitical issues such as corruption patterns, local autonomy, power distribution and interjurisdictional conflicts.

Renewable energy development in Southeast Asia

Electricity consumption varies greatly among Southeast Asian countries. Total electricity consumption is led by Thailand, Indonesia, Malaysia, Vietnam, the Philippines and Singapore, also known as the Association of Southeast Asian Nations (ASEAN)-6 countries. Among them, only the Philippines and Vietnam, and to a lesser extent Indonesia, have a considerable amount of renewables (including hydro) in their electricity mix. The overall energy mix is dominated by coal (Indonesia, the Philippines and Malaysia), oil and natural gas (Vietnam, Thailand and Singapore). The share of renewables is dominated by hydro and to some extent geothermal (Indonesia and the Philippines) or bio-fuels (Malaysia and Thailand), whereas solar power, wind power and tidal energy are only marginal. Figure 7.1 provides an overview of electricity consumption and the electricity mix in Southeast Asian countries.

Southeast Asia's future energy demand will have an enormous global impact. The region is considered to be "the next big growth engine in Asia" (Bower et al. 2012, p. v). The Asian Development Bank (ADB)'s (2013) *Energy Outlook for Asia and the Pacific* shows a high dependence on fossil fuels – with coal meeting the highest share of total primary energy demand (TPED) at 38.3 percent. New and renewable energy sources will represent the fourth largest source, with a share of 11.2 percent in 2030, still behind oil and natural gas. The potential in the Greater Mekong Subregion should allow hydro to grow by 5.2 percent annually despite political resistance (EIA 2013, p. 104).

Renewable energy sources are expected to grow by only 1.3 percent per annum until 2030 – more slowly than oil, coal and natural gas, and especially much more slowly than the overall energy demand in Asia and the Pacific, which will grow by 3.4 percent annually on average, reaching 11,593 TW/h in 2030. Energy demand is expected to increase from 492.1 million tons of oil equivalent (MTOE) in 2005 to 988.2 MTOE in 2030. EE Japan (2011) even expects an annual increase in final energy consumption between 2007 and 2030 at an average rate of 4.4 percent and an increase in demand from 375 MTOE to 1,018 MTOE, based on an assumed annual gross domestic product (GDP) growth rate of 5.2 percent. CO_2 emissions in Asia and the Pacific are expected to increase from about 10 billion tons in 2005 to almost 18 billion tons in 2030 (ADB 2013).

Southeast Asia is also expected to become a net energy importer in the future. Following China, India and the European Union, the region could become "the world's fourth-largest oil importer" (IEA 2013, p. 12). This rising dependency on fossil fuels puts pressure on ASEAN countries to foster renewable energy development "in order to diversify the energy mix and to decrease dependency on imported energy" (Ölz and Beerepoot 2010). Clean energy technologies could play a vital role in reducing energy dependency and negative environmental impacts. Despite positive effects such as air quality, local added-value, job opportunities and rural electrification, their role remains marginal in energy outlooks for the region –in both business-as-usual and alternative policy scenarios (ADB 2013; EE Japan 2011).

Southeast Asia's electricity demand is projected to more than triple from 37.9 MTOE in 2005 to 123.1 MTOE in 2030 (EE Japan 2011). Electricity generation is expected to increase from 506.3 TW/h (2005) to 1,618.4 TW/h (2030) with natural gas remaining the dominant energy source (ADB 2013). The IEA (2013, p. 11) also predicts an enormous increase in coal production. Its "relative abundance and affordability in the region" are expected to increase its share of electricity generation from about one-third in 2013 to almost one-half in 2035.

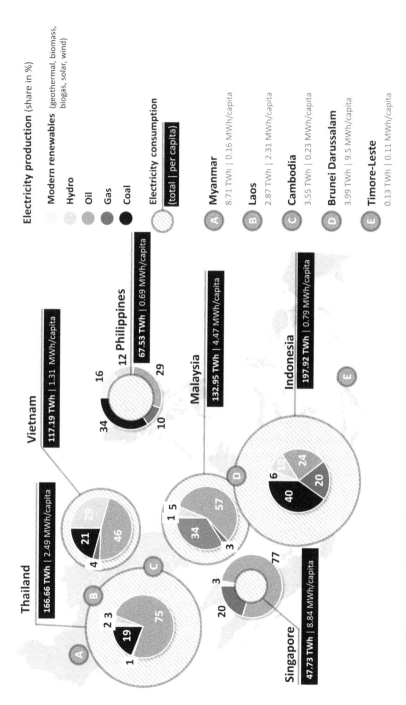

Electricity production (share in %)

Modern renewables (geothermal, biomass, biogas, solar, wind)
Hydro
Oil
Gas
Coal

Electricity consumption (total | per capita)

A Myanmar
8.71 TWh | 0.16 MWh/capita

B Laos
2.87 TWh | 2.31 MWh/capita

C Cambodia
3.55 TWh | 0.23 MWh/capita

D Brunei Darussalam
3.99 TWh | 9.5 MWh/capita

E Timore-Leste
0.13 TWh | 0.11 MWh/capita

Vietnam
117.19 TWh | 1.31 MWh/capita

Thailand
166.66 TWh | 2.49 MWh/capita

12 Philippines
67.53 TWh | 0.69 MWh/capita

Malaysia
132.95 TWh | 4.47 MWh/capita

Indonesia
197.92 TWh | 0.79 MWh/capita

Singapore
47.73 TWh | 8.84 MWh/capita

Figure 7.1 Electricity production and consumption in Southeast Asia (2013).

Source: illustration by the author based on IEA (2016) energy statistics.

While oil-fired electricity generation is expected to be replaced almost completely by coal, the total share of new and renewable energy sources increases only marginally from 3.9 percent in 2005 to 4.5 percent in 2030, although realizable and economically feasible renewable energy potential is high (about 1.8 times the total 2007 electricity consumption), especially for hydro power, but also for biomass, onshore wind, geothermal and solar photovoltaic (PV) (Ölz and Beerepoot 2010). Rapid economic growth is also likely to have negative effects on the region's ambitious renewable energy targets. The increase in modern renewable energy sources such as geothermal, solar and wind is offset by a reduced use of traditional biomass for cooking (IEA 2013, p. 11).

Policy frameworks for renewables vary greatly among Southeast Asian countries (Ölz and Beerepoot 2010). Looking at the economic heavyweights of the region (Indonesia, Malaysia, the Philippines, Singapore, Thailand and Vietnam), nearly all of them have set medium- and long-term targets for renewables and implemented supportive policy frameworks to attract private sector investments. Financial incentives exist in all six countries, with a clear focus on feed-in-tariffs, but also tax exemptions and capital cost grants as well as research and development. Malaysia, Indonesia and Thailand introduced additional non-financial support mechanisms such as standard power purchase agreements, preferential arrangements for small generators, and information support. Further non-economic barriers include infrastructure, grid connection and regulatory hurdles. Gaps in legal frameworks and a lack of authoritative institutions "continue to be a major impediment to the deployment of renewables" (Ölz and Beerepoot 2010, p. 11). And even if supportive legislations exist on paper, a lack of policy implementation remains a major barrier to renewable energy development.

Modern renewables have the potential to play an important role in rapidly developing subtropical and tropical archipelagos like the Philippines and Indonesia. Renewables that have already reached, or are close to, market competitiveness will most likely contribute to energy developments until 2030. To achieve large-scale diffusion, the International Energy Agency (IEA) recommends reducing non-economic barriers, removing distortionary subsidies for fossil fuels, ensuring the social acceptance of renewables, devising predictable and consistent policies, encouraging off-grid applications, promoting sustainable biofuel production, and establishing platforms for knowledge transfer (Ölz and Beerepoot 2010, pp. 10–11).

Energy transitions in the region

Despite positive global developments, achieving a major shift towards renewables in Southeast Asia remains an extraordinarily challenging task. Future energy demand in the region is expected to grow between 2.8 and 4.4 percent annually until 2030, but most added capacity is expected to come from fossil fuels.

> Since 1990, the region's energy demand has expanded two-and-a-half times. The fundamentals suggest that considerable further growth in demand can be

expected, especially considering that per capita energy use of its 600 million inhabitants is still very low, at just half of the global average.

(IEA 2013, p. 10)

The region's energy sector has developed significantly and electricity generation increased fourfold between 1990 and 2007, but targets and policy mechanisms for renewables are either weak or underdeveloped. Political factors influencing this development were underestimated over the last decades, but are highly significant for energy transitions – and their failure – in Southeast Asia. Discussion about the political dimension of energy transitions is often limited to financial incentive schemes and other support mechanisms. These discussions are unlikely to consider whether and how overarching governance frameworks or political developments such as decentralization or local empowerment affect energy transitions in the region.

As an exception, Smits (2015) links Southeast Asian energy transitions to debates about modernity. "Energy-modernity" is largely shaped by international and regional initiatives fostered by ASEAN, the ADB and the United Nations. These activities are embedded into regional plans and programs that aim to better connect the regional energy infrastructure and promote access to energy and rural electrification. Civil society actors and environmental groups all over the region advocate sustainable energy solutions by making a strong link between modern, decentralized and renewable forms of energy and their environmental and social benefits. Implementing renewable energy projects today could avoid lock-in into fossil fuel-based energy systems for decades. Renewables might also allow leapfrogging for substituting traditional energy sources such as biomass. Donors use these arguments when advocating the advantages of renewables (Meller and Marquardt 2013).

Despite increasingly relevant environmental movements, active communities, donor-driven activities, and more and more political incentives for renewables and energy efficiency, energy systems in Southeast Asia are far from being radically transformed. Fossil fuels still dominate most electricity regimes. Existing institutions, power structures, interests and market designs manifest the status quo of a stable fossil fuel-based system, in which renewables might provide some additional capacities but could not substitute for coal, oil and natural gas.

Southeast Asian countries have already witnessed numerous significant shifts in their energy systems. Looking at how people have used energy in everyday life and how patterns have changed over time, Smits (2015) shows how energy transitions in Southeast Asia have developed contingently and in a non-linear way together with economic and social progress. Over the decades, society and the energy sector have significantly influenced each other. Energy and development issues also fostered regional integration (Rigg 2003), with cross-border trading of electricity starting in the 1960s. Natural gas fundamentally changed energy systems when it entered into the markets 20 years later.

International organizations and donors pushed for deregulation and privatization of the energy sectors – with sometimes pervasive and partly devastating effects for renewables. Experiences from the Philippines have shown how electricity prices went up significantly and coal extraction massively expanded due to a more competitive electricity market design with weak political structures. Although donors widely promote clean and sustainable energy sources, an energy transition towards renewables has yet to come. Fossil fuels still dominate Southeast Asian electricity markets.

Donor-driven support for renewables

Bi- and multilateral donors and donor organizations such as the World Bank, the ADB, the Deutsche Gesellschaft für Internationale Zusammenarbeit (GIZ) and United States Assistance for International Development (USAID) have long promoted renewable energy development through pilot projects and advisory activities in Southeast Asia, a global "boom region" (Franz 2010) for renewables. Global trends towards a changing and greening development cooperation landscape also affect these interventions.

Donors support renewable energy technologies by either project-based investments or technical assistance and capacity building. Public finance mechanisms include loan guarantees, loan-softening programs and technical assistance grants. Project-based support and technology transfer need to be accompanied by measures to remove existing barriers and create an enabling environment for renewable energy. Although development cooperation "can play an effective role by supporting the implementation of coherent and comprehensive renewable energy policy frameworks and providing innovative co-financing options" (Ölz and Beerepoot 2010, p. 13), its actual impact remains hard to define.

Despite the donors' commitments to transparency, knowledge management, harmonization and exchange of experiences among each other to increase their overall effectiveness, it is impossible to provide a comprehensive and detailed overview of donor-driven activities related to renewables in Southeast Asia. Reporting, documenting and archiving standards vary greatly among donors and recipient countries alike. Beyond that, the donors' strategies and programs have also changed over time. Knowledge-sharing tools and initiatives such as *Energypedia* are constantly being developed, but cover only a fraction of energy-related activities. Research in this field, as well as extensive project evaluations or overarching program reports, especially from the 1980s or the 1990s, remain fragmented and rare (e.g. Ashworth 1985; Biermann et al. 1992; Böhnke 1992).

The web-based AidData (2016) database provides at least a rough overview of the numbers of donor-driven renewable energy projects. Based on the selection of all projects between 1955 and 2014 that match the keyword "renewable energy" and are located in Southeast Asia, three general conclusions can be drawn:

1   The number of activities promoting renewables has significantly proliferated over time. It has increased from two projects between 1955 and 1959, to 161 projects between 2005 and 2009, and 121 between 2010 and 2014.

Table 7.1 Donor-driven renewable energy projects in Southeast Asia

	1955–1959	1960–1964	1965–1969	1970–1974	1975–1979	1980–1984	1985–1989	1990–1994	1995–1999	2000–2004	2005–2009	2010–2014
Number of projects	2	4	10	28	34	49	24	60	69	82	161	121
ODA-receiving countries	2	3	5	7	5	6	5	7	7	8	9	9
Funding organizations	1	1	3	6	9	7	5	11	14	15	24	24
Total funding (in US$ billion)	0.421	0.798	0.731	1.900	4.000	4.900	2.100	6.800	6.300	2.600	2.300	0.749
Funding per project (in US$ million)	210.5	199.5	73.1	67.9	117.6	100.0	87.5	113.3	91.3	31.7	14.3	6.2

Source: data retrieved from AidData (2016).

2   The donor landscape has become more and more fragmented. The number of donors that are active in the field has increased substantially over time. This is accompanied by a more fragmented distribution of loans and grants, as a decrease in funding per project reveals.
3   The total amount of funding for renewable energy projects has surged, with a peak in the 1990s. Since then, there has been a considerable decline in commitments. A similar development can be seen concerning the average funding per project, showing a significant decrease over the last 15 years.

This reveals a more diversified landscape of donor activities with more and more project interventions at the national level (e.g. policy advice, institution-building, capacity development) that are less capital intensive than technical demonstration projects. Table 7.1 provides an overview of the information retrieved from AidData, showing how the numbers of projects, aid-receiving countries, donors, total amount of funding and funding per project developed between 1955 and 2014.

Development cooperation has promoted renewables in Southeast Asia for decades and has also diversified over that time. The focus has shifted from mainly local technology-specific demonstration projects towards more and more national advisory activities tackling electricity regime components such as policies, research and development, industries, or social and cultural aspects such as acceptance. Today, donors link their renewable energy activities to the broader context of an energy transition in the recipient countries. Following sustainable development as a leading paradigm, donor-driven renewable energy projects aim to combine environmental protection with economic development and social benefits.

References

ADB, 2013. *Energy outlook for Asia and the Pacific*, Manila: Asian Development Bank.
AidData, 2016. AidData 3.0. Open data for international development. Available at: http://aiddata.org/ [accessed March 30, 2016].
Ashworth, J.H., 1985. *Renewable energy systems installed in Asia: Current successes and the potential for future widespread dissemination*, Burlington: Associates in Rural Development.
Biermann, E., Corvinus, F., Herberg, T.C. and Höfling, H., 1992. *Basic electrification for rural households: GTZ's experience with the dissemination of small-scale photovoltaic systems*, Eschborn: Gesellschaft für Technische Zusammenarbeit.
Böhnke, H.-W., 1992. *Opening the PV market: The development of a rural photovoltaic electrification model in the Philippines*, Eschborn: Deutsche Gesellschaft für Technische Zusammenarbeit.
Bower, E.Z., Pumphrey, D.L., Poling, G.B. and Walton, M.A., 2012. *Sustainable energy futures in Southeast Asia*, Washington DC: Center for Strategies and International Studies.
EE Japan, ASEAN Centre for Energy & National ESSPA Project Teams, 2011. *The 3rd ASEAN Energy Outlook*, Tokyo: The Institute of Energy Economics, Japan.

EIA, 2013. *International energy outlook 2013*, Washington, DC: US Energy Information Administration.

Franz, S., 2010. *Renewable energy opportunities in South East Asia*, Berlin: Deutsche Energie-Agentur.

IEA, 2013. *Southeast Asia energy outlook. World energy outlook special report*, Paris: International Energy Agency.

Meller, H. and Marquardt, J., 2013. *Renewable energy in the Philippines: Costly or competitive? Facts and explanations on the price of renewable energies for electricity production*, Manila: Deutsche Gesellschaft für Internationale Zusammenarbeit (GIZ) GmbH.

Ölz, S. and Beerepoot, M., 2010. *Deploying renewables in Southeast Asia. Trends and potentials*, Paris: International Energy Agency.

Rigg, J., 2003. *The human landscape of modernization and development*, London: Routledge.

Smits, M., 2015. *Southeast Asian energy transitions. Between modernity and sustainability*, London: Routledge.

Part III

Setting the scene

Theory and analytical framework

8 The limits of development theory

Introduction

Donor-driven projects are intended to diffuse or scale up results beyond their direct context (Neumann-Silkow 2010; Terrapon-Pfaff et al. 2014). Donors link their activities to the broader goal of a sustainable energy system, although such a system and the transition to renewables are often only vaguely defined. Acknowledging the complexity of the political system is a prerequisite for understanding the challenges of an energy transition and donor-driven support for renewables. Classical development theory can be a starting point for investigating the relation between development activities and renewable energy development, but it falls short of elaborating on fundamental issues related to coordination and power.

More than six decades of modern post-World War II development cooperation has become the focus of a vast body of literature about its purpose, its effectiveness and the best way to achieve its goals. This chapter presents major debates and shifting paradigms in development theory and summarizes the dispute about a grand, universal theory of development. It critically reflects on development cooperation thinking with a focus on two main aspects: the emergence of sustainable development as a leading paradigm, and structural change as the key target of development assistance.

Shifting paradigms and the quest for effective aid

Since its introduction at the end of colonialism, development cooperation has changed fundamentally. In parallel, mainstream theories, paradigms, doctrines and concepts have further developed (Cowen and Shenton 1995; Nuscheler 2004). The history of development assistance and its theory is long, complex and full of breakages. Theory-building is politically and ideologically driven rather than neutral concerning its overarching goals (Akude 2011, p. 69). Key practical challenges such as the micro-macro paradox, sustainable development or upscaling are closely related to theoretical debates (Hauck 2014). Major paradigms such as pro-poor growth in the 1970s, neoliberal structural adjustment programs in the 1990s and sustainable development since the 2000s form the basis for understanding the theoretical development of the field.

The contested terms *development* and *development cooperation* refer to approaches to economic development in non-industrialized countries since the end of World War II. Starting with the paradigm of modernization in the 1950s, development was framed as industrialization and catch-up development. Developing countries strove to reach the economic level of industrialized nations. The corresponding big push theory (Nurkse 1953; Rosenstein-Rodan 1957) concentrated on the necessity to achieve economic growth as the basis for any kind of human development. Since poverty was not eradicated, but even increased during the 1970s, criticism of the modernization paradigm became stronger. Opposing modernization, authors such as Evers and Wogau (1973) and Senghaas (1997) expressed the view that development politics leads to structural heterogeneity and increasing contradictions between the modern and the traditional sectors. These dependence theorists argued that capitalist economies in developing countries (periphery) lack a strong domestic market and therefore remain dependent on industrialized countries (metropolitan economies). This calls for an endogenous domestic market-oriented development, independent of the world market (Leys 1996, p. 12). Claiming that not development alone, but development of the poor, should be the primary goal of development politics, the idea of basic needs became the mainstream paradigm for development cooperation in the 1970s and 1980s (Streeten 1982). This concept was later enhanced with elements of participation and ownership (Uphoff and Cohen 1977) and further developed into people-centered development that criticizes the focus of development cooperation on economic growth and the lack of social and political elements (Korten 1990).

Despite these grassroots interpretations of development, political elites at that time still demanded economic growth and catch-up development (Rauch 2009, p. 71), laying the ground for neoliberal institutionalism. Liberal market designs were enforced in developing countries in the 1990s – pushing for deregulation, privatization, open markets, free movement of goods and capital (Körner et al. 1991; World Bank 1989), and other policy reforms "that all countries should adopt to increase economic growth" (WHO 2014). Known as the *Washington Consensus*, a new development paradigm had emerged, with structural adjustment programs (SAP) being initiated by the Bretton Woods Institutions.[1] Although a relatively small privileged elite was able to benefit from neoliberal institutions, the poor majority became even more excluded from social services such as health care and education (Rauch 2009, p. 71). Since then, development thinking has diversified, and a variety of competing paradigms frame the development discourse (Jakobeit et al. 2014). Current demands range from the creation and empowerment of democratic institutions (North 1992) to good governance (Faust 2005) and the realization of specific and measurable long-term development goals (United Nations 2000).

The idea of sustainable development entered the development theory discourse with a rather normative and teleological approach – having its origin in fundamental reports, such as *Limits to Growth* (Meadows 1973) and *Our Common Future* (WCED 1987), that stressed ecological aspects of development.

Environmental and sustainability issues have more and more "weakened the economic growth paradigm and given a boost to alternative and ecological economics" (Nederveen Pieterse 2009, p. 90). Global events such as the United Nations Conferences on Sustainable Development in 1992 and 2012 further strengthened the nexus between development and the environment (Methmann and Oels 2014).

Development cooperation has seen a constant struggle over concepts, new orientations and paradigm shifts (Jakobeit et al. 2014). Mainstream ideas often moved from one extreme to another. There is a pattern of radical shifts in the dominant schools rather than a process of gradual learning and development (Rauch 2009; Thiel 2001). In the light of global transformation processes and the development of a polycentric world order, the field is subject to constant (political) change (Jakobeit et al. 2014). Development practice and theory have developed over time in a mutually impacting way, with influence from political contexts as well as social sciences (Nederveen Pieterse 2009, p. 5).

Debates in development theory are closely related to aid effectiveness, but empirical evidence for the success of development cooperation is hard to measure. Official development assistance (ODA) activities are generally considered to be potentially effective at the local level but lacking in national, macro-level or structural effects. Most local-level or project-related studies dating back to the 1950s argue that aid had a positive impact, whereas there is still little evidence of positive effects at the macroeconomic level (Hermes and Lensink 2001). This phenomenon has long been described as the "micro-macro paradox" (Mosley 1987). In 1998, a landmark report by the World Bank challenged the micro-macro paradox, outlining that development assistance leads to growth, but its effectiveness depends on the recipient country's policy regimes (World Bank 1998). McGillivray et al. (2006) have surveyed the literature that has emerged in response to the World Bank report. Their results are sobering: "Some studies concluded that this relationship was negative, others concluded it was positive and others found no relationship at all. Aid either worked, or it didn't, it seemed" (McGillivray et al. 2006, p. 1045). Aid effectiveness literature failed "to show that there is a significantly positive effect of aid" (Doucouliagos and Paldam 2009). William Easterly (2007, p. 321) blames "its aspiration to a utopian blueprint" as the biggest problem of development cooperation.

Since the early 1990s, international donors have articulated the aim of streamlining their activities and improving their overall impact. Donors agreed to mutual principles such as ownership, alignment and harmonization (OECD 2008). In 2011, donor countries even proclaimed "a new consensus in development cooperation" (BMZ 2011) with their commitment to ownership, output orientation, inclusive development partnerships, transparency and accountability (OECD 2011). Protecting and regulating global public goods such as climate and fish stocks have become increasingly important (Ashoff and Klingebiel 2014).

Failure of a grand development theory

According to Schuurman (2000), three aspects characterized early development theory: (1) developing countries and their inhabitants were essentialized as homogeneous entities; (2) the strong belief in economic development and human progress remained unquestioned; (3) the nation state was the analytical frame of reference and essential for realizing progress. These widely acknowledged beliefs attracted more and more criticism, starting around the mid-1980s, and have lost their hegemonic status, "being replaced by a loose set of partly descriptive, partly heuristic notions" (Schuurman 2000, p. 7). Development scholars failed to deliver a unifying theoretical body for development studies, and some scholars even rejected the whole idea of development as such, which "stands like a ruin in the intellectual landscape" (Sachs 1992, p. 1).

After decades of shifting development paradigms and changing mainstream ideologies, the development theory discourse was overshadowed by a fundamental debate on the meaning and applicability of development theory in modern times. Menzel (1992) pronounced the failure of a grand, coherent and universal development theory that could explain or even predict patterns of development. He claimed that a macro-theory of development could not be applied to the diversity of settings and country contexts. Nuscheler (2001) and others strongly opposed Menzel's assumption, citing a need for broad development theories and concepts in the light of globalization. Their debate culminated in a wider discourse about the reassessment of development theory as such (Thiel 2001).

In his collection of essays about *The rise and fall of development theory*, Leys (1996) explains the failure of development theory to guide development cooperation by the increasing impact of globalization, which erodes national governmental capacities to effectively manage country-specific priorities. Complexities at the national and local levels need to be taken into account more seriously than before. This reflects a deeply fundamental shift in development thinking, from overarching meta-conceptual theories in the 1960s and 1970s to more empirically based country-specific approaches. As the relation between critical theory and development research has been re-established (Schuurman 2009), development studies have experienced a reinvention – even in the face of fundamental criticism towards development theory pronounced by post-development scholars. The field of development theory is more diverse than ever before, with constant debates, reinventions and paradigm shifts still to come.

Moving beyond development thinking

The plurality of competing theories related to development cooperation is characteristic of all human and social sciences. There are no nomological explanations or absolute generalizations. Nor can we easily contradict or falsify existing theories (Nohlen and Schultze 2009). Arguing that development theory has failed completely shows a rather teleological understanding of theory. This might be true in the sphere of the natural sciences, but political theory able to explain or predict mechanisms of development that can be repeated in different contexts or countries remains unrealistic. Human development is not an experiment under laboratory conditions. On the contrary, it involves human interactions that remain impossible to predict.

Universal theories may always fail to explain and predict social change. Still, theories are desperately needed as broad frameworks to classify, structure and compare phenomena. We should not strive for "grand theories," but rather, for theoretical approaches or frameworks that remain open to critical reflection, learning and alternative thinking (Thiel 2001). Instead of extracting a universal theoretical framework for analyzing energy transitions and donor-driven support, two fundamental normative objectives can be derived from development thinking that guide further theoretical reflections: the paradigm of sustainable development and the aim for structural change.

Human development goes far beyond economic growth. Even the World Bank calls for a "new paradigm for development" (Stiglitz 1998), defining it as economic *and* social transformation (Korten 1990). Economic growth might be a prerequisite for development, but it also needs further enabling social and political conditions to be successful (Nuscheler 2004). Facing the negative effects of industrialization and economic growth, such as environmental degradation or social inequalities, sustainable development has become a critical issue in development theory (Ziai 2006). This approach acknowledges certain limits of growth and goes beyond pure economic figures as indicators for development. Although it has become a guiding principle also for donors (BMZ 2008), its theoretical basis remains relatively weak, unclear and diffuse due to fundamental tensions between environment protection, social development and economic progress (Exenberger 2008).

Be it modernization, basic needs or sustainability, development paradigms emphasize that structural changes, rather than small-scale projects, matter. Mosley (1987), Stockmann (1997) and others revealed the shortcomings of local development activities and a conflict between their ambitious project goals and their actual outcomes. Development policy defines itself as a global structural policy (Klemp 2001). Poverty and other problems should not be eradicated through small-scale demonstration projects in a local context, but through broader programs, institutional changes and structural improvements (Tetzlaff 2005). Development cooperation not only aims to deliver locally successful projects, but is also intended to change overarching structures. This might exaggerate the potential of development projects (Rauch and Lohnert 2010). Advocating "homegrown development based on the dynamics of individuals and firms" Easterly (2007, p. 322) also dismisses widely planned development projects that seek to eradicate poverty. At the same time, the focus of interventions should be brought back to the poor and their needs rather than bureaucracies and other structures.

Modern development thinking is dominated by a discourse between catch-up development and sustainable development, with arguments from different theoretical schools and paradigms. Such a controversial and complex context calls for theory that is capable of guiding research about donor-driven interventions – a theory that is not a mathematical formula, but that helps to clarify the role of political systems in development projects. Such a theory needs to cover and reduce complexity at the same time as it reflects the multiple structures, interactions and power relations found in a complex political environment, and insights from outside development theory can make a fruitful contribution to the field.

Multi-level governance provides a helpful framework for analyzing the links between national and subnational decision-making bodies. They shape the development of a country's energy sector and heavily influence energy-related development assistance. Energy systems were established over decades and require both vertical and horizontal forms of coordination. Any attempt to change the status quo of the system will typically encounter high barriers and requires substantial efforts at various jurisdictional levels. Structural changes cannot be understood without analyzing the distribution of power and power-related struggles in the political system. Power needs to be considered not only in terms of resources such as constitutional, regulatory or political power. It also needs to include the ability or capacity to make use of these resources. Integrating power-related aspects into the multi-level governance framework represents a promising approach for better understanding energy transitions in developing countries and the role of development cooperation.

Knowing the multidimensional political context should be a prerequisite before implementing any development project. This is especially important for countries with complex political systems, high levels of uncertainty and institutional shortcomings, and that have gone through radical transformation processes. Developing countries with different institutional settings and political systems demonstrate that local authorities hold substantial power to block or change the implementation of national energy policies. Power relations and capacities in central–local relations are crucial to renewable energy development. This needs to be reflected in any theoretical framework dealing with donor-driven interventions.

Note

1 The World Bank, the International Bank for Reconstruction and Development, and the International Monetary Fund were established in Bretton Woods, New Hampshire, in 1945.

References

Akude, J.E., 2011. Theorien der Entwicklungspolitik. Ein Überblick. In J. König and J. Thema, eds. *Nachhaltigkeit in der Entwicklungszusammenarbeit*, Wiesbaden: VS Verlag für Sozialwissenschaften, pp. 69–94.

Ashoff, G. and Klingebiel, S., 2014. Transformation eines Politikfeldes: Entwicklungspolitik in der Systemkrise und vor den Herausforderungen einer komplexeren Systemumwelt.

In C. Jakobeit et al., eds. *Entwicklungstheorien: Weltgesellschaftliche Transformationen, entwicklungspolitische Herausforderungen, theoretische Innovationen*, Baden-Baden: Nomos, pp. 166–199.

BMZ, 2008. *Auf dem Weg in die Eine Welt. Weißbuch Entwicklungspolitik*, Bonn: Bundesministerium für wirtschaftliche Zusammenarbeit und Entwicklung.

BMZ, 2011. Busan: A new consensus in development cooperation. *Bundesministerium für wirtschaftliche Zusammenarbeit und Entwicklung*. Available at: www.bmz.de/en/press/ aktuelleMeldungen/2011/December/20111201_pm_220_busan/index.html [accessed April 20, 2012].

Cowen, M. and Shenton, R.W., 1995. *Doctrines of development*, London: Routledge.

Doucouliagos, H. and Paldam, M., 2009. The aid effectiveness literature: The sad results of 40 years of research. *Journal of Economic Surveys*, 23(3), pp. 433–461.

Easterly, W., 2007. *The white man's burden: Why the west's efforts to aid the rest have done so much ill and so little good*, Oxford: Oxford University Press.

Evers, T. and von Wogau, P., 1973. "dependencia": Lateinamerikanische Beiträge zur Theorie der Unterentwicklung. *Das Argument*, 79, pp. 404–454.

Exenberger, A., 2008. *Wachstum – Umwelt – Entwicklung*, Wien: Mandelbaum.

Faust, J., 2005. Good Governance als entwicklungspolitisches Zielsystem: Verteilungskonflikte und Koordinationsprobleme im Transformationsprozess. In D. Messner and I. Scholz, eds. *Zukunftsfragen der Entwicklungspolitik*, Baden-Baden: Nomos, pp. 159–170.

Hauck, G., 2014. Die Aktualität der "großen" entwicklungspolitischen Debatten der 1970er/80er Jahre. In F. Müller, E. Sondermann, I. Wehr, C. Jakobeit and A. Ziai, eds. *Entwicklungstheorien: Weltgesellschaftliche Transformationen, entwicklungspolitische Herausforderungen, theoretische Innovationen2*, Baden-Baden: Nomos, pp. 352–380.

Hermes, N. and Lensink, R., 2001. Changing the conditions for development aid: A new paradigm? *Journal of Development Studies*, 37(6), pp. 1–16.

Jakobeit, C., Müller, F., Sondermann, E., Wehr, I. and Ziai, A., 2014. Einleitung. In F. Müller, E. Sondermann, I. Wehr, C. Jakobeit and A. Ziai, eds. *Entwicklungstheorien: Weltgesellschaftliche Transformationen, entwicklungspolitische Herausforderungen, theoretische Innovationen*, Baden-Baden: Nomos, pp. 5–40.

Klemp, L., 2001. Entwicklungspolitik am Scheideweg: Politische Randerscheinung oder globale Strukturpolitik? *Aus Politik und Zeitgeschichte*, 18–19, pp. 13–20.

Körner, P., Maaß, G. and Siebold, T., 1991. *Im Teufelskreis der Verschuldung: Der Internationale Wahrungsfonds und die Dritte Welt*, 2nd ed., Hamburg: Junius.

Korten, D.C., 1990. *Getting to the 21st century: Voluntary action and the global agenda*, West Hartford: Kumarian.

Leys, C., 1996. *The rise and fall of development theory*, Oxford: James Currey.

McGillivray, M., Feeny, S., Hermes, N. and Lensink, R., 2006. Controversies over the impact of development aid: It works; it doesn't; it can, but that depends.... *Journal of International Development*, 18(7), pp. 1031–1050.

Meadows, D.H., 1973. *The limits to growth : A report for the Club of Rome's project on the predicament of mankind*, New York: Universe Books.

Menzel, U., 1992. *Das Ende der Dritten Welt und das Scheitern der grossen Theorie*, Berlin: Suhrkamp.

Methmann, C. and Oels, A., 2014. Ein neues Klima für Entwicklung? Die Ökologische Gouvernementalität der Entwicklungspolitik. In C. Jakobeit et al., eds. *Entwicklungstheorien: Weltgesellschaftliche Transformationen, entwicklungspolitische Herausforderungen, theoretische Innovationen*, Baden-Baden: Nomos, pp. 464–487.

Mosley, P., 1987. *Overseas development aid: Its defence and reform*, Brighton: University Press of Kentucky.

Nederveen Pieterse, J., 2009. *Development theory: Deconstructions/reconstructions*, Thousand Oaks: Sage.

Neumann-Silkow, F., 2010. *Scaling up in development cooperation. Practical guidelines*, Eschborn: Gesellschaft für Technische Zusammenarbeit.

Nohlen, D. and Schultze, R.-O., 2009. *Lexikon der Politikwissenschaft Bd. 1: A-M: Theorien, Methoden, Begriffe*, 4th ed., München: Beck.

North, D.C., 1992. *Institutionen, institutioneller Wandel und Wirtschaftsleistung*, Tübingen: Mohr Siebeck.

Nurkse, R., 1953. *Problems of capital formation in underdeveloped countries*, Oxford: Blackwell.

Nuscheler, F., 2001. Warum brauchen wir Entwicklungstheorien? In R. Thiel, ed. *Neue Ansätze zur Entwicklungstheorie*, Bonn: Deutsche Stiftung für internationale Entwicklung (DSE). Informationszentrum Entwicklungspolitik (IZEP), pp. 389–399.

Nuscheler, F., 2004. *Lern- und Arbeitsbuch Entwicklungspolitik*, Berlin: Dietz Verlag J.H.W. Nachf.

OECD, 2008. *The Paris declaration on aid effectiveness and the Accra agenda for action*, OECD, ed., Paris: Organisation for Economic Co-operation and Development.

OECD, 2011. *The Busan partnership for effective development co-operation*, Paris: Organisation for Economic Co-operation and Development.

Rauch, T., 2009. *Entwicklungspolitik. Theorien, Strategien, Instrumente*, Braunschweig: Westermann.

Rauch, T. and Lohnert, B., 2010. Live Aid – Dead Aid – Better Aid? Die Neuerfindung der Entwicklungszusammenarbeit. *Geographische Entwicklungsforschung*, (10), pp. 46–50.

Rosenstein-Rodan, P.N., 1957. *Notes on the theory of the "big push"*, Cambridge: Center for International Studies, Massachusetts Institute of Technology.

Sachs, W., 1992. *The development dictionary: A guide to knowledge as power*, London: Zed Books.

Schuurman, F.J., 2000. Paradigms lost, paradigms regained? Development studies in the twenty-first century. *Third World Quarterly*, 21(1), pp. 7–20.

Schuurman, F.J., 2009. Critical development theory: Moving out of the twilight zone. *Third World Quarterly*, 30(5), pp. 831–848.

Senghaas, D., 1997. *Peripherer Kapitalismus. Analysen über Abhängigkeit und Unterentwicklung*, München: Suhrkamp.

Stiglitz, J.E., 1998. Towards a new paradigm for development. Strategies, policies and processes. 9th Raúl Prebisch Lecture, UNCTAD, (October), p. 34. Available at: http://unctad.org/en/Docs/prebisch9th.en.pdf [accessed May 29, 2015].

Stockmann, R., 1997. The sustainability of development projects: An impact assessment of German vocational-training projects in Latin America. *World Development*, 25(11), pp. 1767–1784.

Streeten, P., 1982. *First things first: Meeting basic human needs in the developing countries*, Oxford: Oxford University Press.

Terrapon-Pfaff, J., Dienst, C., König, J. and Ortiz, W., 2014. How effective are small-scale energy interventions in developing countries? Results from a post-evaluation on project-level. *Applied Energy*, 135, pp. 809–814.

Tetzlaff, R., 2005. Armutsbekämpfung durch globale Entwicklungspolitik. *NORD-SÜD aktuell*, 2, pp. 228–238.

Thiel, R., 2001. Einleitung. Zur Neubewertung der Entwicklungstheorie. In R. Thiel, ed. *Neue Ansätze zur Entwicklungstheorie*. Bonn: Deutsche Stiftung für internationale Entwicklung, Informationszentrum Entwicklungspolitik, pp. 9–34.

United Nations, 2000. United Nations Millennium Declaration (A/res/55/2).

Uphoff, N.T. and Cohen, M.J., 1977. *Rural development participation. Concepts and measures for project design. Implementation and evaluation*, Ithaca: WAERSA, Cornell University.

WCED, 1987. *Our common future*, New York: World Commission On Environment and Development.

WHO, 2014. Washington consensus. *Trade, foreign policy, diplomacy and health*. Available at: www.who.int/trade/glossary/story094/en/ [accessed August 19, 2014].

World Bank, 1989. *Adjustment lending: An evaluation of ten years of experience*, Policy and Research Series, Washington, DC: World Bank.

World Bank, 1998. *Assessing aid: What works, what doesn't, and why*, Washington, DC: World Bank.

Ziai, A., 2006. *Zwischen Global Governance und Post-Development. Entwicklungspolitik aus diskursanalytischer Perspektive*, Münster: Westfälisches Dampfboot.

9 Taking a multi-level governance perspective

Multi-level governance and central–local relations

Although a variety of scholars consider multi-level governance a theory (Piattoni 2010; Stephenson 2013) or combine it with other theories in multi-level systems (Benz et al. 2009), it is applied here in its basic sense as a framework for mapping complexity in governance systems. Taking advantage of its conceptual, analytical and theoretical openness (Brunnengräber and Walk 2007, p. 19), multi-level governance is used as a starting point for constructing a theoretical framework. Taking a multi-level governance perspective means understanding political decision-making as a process of coordination between different jurisdictional levels, rather than autonomous forms of government within these levels. This approach allows the scale and functionality of mechanisms for coordination between at least partly interdependent levels in complex governance systems to be investigated (Benz et al. 2009).

Rhodes (2000, pp. 56–61) identifies at least seven separate definitions and types of governance, but the term is used here in its rather simple meaning of "binding decision-making in the public sphere" (Marks and Hooghe 2004, p. 15). Governance describes "the sum of regulations [...] designed to remedy a public problem via a collective course of action" (Enderlein et al. 2011, p. 2). An energy transition clearly describes such a public problem, as the participating actors "claim to act in the name of a collective interest or the common good," that is, for environmental protection, rural electrification, energy security or – combining multiple aims – sustainable development. Governance covers the actors, processes and structures that shape political decision-making (Enderlein et al. 2011, pp. 2–3). This is particularly relevant for governments and their changing role "in the coordination process of different social systems" (Eckerberg and Joas 2004, p. 406).

> Governance refers to sustaining coordination and coherence among a wide variety of actors with different purposes and objectives such as political actors and institutions, corporate interests, civil society, and transnational organizations. What previously were indisputably roles of government are now increasingly seen as more common, generic, societal problems which can be resolved by political institutions but also by other actors.
>
> (Pierre 2000, pp. 4–5)

Changes in central–local relations are key to multi-level governance concepts, which hold the potential to capture "the dispersion of central government authority both vertically to actors located at other territorial levels, and horizontally to non-state actors" (Bache and Flinders 2004). Even a state-centered perspective cannot overlook the role of various non-state actors in interactions across jurisdictional levels. "Subnational governmental authorities are all the more successful at claiming greater powers from their national governments the more they can plausibly demonstrate that they represent their local civil society" (Piattoni 2010, p. 266). Stating the nation state's declining institutional strength, Pierre (2000, p. 1) defines "the erosion of traditional bases of political power" as the core element of governance. Policy outcomes are not the result of actions taken by the central government alone; they reflect interactions between the national government and local authorities as well as other actors during the implementation process (Rhodes 1996, p. 657).

Multijurisdictionality

Differentiating between various jurisdictional levels is a key concept behind multi-level governance. These levels refer to political-territorial, administrative units with defined vertical hierarchies or horizontal coordination (Brunnengräber and Walk 2007, p. 18) in which the defined and undefined processes of decision-making – such as institutional arrangements, interactions and efforts of coordination – are the starting point for any empirical analysis. Multi-level governance arrangements are linked to a number of advantages: multiple jurisdictions can facilitate the credibility of policy commitments (Majone 1997; Pollack 1997), competition between jurisdictions can foster effective governance (Frey and Eichenberger 2004; Weingast 1995) and multijurisdictional arrangements improve learning, innovation and experimentation (Gray 1973).

Hooghe and Marks (2001) differentiate between two types of multi-level governance arrangements: whereas type 1 describes "territorially mutually exclusive jurisdictions in a relatively stable system with limited jurisdictional levels and a limited number of units," type 2 refers to rather "specialized, territorially overlapping jurisdictions in a relatively flexible, non-tiered system with a large number of jurisdictions" (Hooghe and Marks 2001, p. 1). Investigating the interplay between different jurisdictional levels of government in a developing country means looking at a type 1 multi-level governance system with non-intersecting jurisdictions at any particular territorial scale. Each level is responsible for policies, provides a court system and bundles representative institutions.

Type 1 governance systems are general-purpose jurisdictions. Decision-making powers are distributed across a limited number of jurisdictional levels and involve only a small number of packages. "The membership boundaries of such jurisdictions do not intersect" (Marks and Hooghe 2004, p. 16). A member of one jurisdiction cannot hold membership of another jurisdiction. Competencies are bundled at just a few territorial levels, where power is shared "among a limited number of governments" (Hooghe and Marks 2003). Jurisdictional levels can be distinguished between a central, an intermediate and a local level (John 2001). These jurisdictions "form part of a systemwide plan" (Hooghe and Marks 2003) whereby governance structures are systematically institutionalized and guarantee a system-wide, durable architecture, for example through a legislature, an executive and a court system at the national and subnational levels.

Coordination between various jurisdictional levels is a key interest for multi-level governance scholars, but also the primary dilemma in multi-level governance systems, where the need for coordinating multiple jurisdictions can increase transaction costs. "To the extent that policies of one jurisdiction have spillovers (i.e. negative or positive externalities) for other jurisdictions, so coordination is necessary to avoid socially perverse outcomes" (Hooghe and Marks 2003). The more jurisdictions are involved in a decision-making process, the higher are the costs for coordination. Defectors become harder to control or to sanction, and problems related to free riding become more likely. Such a perception draws on Scharpf's (1997, p. 70) law about the conditions for interjurisdictional coordination: "As the number of affected parties increases [...] negotiated solutions incur exponentially rising and eventually prohibitive transaction costs." To minimize the coordination dilemma, Hooghe and Marks (2003) propose to bundle competencies together to gain "the benefits of varying territorial scale while minimizing the number of jurisdictions that have to be coordinated." Such a formation of multi-level governance systems can emerge from bottom-up or top-down processes, and often leads to "nested institutional structures" (Paavola 2007, p. 99).

Development cooperation and multi-level governance

As multi-level governance arrangements emerge, and the relation between local governments and a central government become increasingly important, policy-making and implementation related to the environment and sustainable development are "becoming more and more complex and diversified" (Eckerberg and Joas 2004, p. 409). Multi-level governance is widely used for public policy fields such as energy or climate, and provides a useful framework for investigating "structural transformations" (Piattoni 2010, p. 17) such as energy transitions. The approach is particularly helpful for understanding the multidimensionality of structural change and sustainable development beyond single development projects or environmental innovations (Anderson and Tushman 1990; Christensen 1997; Hekkert et al. 2007) within complex governance arrangements.

At the same time, multi-level governance can be narrowed down to a practical modeling instrument for specific activities, making it a useful analytical tool for development interventions (Neumann-Silkow 2010). Donor-driven renewable energy projects either are implemented at the local level (e.g. solar mini grids as a demonstration project in remote areas) or promote supportive conditions for renewables at the national level (e.g. through policy advice for a feed-in tariff system). At both levels, donors intend to trigger structural change beyond the actual project boundaries through paths of upscaling, diffusion, learning or institutionalizing outcomes. Taking a multi-level governance perspective provides an analytical framework for elaborating on the patterns of interaction between jurisdictional levels that also determine the potential for structural effects from development cooperation.

Transformative change heavily depends on sociotechnical innovations or local initiatives that function as role models for change and further development. Development projects are widely considered at least to have the potential to be these models for system innovations. This perspective can be found not only in mainstream development theories such as modernization (e.g. Anderson 2012) or institution-building approaches (e.g. Rondinelli 1992), but even among fundamental development cooperation critics such as post-development scholars (e.g. Rahnema and Bawtree 1997, p. 381). A much-discussed question within this discourse remains whether and how any local- or national-level development project can achieve this ideal of a model with potential for scaling up or diffusing results beyond its project environment.

Also taking a multi-level perspective, sustainability transitions research largely reflects on the relation between niche experiments (e.g. innovative renewable energy projects), the regime context (e.g. the electricity system) and broader landscape conditions (e.g. the political system or market structure). There is no doubt that concepts such as transition management also hold the potential for better understanding the link between systemic or structural change and donor-driven interventions (Marquardt 2015). Yet, the multi-level perspective and multi-level governance cannot and should not be mixed up here. Both approaches apply distinct analytical categories and conceptualize terms such as "levels" in a fundamentally different way. To avoid confusion, this chapter concentrates on multi-level governance.

Multi-level governance helps to better understand the relation between local-level projects and their national-level environment, and vice versa. This approach can inform development cooperation about obstacles and challenges to upscaling and diffusing results in the recipient country's complex political system. These insights could eventually contribute to a fundamental critique of development cooperation, with its small-scale projects but large-scale ambitions, also known as the "micro-macro paradox" (Mosley 1987). More precisely, multi-level governance seems to be a promising starting point for better understanding the complex governance systems for renewables in developing countries and for analyzing the role of development projects.

Literature that links sustainability topics such as water supply (Barbosa and Brusca 2015), resilience (Larsen et al. 2011), climate change (Bisaro et al. 2010) or health (Ciccone et al. 2014) to multi-level governance frameworks in developing countries is sparse. Scholars investigate innovation processes (Daniell et al. 2014), conceptualize stakeholder agency (Larsen et al. 2011) or shed light on the challenges for multi-level coordination (Chang Seng 2013). Probably the strongest link between multi-level governance and development cooperation can be seen in development projects that promote decentralization (Bardhan 2002; Litvack et al. 1998; Manor 1999; Shiraishi 2014).

Donors promote decentralized governance structures to empower local governments, strengthen the role of non-governmental organizations or foster democratization. If designed well, decentralization "can have significant repercussions for resource mobilization and allocation and ultimately for macroeconomic stability, service delivery, and equity" (Litvack et al. 1998, p. v). Not surprisingly, international donors often describe decentralization as one of their major goals (Shiraishi 2014). According to Marks and Hooghe (2004, p. 22), decentralization includes fiscal (independent forms of taxation and spending), regulatory (formal power to overrule subnational decisions) and political elements (election of local governments). Sixty-three out of 75 developing countries went through some form of decentralization of authority (Garman et al. 2001, p. 205). They have "given way to new forms of governing" (Marks and Hooghe 2004, p. 15), underlining the need for a multi-level governance perspective.

A framework for renewable energy development

Multi-level governance might not provide a coherent concept, or even a theory, but it acts as a promising starting point for analyzing renewable energy development. The approach is used here in its rather narrow definition, concentrating on the differentiation between a limited number of jurisdictional levels that are involved in the decision-making process, relevant actors and their interaction with each other. Energy transitions represent a relevant field for a multi-level governance analysis due to their complexity, the number of competing interests and the role of externalities spreading across different levels. A multi-level perspective is also taken in development cooperation, which promotes renewables not only at national, but also at subnational levels. Structural effects beyond a project's context represent a major concern in development thinking – and are closely related to multi-level governance structures.

Theories related to multi-level governance need to illuminate the functional logic (rules, institutions, actors and patterns of interaction) and mechanisms behind governance (Benz et al. 2009). Institutions and actors at various jurisdictional levels shape decision-making related to renewable energy development. How they interact with each other depends on various social mechanisms. These mechanisms deliver information about the processes and patterns of interaction behind a specific system. Such an approach raises three fundamental questions: (1) How are different levels of government involved in renewable energy policy-making and implementation? (2) What are the relevant actors and institutions at various administrative levels? (3) How do levels and actors interact with each other (conflicts and coordination)?

Figure 9.1 summarizes the basic idea behind the use of multi-level governance as a framework for renewable energy development. Identifying relevant actors at the national and subnational levels, as well as their patterns of interaction, is the first step for understanding and analyzing governance structures that shape renewable energy development. Being clearly defined as type I

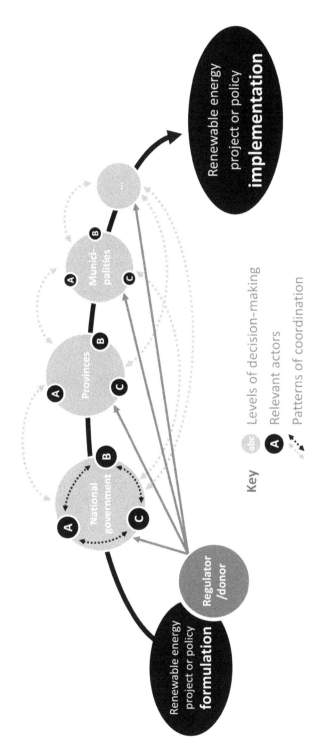

Figure 9.1 Renewable energy development from a multi-level governance perspective.

Source: illustration by the author.

governance, the national, provincial and municipal levels are particularly interesting. Further subnational levels, as well as the international dimension, are excluded here due to the field's overwhelming complexity.

Issues of power play a central role in complex governance arrangements, but are weakly conceptualized in multi-level research. Incorporating insights from power theory and ideas about power in central–local relations into the multi-level governance framework provides a promising approach to better understanding not only development cooperation for renewables, but also the relevant governance structures in the recipient country.

References

Anderson, I., 2012. *Scaling up development results: A literature review and implications for Australia's aid program*, Canberra: Commonwealth of Australia.

Anderson, P. and Tushman, M.L., 1990. Technological discontinuities and dominant designs: A cyclical model of technological change. *Administrative Science Quarterly*, 35, pp. 604–633.

Bache, I. and Flinders, M., 2004. *Multi-level governance*, Oxford: Oxford University Press.

Barbosa, A. and Brusca, I., 2015. Governance structures and their impact on tariff levels of Brazilian water and sanitation corporations. *Utilities Policy*, 34, pp. 94–105.

Bardhan, P., 2002. Decentralization of governance and development. *Journal of Economic Perspectives*, 16(4), pp. 185–205.

Benz, A., Breitmeier, H., Schimank, U. and Simonis, G., 2009. *Politik in Mehrebenensystemen*, Wiesbaden: VS Verlag für Sozialwissenschaften.

Bisaro, A., Hinkel, J. and Kranz, N., 2010. Multilevel water, biodiversity and climate adaptation governance: Evaluating adaptive management in Lesotho. *Environmental Science and Policy*, 13(7), pp. 637–647.

Brunnengräber, A. and Walk, H., 2007. *Multi-Level-Governance. Klima-, Umwelt- und Sozialpolitik in einer interdependenten Welt*, Baden-Baden: Nomos.

Chang Seng, D.S., 2013. Tsunami resilience: Multi-level institutional arrangements, architectures and system of governance for disaster risk preparedness in Indonesia. *Environmental Science and Policy*, 29, pp. 57–70.

Christensen, C., 1997. *The innovator's dilemma: When new technologies cause great firms to fail*, Boston: Harvard Business School Press.

Ciccone, D.K., Vian, T., Maurer, L. and Bradley, E.H., 2014. Linking governance mechanisms to health outcomes: A review of the literature in low- and middle-income countries. *Social Science and Medicine*, 117(0), pp. 86–95.

Daniell, K.A., Coombes, P.J. and White, I., 2014. Politics of innovation in multi-level water governance systems. *Journal of Hydrology*, 519, pp. 2415–2435.

Eckerberg, K. and Joas, M., 2004. Multi-level environmental governance: A concept under stress? *Local Environment*, 9(5), pp. 405–412.

Enderlein, H., Wälti, S. and Zürn, M. eds., 2011. *Handbook on multi-level governance*, Cheltenham: Edward Elgar.

Frey, B.S. and Eichenberger, R., 2004. *The new democratic federalism for Europe: Functional, overlapping and competing jurisdictions*, Cheltenham: Edward Elgar.

Garman, C., Haggard, S. and Willis, E., 2001. Fiscal decentralization. A political theory with Latin American cases. *World Politics*, 53(2), pp. 205–236.

Gray, V., 1973. Innovation in the States: A diffusion study. *The American Political Science Review*, 67(4), pp. 1174–1185.

Hekkert, M.P., Suurs, R.A.A., Negro, S.O., Kuhlmann, S. and Smits, R.E.H.M., 2007. Functions of innovation systems: A new approach for analysing technological change. *Technological Forecasting and Social Change*, 74(4), pp. 413–432.

Hooghe, L. and Marks, G., 2001. Types of multi-level governance. *European Integration Online Papers*, 5(11). Available at: http://eiop.or.at/eiop/texte/2001-011a.htm [accessed August 16, 2016].

Hooghe, L. and Marks, G., 2003. Unraveling the central state, but how? Types of multi-level governance. *American Political Science Review*, 97(02), pp. 233–243.

John, P., 2001. *Local governance in Western Europe*, London: Sage.

Larsen, R.K., Calgaro, E. and Thomalla, F., 2011. Governing resilience building in Thailand's tourism-dependent coastal communities: Conceptualising stakeholder agency in social-ecological systems. *Global Environmental Change*, 21(2), pp. 481–491.

Litvack, J., Ahmad, J. and Bird, R., 1998. *Rethinking decentralization in developing countries*, Washington, DC: The International Bank for Reconstruction.

Majone, G., 1997. From the positive to the regulatory state: Causes and consequences of changes in the mode of governance. *Journal of Public Policy*, 17(2), pp. 139–167.

Manor, J., 1999. *The political economy of democratic decentralization*, Washington, DC: World Bank.

Marks, G. and Hooghe, L., 2004. Contrasting visions of multi-level governance. In I. Bache and M. Flinders, eds. *Multi-level governance*. Oxford: Oxford University Press.

Marquardt, J., 2015. How transition management can inform development aid. *Environmental Innovation and Societal Transitions*, 14, pp. 182–185.

Mosley, P., 1987. *Overseas development aid: Its defence and reform*, Brighton: University Press of Kentucky.

Neumann-Silkow, F., 2010. *Scaling up in development cooperation. Practical guidelines*, Eschborn: Gesellschaft für Technische Zusammenarbeit.

Paavola, J., 2007. Institutions and environmental governance: A reconceptualization. *Ecological Economics*, 63, pp. 93–103.

Piattoni, S., 2010. *The theory of multi-level governance. Conceptual, empirical, and normative challenges*, Oxford: Oxford University Press.

Pierre, J., 2000. Introduction: Understanding governance. In J. Pierre, ed. *Debating governance authority, steering and democracy*. Oxford: Oxford University Press, pp. 1–10.

Pollack, M.A., 1997. Delegation, agency, and agenda setting in the European Community. *International Organization*, 51(1997), pp. 99–134.

Rahnema, M. and Bawtree, V., 1997. *The post-development reader*, London: Zed Books.

Rhodes, R.A.W., 1996. The new governance: Governing without government. *Political Studies*, 44, pp. 652–667.

Rhodes, R.A.W., 2000. Governance and public administration. In J. Pierre, ed. *Debating governance authority, steering and democracy*. Oxford: Oxford University Press.

Rondinelli, D.A., 1992. *Development projects as policy experiments: An adaptive approach to development administration*, London: Routledge.

Scharpf, F.W., 1997. *Games real actors play: Actor-centered institutionalism in policy research*, Boulder: Westview.

Shiraishi, K., 2014. Decentralization and local governance for sustainable development. In K. Ueta and Y. Adachi, eds. *Transition management for sustainable development*. Tokyo: United Nations University Press, pp. 234–248.

Stephenson, P., 2013. Twenty years of multi-level governance: "Where does it come from? What is it? Where is it going?" *Journal of European Public Policy*, 20(6), pp. 817–837.

Weingast, B.R., 1995. The economic role of political institutions: Market-preserving federalism and economic development. *Journal of Law, Economics, and Organization*, 11(1), pp. 1–31.

10 Integrating power theory

Introduction

Concepts of power are central to energy transitions and the role of development cooperation. If we understand power as "the production of causal effects" and the "transformative capacity" hold by human agents to produce effects (Scott 2001, p. 1), its conceptualization should provide answers to the question of how development assistance affects renewable energy development and how donor agencies push or make use of the transformative power in a given governance arrangement.

Multi-level analytical frameworks such as multi-level governance and the multi-level perspective in transitions studies have been criticized for ignoring power-related aspects (Geels 2010; Hendriks and Grin 2007; Shove and Walker 2007, 2008; Voß et al. 2007). This stands in sharp contrast to empirical findings from around the world. Incorporating power into reflections about energy transitions should therefore not only be empirically fruitful, but also further advance theoretical discussions in the field (Smith and Stirling 2005).

Concepts of power

Energy transitions can be studied from various angles by different disciplines. Every approach is underpinned by ontologies, that is, foundational assumptions about the nature of the (social) world and its causal relations (Burrell and Morgan 1979; Collins 1994; Ritzer 1980). Collective actors with conflicting interests are the causal agents in power theory approaches (Mahoney 2004); conflict and power struggles between them are the core causal mechanism (Geels 2010). Combining power theory with multi-level governance implies investigating how collective actors at different jurisdictional levels compete with each other and shape outcomes related to renewables.

Power is probably one of the most critical and "essentially contested" (Lukes 1995, p. 26) concepts in political science. Definitions of power are extraordinary diverse. They depend on the context and vary greatly when it comes to aspects related to agency, interests, discourses and resources (Haugaard 2002, p. 1). "It seems as if there are as many definitions and approaches as there are power analysts" (Arts and van Tatenhove 2004, p. 346). Lasswell and Kaplan (1950, p. 75) describe the political process as "the shaping, distribution, and exercise of power."

Weber (1978, p. 53) defines power as "the probability that one actor within a social relationship will be in a position to carry out his own will despite resistance, regardless of the basis on which this probability rests." Scott (2001, p. 3) summarizes the key dialectic behind power as "the exercise of power and the possibility of resistance to it [...], a balance of power that limits the actions of the participants in their interplay with each other." Quiescence and rebellion are the key terms of power for Gaventa (1980); Bacharach and Lawler (1980) distinguish between authority (formal rights, structures, sanctions) and influence (personal dynamics, expertise, tactics). For Parsons (1967, p. 331), power is "conceived as a generalized medium of mobilizing commitments or obligation for effective collective action" that "depends on the institutionalization of authority." Whereas elite power theorists such as Schattschneider (1960), Mills (1956) and Putnam (1976) focus their attention on how power is concentrated among elites, pluralists such as Bachrach and Baratz (1962), Gaventa (1980) and Lukes (1995) investigate how power is distributed among actors, leading to power struggles and conflicts. Framing political power as dispersed and highly fragmented makes political decisions the product of bargaining and compromise between different groups. Energy transitions can be conceptualized as the result of "a struggle between plural interest groups" (Avelino and Rotmans 2009, p. 547).

Various power concepts distinguish between different faces, dimensions or circuits of power. Dahl (1957) criticized the ruling elite model by presenting a pluralistic explanation of who rules politics in the United States. He argued that political power is shared among various groups in broad decision-making processes. Adding a "second dimension of power," Bachrach and Baratz (1962) highlighted the role of agenda-setting by elites and their ability to keep aspects off the agenda. Consequently, not only decisions but also non-decisions as well as potential political issues, are the result of power struggles. Lukes (1995) further developed that perspective by adding a third face of power that considers processes of preference-shaping. Not only can issues be kept off the agenda; they can even be prevented from emerging in people's minds when actors shape the preferences and interests of others through efforts of manipulation, information, or the propagation of specific norms and values. Power can then be defined as the ability to get someone else to do something that he/she would otherwise not have done (Lukes 1995). Beyond these "three faces," power can be understood either as conflictual and as the result of (violent) power struggles (Mann 2002), or as consensual, with negotiations and a consensus as a necessary condition of power (Parsons 2002). Clegg (1989) differentiates between episodic, dispositional and facilitative forms of power (circuits).

Whereas instrumental interpretations view power as "actor-specific resources used in the pursuit of self-interests" (Avelino and Rotmans 2009, p. 546) even against resistance (power of one actor over another), structuralists highlight the role of structures, institutions and processes that already determine options and alternatives for decision-makers. Investigating "the ability that actors have to facilitate certain things" (Scott 2001, p. 6) is central to structuralists' analyses. Morris (2002, p. 299) claims that "everything that needs to be said about power can be said by using the idea of the capacity to affect outcomes." If "power is, at root, a capacity" (Scott 2001, p. 5), it can be conceptualized as "the capacity of actors to mobilize resources to realize a certain goal" (Avelino 2011, p. 69).

Three dimensions of power

The complex phenomenon of power can be analyzed from various angles. Three dimensions of power seem to be most relevant for understanding energy transitions: resources, capacities and structures. The power to achieve outcomes depends on hard and soft resources (money, political power, agenda-setting, framing), the capacity to make use of these resources (knowledge, personnel, money) and the macrosocietal structure of a policy setting (governance framework). The policy arrangement approach (Arts and van Tatenhove 2000; Van Tatenhove et al. 2000) helps us to understand the interplay between all three dimensions.

A policy arrangement can be described as "the ordering of a specific policy field in terms of agents, resources, rules and discourses" (Arts and van Tatenhove 2004, p. 341) that influences decision-making. Policy decisions are the result of the interplay between structural changes (political modernization) and day-to-day practice (policy innovation). To analyze substantial characteristics of a policy arrangement (like an electricity system), Arts and van Tatenhove (2004) stress the role of power. Similarly to Scott's (2001, p. 4) differentiation between holding power (resources) and exercising power (capacities), Arts and van Tatenhove (2004, p. 343) distinguish between "the asymmetrical distribution of resources in a society" (dispositional power) and "the ability of actors to mobilise resources in order to achieve certain outcomes in social relations" (relational power). A structural dimension of power describes overarching arrangements that structure a decision-making process. These three layers of power are an important inspiration for this book. Adapted to the context of this research, *dispositional power* is linked to hard and soft power resources, *relational power* relates to capacities and *structural power* refers to broader governance structures.

Power depends on resources (first dimension of power)

Mobilizing resources is essential for agents to be able to achieve certain outcomes (Arts and van Tatenhove 2004, p. 346). In line with the three faces of power (Lukes 1995), resources include not only hard – and obvious – resources such as financial or political power, but also soft resources such as the power of arguing and persuasion. "Policy agents may become influential not only by organizational resources, like money, personnel, tactics, but also by arguments and persuasion, or by both" (Arts and van Tatenhove 2004, p. 347). Any actor's autonomy or dependency in a certain position is determined by the division of resources.

Rhodes (1986) distinguishes between five sets of resources that provide a useful categorization for analyzing interjurisdictional relations: *constitutional-legal resources* (formally granted by constitution), *regulatory resources* (administrative rules, control, enforcement), *financial resources* (expenditure, taxes, grants, borrowing), *political resources* (public support, representation), and *professional* or *informational resources* (skills, material, land). These resources fundamentally shape competition, conflicts and cooperation among actors (Bacharach and Lawler 1980). Whereas constitutional, regulatory and political resources are considered to be hard resources for decision-making, financial and professional resources should be used, rather, as forms of capacity that enable agents to make use of their resources to achieve outcomes.

Beyond these hard power resources, less obvious, but nonetheless important, soft forms of power resources influence the decision-making process. Although mainly discussed in international relations (Keohane and Nye 1998; Nye 1990, 2005), soft power resources also shape domestic policy-making. They include factors that cover decision-making and "control over the agenda of politics and of the ways in which potential issues are kept out of the political process" (Lukes 1995, p. 25), such as *agenda-setting* (bringing topics on or keeping them off the agenda) and *framing* (associating and linking certain aspects with a topic).

Power depends on capacities (second dimension of power)

The distribution of resources in a given system does not say a lot about the power relations between agents and their ability to achieve certain outcomes in a specific decision-making process. Giddens (1984) argues that power goes far beyond the mere existence and accumulation of resources. He explains the duality of power by describing power as something that is both a quality of resource and also a social factor influencing resources (Sadan 1997, p. 38).

Capacities describe an agent's ability to make use of available power resources (Polsby 1963, pp. 3–4). The capacity of agents to achieve outcomes is not equivalent to their resources (Keohane and Nye 1989). As long as actors are not able to make effective use of their resources, they cannot execute power. Investigating resources alone is thus not sufficient to analyze power relations. Although Arts and van Tatenhove (2004, p. 350) prefer the term *relational power* over *capacity* or *agent power*, capacity is used here for aspects such as knowledge, skills or personnel. These are also framed as forms of capacity in development cooperation when it comes to projects for or capacity development.

Personnel capacity (staff, skills, training, education), *information capacity* (data) and *financial capacity* (funds) are the main categories used here. One can clearly see the link and overlaps between power resources and capacities. Money, skills or knowledge could also be considered as resources, showing that a sharp distinction between resources and capacities is not always possible and depends on the context. Gaventa (1980, pp. 14–16) distinguishes between three mechanisms of power (observable resources, rules of the game, power process). Both resources and capacities could be described as "observable resources" that shape the decision-making process. The ability to inform, communicate or even manipulate other agents' bias towards a specific topic such as renewables would fall into Gaventa's second and third dimensions of power.

Power depends on macrosocietal structures (third dimension of power)

Beyond the availability of resources and the ability of agents to make use of these resources in order to influence policy outcomes in one or the other direction, power is embedded into overarching historical and societal structures, institutions and discourses. These macrosocietal structures "enable and constrain certain types of behaviour more than others" (Arts and van Tatenhove 2004, p. 347). For Weber (1978), "structures of domination" based on the unequal distribution of political authority, social contexts and economic resources form the essential context for exercising power. Structural power refers to "the way macro-societal structures shape the nature and conduct of agents [due to an] uneven access to the constitution and use of resources" (Arts and van Tatenhove 2004, pp. 350–351). Such a perspective underlines that power also relates to interdependencies between actors and levels that are involved in a decision-making process due to structural elements.

Two categories of structural power summarize the elements of interest in multi-level governance systems: *jurisdictional levels* (i.e. national, provincial and local authorities involved in the decision-making process) and *central–local relations* (conflicts, competition and coordination between agents at different levels).

Power in central–local relations

For decades, local government issues were rather underresearched and weakly theorized. In 1980, "the comparative study of local government, in its widest sense, has not existed and does not exist" (Rhodes 1980a, p. 563). Since then, researchers have invested substantial efforts in central–local government relations (Boddy 1983; Hinings et al. 1985; Rhodes 1980b), decentralization (Rondinelli et al. 1989; Schneider 2003) and multi-level governance (Bache and Flinders 2004; Enderlein et al. 2011; Hooghe and Marks 2003). Yet, systematic and comparative frameworks and concepts for analyzing these relations are relatively rare – and mostly limited to industrialized countries (Blom-Hansen 1999; Elander 1991; Rhodes 1999). Agranoff (2013) and Laffin (2009) link the topic of central–local relations to issues of (multi-level) governance and detect a "changed nature of these relations in an era of govern-ance" (Laffin 2009, p. 35) due to increasingly important local bureaucracies and networks.

Investigating central–local relations requires asking for the local govern-ments' share and influence in a country's national governmental decision-making, and vice versa. Relevant factors are not easy to conceptualize, and even quantifiable indicators such as expenditure are hard to measure (Elander 1991, p. 33). In addition to this, central–local relations may vary from one policy area to another. Rhodes (1986, pp. 98–111) developed a resource-based framework for analyzing central–local relations in Great Britain by making use of a power–dependence framework and defining a local authority's dependency upon a central department "to the extent that it needs the resources controlled by the department and cannot obtain them elsewhere" (Rhodes 1986, p. 99). No matter how powerful a central department might be, to some degree it depends on local authorities. To understand the relative power of interaction between central and local authorities, it is important to analyze "the avail-ability, distribution and substitutability of resources" (Rhodes 1986, p. 100). The relation between the goals of central and local authorities is another factor influencing political decision-making. Rhodes (1986, p. 103) describes goal-setting as a constrained political process in which central departments might "view a local authority's goals as 'illegitimate' and deny it needed resources," forcing local authorities to negotiate their goals. In contrast, domain consensus should lead to better access to needed resources – such as subsidies for renewables.

Interests, expectations and values form the appreciative system of decision-makers that "influences the goals pursued, perceptions of what is a problematic relationship and the definition of the resources required" (Rhodes 1986, p. 104). Central–local relations thus depend not solely on resources, but also on the decision-makers' perceptions. Similar local and national appreciative systems explain why local authorities accept central interventions. Central–local rela-tionships also cover more procedural perspectives, including rules of the game and strategies of agents. Although these rules can be extensive and hard to specify, it is important to stress "that such rules do exist" (Rhodes 1986, p. 103). The agents' strategies "for imposing upon the other level of government its pref-erences concerning the time of, the conditions for, and the extent of the exchange of resources" (Rhodes 1986, p. 106) sheds light on these (often unwritten) rules of the game for political decision-making. Discretion, defined as "the room for decisional manoeuvre possessed by a decision-maker," is another important factor that influences central–local relations (Rhodes 1986, p. 108).

Power and decentralization

Defined as "the transfer of authority and responsibility for public functions from the central government to subordinate or quasi-independent government organizations" (Shiraishi 2014, p. 234), decentralization has significantly shaped central–local relations in numerous developing countries. Decentralized political structures together with local empowerment are considered to be an important prerequisite for democracy, good governance and sustainable development (Bakir 2009; Jessop 2007; Pierre and Stoker 2000). Donors such as the World Bank (Litvack et al. 1998) and the United Nations Development Programme (UNDP 1999) actively pushed reforms towards decentralized statehood from the early 1990s, calling it "a fashion of our time" (Manor 1999, p. 1). Despite its vague conceptualization, expectations related to decentralization are extraordinarily high when scholars argue that decentralized government frameworks can deliver policies more effectively and more efficiently (Oates 1972; Tiebout 1956; Weingast 1995). Critical studies warn against an overhasty and widespread devolution of power to subnational authorities. They point out perverse macroeconomic incentives, lack of local expertise, increasing patronage, subnational authoritarianism and a lack of citizen information (Cornelius et al. 1999; Davoodi and Zou 1998; Rodden 2005; Rodden and Wibbels 2002; Samuels 2003; Treisman 2007).

UNDP (1997, pp. 5–6) distinguishes between various arrangements of decentralization. Whereas "devolution" describes a shift of functions from the central government to autonomous lower-level units or the creation of new units of government outside its direct control, "delegation" leads to semi-autonomous lower-level units that are either under indirect government control or semi-independent. "Deconcentration" encompasses the transfer of authority by administrative means to subordinate lower-level units or subunits under the same jurisdictional authority of the central government. "Divestment" or privatization can be seen as a fourth form of decentralization that shifts power to organizations outside the formal government structure, such as non-governmental organizations (NGOs) or corporations. A more power-related differentiation distinguishes between fiscal (tax collection and expenditures), political (the extent to which political decisions reflect the multiplicity of citizen interests) and administrative (the power of political institutions to turn policy decisions into allocative and distributive outcomes) decentralization (Manor 1999; UNDP 1999). Although power is obviously inherent in concepts of decentralization, the process does not necessarily lead to powerful local authorities if they do not have the capacity to use certain legislative resources or are not aware of them. Decentralization can even expand a central government's power and resources due to the absolute increase in political control (Falleti 2005; Mcconaughey 2013).

Power and multi-level governance

Energy transition can be understood as a power struggle between an existing (stable) regime structure (in favor of fossil fuels) and upcoming competing interests together with contesting sociotechnological innovations (renewables). Although power struggles are an intrinsic part of transition processes (Grin

2010), explicit power-related references are marginal and a "conceptual weakness" (Avelino and Rotmans 2009, p. 545) in energy transitions literature. Framing and agenda-setting as well as the role of veto players and responsibilities for policy implementation are inextricably linked to questions of power, resources and capacities. Governance and multi-level governance handbooks highlight this connection, but often fall short of stressing it explicitly (Benz et al. 2009). Or, in other words, power is "often neglected in the governance literature" (Arts and van Tatenhove 2004, p. 340).

In complex multi-level governance systems, power resources and capacities can vary greatly across different levels. Veto players can block decisions; competition and conflicting interests shape policy outcomes. Power and agency depend on the membership of sociotechnical regimes, resource interdependencies between actors, and expectations about future sociotechnical developments (Smith et al. 2005). Resources that are required to induce significant sociotechnical change (i.e. to rewrite the rule sets) are unevenly distributed across different actors and levels. For the field of energy transitions, some researchers already incorporate power theories into their empirical investigations, but these efforts remain rather exceptional (Nastar and Ramasar 2012).

Summary

Power theories enhance our understanding of the role of structures, agency and resources when it comes to decision-making in complex multi-level governance arrangements. There is no doubt that power matters, but it needs to be explicitly conceptualized in multi-level governance research so that it can be systematically investigated. Analyzing central–local relations is a complex, multilayered process. The framework developed here needs to reduce that complexity with the help of manageable analytical categories. Political decision-making in central–local relations depends on resources, goals, interests, expectations and values, processes of exchange, and strategies as well as discretion. Central–local relations have substantial effects on the potential for scaling up and diffusing results from development projects.

Theoretical concepts about central–local relations and decentralization are clearly related to power. They emphasize the distribution of resources, the ability to use these resources, and the balance of power between different jurisdictional levels within a political system. The power-based multi-level governance framework developed here takes into account the roles of systemic and structural developments (decentralization), institutional arrangements (multi-level governance framework) and different forms of power (resources and capacities). Table 10.1 summarizes the three main dimensions of power that are expected to shape energy transitions and donor-driven support.

Development theory is considered to be ineffective in providing plausible and generalizable explanations or predictions for successful developments and structural changes initiated by donor-driven interventions. Taking a multi-level governance perspective allows us to investigate the effects of development

Table 10.1 Three dimensions of power: structures, resources, capacities

Power dimension	Macrosocietal structures	Resources	Capacities
Key question	What are the relevant governance structures for decision-making related to renewable energy development?	How are power resources distributed among different jurisdictional levels?	How is the ability to make use of power resources distributed among different jurisdictional levels?
Focus of analysis	Governance structures	Distribution of resources	Ability to mobilize resources
Elements of interest	Jurisdictional levels • national government • provincial government • municipal government Central–local relations • interjurisdictional coordination • conflicts/cooperation	Hard power resources • constitutional resources • regulatory resources • political resources Soft power resources • agenda-setting • framing	Capacities • trained staff • financial capacity • information

Source: compiled by the author.

cooperation by looking at political decision-making as a process of coordination between different jurisdictional levels. The approach provides a fruitful analytical framework for exploring the scale and functionality of mechanisms for coordination between at least partly interdependent levels of government, but often remains silent about power relations, which do shape energy transitions and need to be explicitly theorized.

Distinguishing between different dimensions, power covers the asymmetric distribution of resources in a society, the ability of actors to mobilize these resources in order to achieve certain outcomes in social relations, and the overarching structures that determine societal interactions and decision-making. Figure 10.1 schematically outlines the analytical framework that incorporates power into multi-level governance.

Acknowledging the complexity of governance arrangements and coordination across jurisdictional levels as well as the distribution of resources and capacities, the framework should help to better understand how power in its various forms shapes energy transitions in developing countries. Shedding light on these contextual elements provides substantial information about the effectiveness of donor-driven interventions for renewable energy development.

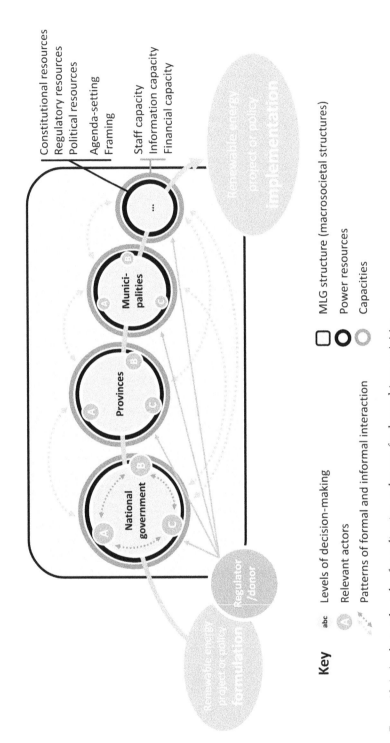

Constitutional resources
Regulatory resources
Political resources

Agenda-setting
Framing

Staff capacity
Information capacity
Financial capacity

Renewable energy
project or policy
implementation

Municipalities

Provinces

National government

Regulator/donor

Renewable energy
project or policy
formulation

Key

abc   Levels of decision-making

Ⓐ   Relevant actors

      Patterns of formal and informal interaction

☐   MLG structure (macrosocietal structures)

◉   Power resources

○   Capacities

Figure 10.1 Analyzing the role of coordination and power for donor-driven activities.

Source: illustration by the author.

References

Agranoff, R., 2013. Local governments in multilevel systems: Emergent public administration challenges. *The American Review of Public Administration*, 44(4S), pp. 47S–62S.

Arts, B. and van Tatenhove, J., 2000. Environmental policy arrangements: A new concept. In H. Goverde, ed. *Global and European polity? Organizations, policies, contexts*. Aldershot: Ashgate, pp. 223–237.

Arts, B. and van Tatenhove, J., 2004. Policy and power: A conceptual framework between the "old" and "new" policy idioms. *Policy Sciences*, 37(3–4), pp. 339–356.

Avelino, F., 2011. *Power in transition. Empowering discourses on sustainability transitions*. Rotterdam: Erasmus University Rotterdam.

Avelino, F. and Rotmans, J., 2009. Power in transition: An interdisciplinary framework to study power in relation to structural change. *European Journal of Social Theory*, 12(4), pp. 543–569.

Bacharach, S.B. and Lawler, E.J., 1980. *Power and politics in organizations*, London: Jossey-Bass.

Bache, I. and Flinders, M., 2004. *Multi-level governance*. Oxford: Oxford University Press.

Bachrach, P. and Baratz, M.S., 1962. Two faces of power. *The American Political Science Review*, 56(4), pp. 947–952.

Bakir, C., 2009. The governance of financial regulatory reform: The Australian experience. *Public Administration*, 87(4), pp. 910–922.

Benz, A., Breitmeier, H., Schimank, U. and Simonis, G., 2009. *Politik in Mehrebenensystemen*, Wiesbaden: VS Verlag für Sozialwissenschaften.

Blom-Hansen, J., 1999. Policy-making in central-local government relations: Balancing local autonomy, macroeconomic control, and sectoral policy goals. *Journal of Public Policy*, 19(3), pp. 237–264.

Boddy, M., 1983. Central-local government relations: Theory and practice. *Political Geography Quarterly*, 2(2), pp. 119–138.

Burrell, G. and Morgan, G., 1979. *Sociological paradigms and organizational analysis*, Portsmouth: Heinemann.

Clegg, S.R., 1989. *Frameworks of power*, London: Sage.

Collins, R., 1994. *Four sociological traditions*, Oxford: Oxford University Press.

Cornelius, W.A., Eisenstadt, T.A. and Hindley, J., eds., 1999. *Subnational politics and democratization in Mexico*, La Jolla, CA: Center for U.S.-Mexican Studies, UCSD.

Dahl, R.A., 1957. The concept of power. *Behavioral Science*, 2(3), pp. 201–215.

Davoodi, H. and Zou, H., 1998. Fiscal decentralization and economic growth. A cross-country study. *Journal of Urban Economics*, 43, pp. 244–257.

Elander, I., 1991. Analysing central-local government relations in different systems: A conceptual framework and some empirical illustrations. *Scandinavian Political Studies*, 14(1), pp. 31–58.

Enderlein, H., Wälti, S. and Zürn, M., eds., 2011. *Handbook on multi-level governance*, Cheltenham: Edward Elgar.

Falleti, T.G., 2005. A sequential theory of decentralization: Latin American cases in comparative perspective. *American Political Science Review*, 99(03), pp. 327–346.

Gaventa, J., 1980. *Power and powerlessness: Quiescence and rebellion in an Appalachian valley*, Urbana: University of Illinois Press.

Geels, F.W., 2010. Ontologies, socio-technical transitions (to sustainability), and the multi-level perspective. *Research Policy*, 39(4), pp. 495–510.

Giddens, A., 1984. *The constitution of society. Outline of the theory of structuration*, Cambridge: Polity.

Grin, J., 2010. Understanding transitions from a governance perspective. In J. Grin, J. Rotmans and J. Schot, eds. *Transitions to sustainable development: New directions in the study of long term transformative change*. New York: Routledge, pp. 221–337.

Haugaard, M., 2002. *Power: A reader*, Manchester: Manchester University Press.

Hendriks, C.M. and Grin, J., 2007. Contextualizing reflexive governance: The politics of Dutch transitions to sustainability. *Journal of Environmental Policy and Planning*, 9(3–4), pp. 333–350.

Hinings, B., Leach, S., Ranson, S. and Skelcher, C., 1985. Policy planning and central-local relations. *Long Range Planning*, 18(2), pp. 38–45.

Hooghe, L. and Marks, G., 2003. Unraveling the central state, but how? Types of multi-level governance. *American Political Science Review*, 97(02), pp. 233–243.

Jessop, B., 2007. *State power: A strategic-relational approach*, Cambridge: Polity.

Keohane, R. and Nye, J.S., 1998. Power and interdependence in the information age. *Foreign Affairs*, 77(5), pp. 81–94.

Keohane, R.O. and Nye, J.S. eds., 1989. *Power and interdependence. World politics in transition*, Glenview: Scott Foresman and Company.

Laffin, M., 2009. Central-local relations in an era of governance: Towards a new research agenda. *Local Government Studies*, 35(1), pp. 21–37.

Lasswell, H.D. and Kaplan, A., 1950. *Power and society. A framework for political inquiry*, New Haven: Yale University Press.

Litvack, J., Ahmad, J. and Bird, R., 1998. *Rethinking decentralization in developing countries*, Washington, DC: The International Bank for Reconstruction.

Lukes, S., 1995. *Power: A radical view*, London: Longman.

Mahoney, J., 2004. Revisiting general theory in historical sociology. *Social Forces*, 83(2), pp. 459–489.

Mann, M., 2002. The sources of social power. In M. Haugaard, ed. *Power: A reader*. Manchester: Manchester University Press.

Manor, J., 1999. *The political economy of democratic decentralization*, Washington, DC: World Bank.

Mcconaughey, M., 2013. Decentralization and power: The political geography of sharing, maintaining, and expanding resources and coercion. *APSA 2013 Annual Meeting Paper*, American Political Science Association. Available at http://ssrn.com/abstract=2300587 [Accessed August 16, 2016].

Mills, C.W., 1956. *The power elite*, Oxford: Oxford University Press.

Morris, P., 2002. Power: A philosophical analysis. In M. Haugaard, ed. *Power: A reader*. Manchester: Manchester University Press, pp. 274–303.

Nastar, M. and Ramasar, V., 2012. Transition in South African water governance: Insights from a perspective on power. *Environmental Innovation and Societal Transitions*, 4, pp. 7–24.

Nye, J.S., 1990. Soft power. *Foreign Policy*, 80, pp. 153–171.

Nye, J.S., 2005. *Soft power: The means to success in world politics*, New York: Perseus Books Group.

Oates, W.E., 1972. *Fiscal federalism*, New York: Harcourt Brace Jovanovich.

Parsons, T., 1967. *Sociological theory and modern society*, New York: The Free Press.

Parsons, T., 2002. On the concept of political power. Sociological theory and modern society. In M. Haugaard, ed. *Power: A reader*. Manchester: Manchester University Press.

Pierre, J. and Stoker, G., 2000. Towards multi-level governance. In P. Dunleavy, A. Gamble and I. Holliday, eds. *Developments in British politics 6*. Basingstoke: Palgrave Macmillan, pp. 29–44.

Polsby, N.W., 1963. *Community power and political theory*, New Haven: Yale University Press.

Putnam, R.D., 1976. *The comparative study of political elites*, Englewood Cliffs: Prentice Hall.

Rhodes, R.A.W., 1980a. Developed countries. In D.C. Rowat, ed. *International handbook on local government reorganization. Contemporary developments*. London: Aldwych, pp. 563–581.

Rhodes, R.A.W., 1980b. Some myths in central-local relations. *The Town Planning Review*, 51(3), pp. 270–285.

Rhodes, R.A.W., 1986. *Control and power in central-local government relations*, Aldershot: Gower.

Rhodes, R.A.W., 1999. *Control and power in central-local relations*, 2nd ed., Aldershot: Ashgate.

Ritzer, G., 1980. *Sociology: A multiple paradigm science*, Boston: Allyn and Bacon.

Rodden, J., 2005. *Hamilton's paradox: The promise and peril of fiscal federalism*, New York: Cambridge University Press.

Rodden, J. and Wibbels, E., 2002. Beyond the fiction of federalism: Macroeconomic management in multi-tiered systems. *World Politics*, 54, pp. 494–531.

Rondinelli, D.A., McCullough, J.S. and Johnson, R.W., 1989. Analysing decentralization policies in developing countries: A political-economy framework. *Development and Change*, 20(1), pp. 57–87.

Sadan, E., 1997. Theories of power. In E. Sadan, ed. *Empowerment and community planning: Theory and practice of people-focused social solutions*, Tel Aviv: Hakibbutz Hameuchad, pp. 33–71.

Samuels, D., 2003. *Ambition, federalism, and legislative politics in Brazil*, New York: Cambridge University Press.

Schattschneider, E.E., 1960. *The semisovereign people: A realist's view of democracy in America*, New York: Holt, Rinehart and Winston.

Schneider, A., 2003. Decentralization: Conceptualization and measurement. *Studies in Comparative International Development*, 38(3), pp. 32–56.

Scott, J., 2001. *Power*, Cambridge: Polity.

Shiraishi, K., 2014. Decentralization and local governance for sustainable development. In K. Ueta and Y. Adachi, eds. *Transition management for sustainable development*, Tokyo: United Nations University Press, pp. 234–248.

Shove, E. and Walker, G., 2007. CAUTION! Transitions ahead: Politics, practice, and sustainable transition management. *Environment and Planning A*, 39(4), pp. 763–770.

Shove, E. and Walker, G., 2008. Transition management and the politics of shape shifting. *Environment and Planning*, 40, pp. 1012–1014.

Smith, A. and Stirling, A., 2005. *Social-ecological resilience and socio-technical transitions: Critical issues for sustainability governance*, Brighton: STEPS Centre.

Smith, A., Stirling, A. and Berkhout, F., 2005. The governance of sustainable socio-technical transitions. *Research Policy*, 34(10), pp. 1491–1510.

Tiebout, C.M., 1956. A pure theory of local expenditures. *Journal of Political Economy*, 64, pp. 416–424.

Treisman, D., 2007. *The architecture of government: Rethinking political decentralization*, Cambridge: Cambridge University Press.

UNDP, 1997. *Decentralized governance programme: Strengthening capacity for people-centered development*, New York: United Nations Development Programme.

UNDP, 1999. *Decentralization: A sampling of definitions*, New York: United Nations Development Programme.

van Tatenhove, J., Arts, B. and Leroy, P. eds., 2000. *Political modernisation and the environment. The renewal of environmental policy arrangements*, Dordrecht: Kluwer Academic.

Voß, J.-P. et al., 2007. Steering for sustainable development: A typology of problems and strategies with respect to ambivalence, uncertainty and distributed power. *Journal of Environmental Policy and Planning*, 9(3–4), pp. 193–212.

Weber, M., 1978. *Economy and society*, G. Roth and C. Wittich, eds., Berkeley: University of California Press.

Weingast, B.R., 1995. The economic role of political institutions: Market-preserving federalism and economic development. *Journal of Law, Economics, and Organization*, 11(1), pp. 1–31.

Part IV
The Philippines

11 Energy situation in the Philippines

Introduction

Located in the heart of Southeast Asia, the Philippines comprises more than 7,000 islands, stretching across 300,000 km², with a population of more than 100 million people and a gross domestic product (GDP) of more than US$272 billion in 2015. The unitary state consists of about 1,000 inhabited islands varying in size, culture, language and resource base, where "strong provincial and regional identities co-exist with the national identity" (Yilmaz and Venugopal 2013, pp. 2–3), making local politics highly significant. The country is comprised of the three major regions of Luzon in the north, the central Visayas, and Mindanao in the south. The country "stands at the crossroads of the developed western world and the Orient" (IGES 2006, p. 9) with indigenous, Spanish and US influences (Pilny 2008, p. 261). Due to its historical background and strong ties to the United States, the Philippines' government and population show a strong belief in the Western way of development (David 2004).

The Philippines' modern political system is closely related to its historical development (Croissant 2015). The arrival of the Spanish in 1521 initiated a centuries-long colonial rule of the archipelago, laying the ground for a small, but powerful, elite that still dominates political, social and economic life. The dominance of a few influential families and clans, clientelism and patronage, and high levels of corruption as well as the weakness of the democratic system can be traced back to a long history of elitist rule. At the same time, democratic institutions do exist – together with regular elections, a system of checks and balances, and constitutional rights. US colonial rule between 1902 and 1946 resulted in a political system similar to that of the United States, but with massive deficiencies concerning issues of political competition, representativeness and problem-solving capacity. The Philippine people overthrew their last authoritarian leader, Ferdinand Marcos, in 1986, but ineffective governance structures and the dominance of the elite still exclude especially the poor majority of the country from economic progress and human development. This also affects access to sufficient, affordable and modern forms of energy.

An increase in energy demand of almost 5 percent annually, a relatively high share of renewables in the electricity mix, a highly decentralized political system after experiencing an authoritarian regime under former president Ferdinand Marcos (1972–1986), and an active development cooperation landscape in the field of renewables make the Philippines a highly significant case for investigating the link between the country's governance structures, renewable energy development and development assistance.

Energy situation

The Philippines' energy situation is traditionally characterized by a high dependency on fossil fuel imports. According to data from the International Energy Agency (IEA 2016), the country produced 24.5 million tons of oil equivalent (MTOE) in 2013, but had to import 20.87 MTOE at the same time. Total primary energy supply was 44.6 MTOE. Since the early 2000s, the share of fossil fuels in the energy mix has gradually risen – mainly covered by imported sources. Comparatively high energy prices, regular and forced power cutoffs, and large coal power expansions also characterize the energy situation. For the future, the *2009–2030 Philippine Energy Plan* highlights three fundamental policy goals: energy security, implementation of reforms, and social mobilization and cross-sector monitoring mechanisms. Renewables and clean energy technologies should be expanded and their capacity should be doubled by 2030 to contribute to the fulfillment of these goals (DOE 2009, p. 3). At the same time, conventional fuels should be further developed. Energy access and electrification rates should be improved through higher energy security, optimal energy pricing and the development of sustainable energy systems.

The situation of the Philippine electricity sector can be summarized as complex and tense (Larona et al. 2013). While a variety of government authorities regulate the sector, a process of ongoing liberalization and privatization started in the 1990s. At the same time, parts of the archipelago (especially in the southern province of Mindanao) suffer from electricity scarcity and blackouts due to a constant national annual growth in energy demand between 4.4 and 5.5 percent (ADB 2013). Daily power cuts and limited electricity supply are common in most remote off-grid communities (DOE 2012). In some parts, electricity is provided for no more than 4 hours a day. If connected to the electricity grid, average electricity rates are already among the highest in Southeast Asia (Suryadi 2011).

The electricity mix is dominated by oil and coal, but still with relatively high amounts of geothermal and hydro power. Other renewable energy sources are of minor (biomass) or negligible importance (wind and solar). Whereas the use of coal and natural gas increased, the amount of biomass and oil shows a decrease between 1990 and 2013 (IEA 2016). Large-scale hydro and geothermal projects account for the largest share of renewables in the electricity mix. The ADB (2013) predicts that the share of renewables in the country's electricity mix will decrease over the coming years. By 2030, renewable energy sources are expected to contribute only 15 percent of the Philippine electricity mix. A nuclear power plant was constructed by a US company in Bataan, about 100 km west of

Manila. Although completed in 1985, the facility was never put into service due to geographical risks, political power shifts and the people's resistance. Despite high energy demand and insecurity of supply, the majority of the Philippine population reject nuclear energy (Garcia, J. 1998: p. 7).

Table 11.1 summarizes numerous key data from the electricity sector.

Rapid population growth and robust economic development (UNDP 2007b, p. 244) massively pushed electricity demand upward. Per capita electricity consumption significantly increased from 360 KW/h in 1990 to 500 KW/h in 2000 and 675 KW/h in 2013, which means an increase of 86 percent compared with 1990. Yet, these numbers still remain relatively low compared with member countries of the Organisation for Economic Co-operation and Development (OECD). Electrification rates improve only marginally in the light of demographic developments. Whereas 16.2 million inhabitants lived without a modern electricity supply in 2005 (UNDP 2007b, p. 303), 16.0 million people still had no access to electricity in 2010 (Navarro et al. 2013, p. 3).

Renewable energy

Historically, renewables have played an important role in the Philippines. After the oil crises in the 1970s, the country was struck by regular power shortages due to high oil prices and the dependency on crude oil imports. Afterwards, the national government announced the goal of becoming independent of foreign fuel imports. Never again did the Philippines want to go through such an experience, with negative effects on human and economic development due to energy dependency. The country managed to establish substantial know-how, manpower and generation capacity for hydro and geothermal electricity production over the 1980s and 1990s. However, new power shortages occurred due to economic progress and increasing demand. International donors pushed the government to liberalize the electricity market and open it to private actors in 2001

Table 11.1 Key indicators about the Philippine electricity sector

Key indicator	Value (2013)
Electricity production	Coal: 32,081 GW/h; gas: 18,791 GW/h; hydro: 10,019 GW/h; geothermal: 9,605 GW/h; oil: 4,491 GW/h; biofuels: 152 GW/h; wind: 66 GW/h; waste: 60 GW/h; solar PV: 1 GW/h
Total primary energy supply	44.60 MTOE
Total electricity consumption	67.53 TW/h
Per capita electricity consumption	0.69 MW/h
Total CO_2 emissions	89.63 million tons
Total household electrification	79.9% (2014)

Source: data from IEA (2016).

(Government of the Philippines 2001). Since then, especially the use of coal for electricity production has increased significantly – leading to an electricity mix that is more and more dominated by oil and coal despite relatively high amounts of hydro and geothermal (Marquardt 2014).

Decentralized, small-scale renewable energy facilities such as solar photovoltaic (PV) and micro hydro are mainly used for off-grid electrification in remote areas in order to substitute for electricity generation from diesel generators. Beyond energy security and rural electrification, environmental non-governmental organizations (NGOs) make use of climate change as another argument for pushing renewables. Renewable energy sources should be developed in order to reduce greenhouse gas emissions in a country that is severely affected by global warming and considered to be a global "climate change hotspot." Having published a *Sustainable Philippine energy outlook*, Greenpeace and the European Energy Council (Greenpeace and EREC 2008) have simulated how 60 percent of its energy needs could be covered by renewable energy sources in 2050. This, however, would require substantial political incentives.

> Implement a legally binding target for renewable energies, introduce a renewable energy legislation to enable investments in renewable energy technologies [and] provide strict and detailed regulations on how to implement renewable energy projects to minimize bureaucracy and avoid ambiguous interpretation for existing regulation.
>
> (Greenpeace and EREC 2008, p. 5)

According to renewable energy project developers, the Philippine archipelago has "abundant agricultural and renewable resources and access to local and global technology" (IGES 2006, p. 39) – especially for electricity from solar, wind, hydro and biomass. Various detailed studies and initiatives have long discussed the technical and economic potential of renewables and opportunities for project developers (DENA 2013, 2014; IGES 2006), underlining the positive geographical and economic conditions for modern renewable energy sources.

Despite ambitious plans of the Philippine government "to be the world leader in geothermal energy, the largest producer of wind power, and the solar manufacturing hub in Southeast Asia" (Senate of the Philippines 2014, p. 1), the development of wind turbines (Elliott 2000), small-scale hydro plants (IGES 2006), bioenergy facilities and solar PV projects, especially in remote areas, is extraordinarily slow. Only large-scale hydro and geothermal power facilities make a significant contribution to the overall electricity mix. According to the National Renewable Energy Program (NREP), installed renewable energy capacity should be tripled by 2030, with additional capacity especially coming from hydro (5,394 MW), wind (2,345 MW), geothermal (1,495 MW), biomass (277 MW) and solar power (284 MW) over the next 15 years (Senate of the Philippines 2014, p. 3).

Organizations such as Greenpeace (2008, 2011) have long demanded a stronger governmental commitment to increasing the share of renewables in the energy mix. They call for the provision of supportive legislation as well as clear and binding targets, priority access to the grid for renewable electricity generators and an end to the construction of coal-fired power plants (Jabines and Inventor 2007, p. 17). Indigenous energy resources should be given a priority focus. Due to geographical conditions, NGOs also demand a decentralized and community-based development approach to promote an energy transition towards renewables to meet the people's energy needs, empower communities and protect the environment at the same time (Greenpeace and EREC 2008, pp. 4–7).

References

ADB, 2013. *Energy outlook for Asia and the Pacific*, Manila: Asian Development Bank.

Croissant, A., 2015. *Die politischen Systeme Südostasiens*, Wiesbaden: VS Verlag für Sozialwissenschaften.

David, R., 2004. *Reflections on sociology and Philippine society*, Quezon City: University of the Philippines Press.

DENA, 2013. *Länderprofil Philippinen*, Berlin: German Energy Agency.

DENA, 2014. *Market info Philippines: Photovoltaics*, Berlin: German Energy Agency.

DOE, 2009. *Highlights of the 2009–2030 Philippine energy plan*, Manila: Philippines Department of Energy (DOE).

DOE, 2012. *2012–2016 Missionary electrification development plan (2012 MEDP)*, Manila: Philippine Department of Energy.

Elliott, D., 2000. *Philippines wind energy resource atlas development*, Golden: National Renewable Energy Laboratory.

Garcia, J.L.L., 1998. Mitigating climate change: The Philippine case. In P.R. Shukla and P. Deo, eds. *Climate change mitigation in Asia and financing mechanisms. Proceedings of a regional conference*. Roskilde: Risoe National Laboratory.

Government of the Philippines, 2001. *An act ordaining reforms in the electric power industry, amending for the purpose certain laws and for other purposes. Republic Act No. 9136.*, Manila.

Greenpeace, 2011. *The Philippine energy [r]evolution roadmap to 2020*, Quezon City: Greenpeace International.

Greenpeace and EREC, 2008. *Energy [r]evolution. A sustainable Philippine energy outlook*, Quezon City: Greenpeace International, European Renewable Energy Council.

IEA, 2016. Philippines: Indicators for 2013. *International Energy Agency Statistics*. Available at: www.iea.org/statistics/statisticssearch/report/?country=PHILIPPINE&product=indicators [accessed May 4, 2016].

IGES, 2006. *Clean development mechanism. CDM country guide for the Philippines*, Kamiyamaguchi: Institute for Global Environmental Strategies.

Jabines, A. and Inventor, J., 2007. *The Philippines: A climate hotspot. Climate change impacts and the Philippines*, Quezon City: Greenpeace Southeast Asia.

Larona, F., Meller, H. and Marquardt, J., 2013. *Renewable energies for off-grid power generation in the Philippines. Avenues and examples for private sector participation in the off-grid power sector*, Manila: Deutsche Gesellschaft für Internationale Zusammenarbeit GmbH.

Marquardt, J., 2014. How sustainable are donor-driven solar power projects in remote areas? *Journal of International Development*, 26(6), pp. 915–922.

Navarro, A., Sambodo, M.T. and Todoc, J., 2013. *Energy market integration and energy poverty in ASEAN*, Manila: Philippine Institute for Development Studies.

Pilny, K., 2008. *Tiger auf dem Sprung. Politik, Macht und Märkte in Südostasien.*, Frankfurt am Main: Campus.

Senate of the Philippines, 2014. *Renewable energy at a glance*, Manila: Senate of the Philippines.

Suryadi, B., 2011. Electrical tariff in ASEAN member countries. *TalkEnergy*. Available at: http://documents.mx/documents/asean-electricity-tariffs-2011.html [accessed April 29, 2013].

UNDP, 2007. *2007/2008 Human development report. Country fact sheet Philippines*, New York: United Nations Development Programme.

Yilmaz, S. and Venugopal, V., 2013. Local government discretion and accountability in Philippines. *Journal of International Development*, 25(2), pp. 227–250.

12 Sociopolitical framework

Political context

The end of authoritarian leadership under Ferdinand Marcos (SarDesai 1989, p. 200) in 1986 can be described as a turning point in the Philippines' development towards a modern democracy (Hedman and Sidel 2001, p. 13) that also "marked the commencement of the third wave of democratization in Asia" (Croissant 2004, p. 161). Until then, the country had "witnessed periods of both development and decay" (Wurfel 1988, p. 325) due to a soft state with a lack of constitutional legitimacy and institutional capacity, but with ongoing neopatrimonial and neocolonial styles of rule (Wurfel 1988, p. 340). The constitution guarantees personal liberties and civil rights, but everyday life is still characterized by violent political conflicts, human rights violations and the abuse of fundamental civil rights (Werning and Reese 2007). The legacy of the system is still relevant to current politics. Although free and democratic elections are held regularly, the country's economy and political system are dominated by a few traditionally influential families (Croissant 2002; Kreuzer 2009). In this political oligarchy, key families rule economic and social structures. Political parties do exist, but their power and competition in the political system are limited. Many of them only exist to support candidates during elections.

Based on its constitution of 1987, the Philippines is a presidential republic with a parliamentary system. At least in theory, a robust system of checks and balances was established, with the president being both head of state and head of government (executive branch). The Congress (bicameral legislature) consists of the Senate (24 members elected by popular vote to serve 6-year terms) and the House of Representatives (212 members representing the country's districts and 24 sectoral party-list members, elected by popular vote to serve 3-year terms). The Supreme Court (judiciary) represents the highest court in the country (Croissant 2015; Croissant and Schächter 2010; Gonzales 2001).

The Philippines can be described as a "stable, but low quality democracy" (Case 2002, pp. 201–244) or even a defective democracy (Croissant 2015), characterized by low participation, political violence and a lack of political awareness. Local warlords and the complexity of local–national political interactions already shaped the political system before political reforms in 1991

(Sidel 1989), but even since then, different local elite structures have developed all over the Philippines, with similar institutional infirmities and capacity constraints having a significant impact on political decision-making (Lange 2010). Kreuzer (2009, p. 28) sees a "criminalized polity" with similarities to Mafia attitudes and structures, in which state institutions are open to criminal activities and are being transformed into resources for private governance. Corruption, lobbyism and political oppression lead to often non-transparent decisions. This is also true for renewable energy legislation and development, in which an unclear distribution of responsibilities, changing administrative rules and regulations, and the creation of new institutions are identified as major barriers to stronger policy outcomes.

Many challenges to democratic governance are inherent in the Philippine political system and persist over decades – such as vote-buying (electoral clientelism) and the dominance of a few influential families (Quimpo 2005). Private and public interests overlap, and corruption and tax evasion have weakened the state (Reese 2007). Today's widespread corruption and nepotism are also linked to the history of the Philippines, where colonial rule established a system of powerful local elites and families to exercise control over the population.

> Some blame the past and a history of colonialism that has never been completely effaced from the body politic of nation. The more radical accuse capitalism and the failure to realise proper "cultural consciousness." Others blame culture, a tradition of gift-giving and reciprocity that places family and kinship above community and nationhood. Still others see poverty as the root of the cause of all evil, small salaries, and a bloated bureaucracy that promote graft and malfeasance as a survival strategy.
>
> (Bankoff 2007, p. 178)

After decades of dictatorship, a weak state, a poorly evolved and mostly symbolic democracy along with often corrupt political elites, and a fundamental lack of well-functioning and effective good governance structures can be observed (Reese 2007). Quimpo (2009, p. 335) calls the Philippines a "predatory regime, controlled by a rapacious elite," where clientelism and corruption led to "a systematic plunder of government resources and the rapid corrosion of public institutions into tools for predation." Kerkvliet (1995, p. 404) identifies a "great inequality, absence of impersonal guarantees for physical and economic security, and the need for personal linkages beyond immediate kin as part of effort to have more security" as the fundamental conditions for clientelism. Patron–client relations are prevalent all over the Philippines. The term describes a relationship

> in which an individual of higher socio-economic status (patron) uses his own influence and resources to provide protection or benefits, or both, for a person of lower status (client) who, for his part, reciprocates by offering generous support and assistance […] to the patron.
>
> (Scott 1972, p. 92)

Local governance is considered to be inefficient and ineffective due to weak "concurrent upward and downward accountability mechanisms" (Yilmaz and Venugopal 2013, p. 1). Personal relations play a vital role in local-level politics. The importance of families and patron–client dependencies led to an influential "patron-client, factional framework" (Kerkvliet 1995, p. 401). The characteristics of a well-developed patron–client democracy (Sidel 1989, p. 19) can also explain the absence of major societal conflicts despite the ethnic diversity and huge income inequalities. These patron–client relationships, together with an elitist political system, affect all kinds of resources. "They reinforce class and status differences and help to perpetuate a political system in which inequalities, personal relationships and dependencies are endemic" (Kerkvliet 2009, p. 236).

Decentralization and growing local autonomy shape the modern political system of the Philippines, in contrast to the centralization of power under the Marcos regime. Local autonomy was enforced with the Local Government Code in 1991, which also led to "paradoxes of decentralization" (Hutchcroft 2003), because it provides a strong framework for local government discretion and downward accountability, but "a history and culture of patronage and subservience to hierarchy ensures that the discretion on paper does not translate into downward accountability" (Yilmaz and Venugopal 2013, p. 20). The country is divided into a hierarchy of local government units (LGUs) with the province as the primary unit (DILG 1991). As of December 2013, the 81 provinces were further subdivided into 1,634 cities and municipalities, which are in turn, composed of about 42,000 *barangays* headed by *barangay* captains. Local governments are subordinated to the national government, but need to provide official approval and clearances for project developers. Strong societal elites are responsible for a sharp contrast between "powerful oligarchy and a weak state" (Bowie and Unger 1997, p. 127).

> Where local power-holders controlled their resources with weapons and private armies, or could simply withhold votes or switch allegiance, state actors were forced to think twice before imposing central control or demanding professional, efficient, and corruption-free governance.
>
> (Abinales and Amoroaso 2005, p. 190)

Political decision-making does not only involve the national government and local authorities. A strong civil society and private business actors with ties to politicians also influence decision-making. The "people power movement" with mass protests culminating in 1986 successfully ended the authoritarian regime under Marcos. This peasants' revolution should be seen not only as the result of economic decline and international pressure, but also as an answer to local politics and social inequalities (Hawes 1990). A vibrant, diverse and strong non-governmental organization (NGO) community still exists today, and Filipino people show a "spirit of people power" (Abinales and Amoroaso 2005, pp. 266–290) when protesting against presidents and other political leaders.

The business community plays an increasingly important role – especially since formerly government-owned corporations were privatized. Public–private partnerships and joint ventures were established in sectors such as infrastructure and telecommunications. The complete energy sector went through a radical process of liberalization. This "new governance system" aims to promote "genuine cooperation between government, business, and society" (Gonzales 2001, p. 287) to address the country's basic needs and development goals.

Economic development

The Philippine economy is characterized by relatively low productivity and high importance of the electronics industry and the service sector (Pilny 2008, pp. 274–283). Agriculture and fisheries are the most important economic sectors, although their contribution to the overall gross domestic product (GDP) is relatively low. Economic development since the 1950s was less impressive than in other commodity-rich Southeast Asian countries (Bowie and Unger 1997, pp. 98–128), but the Philippines managed to reach a sustainable economic growth of 5–7 percent per annum over the last years. It "escape[d] the 'Asian Crisis' relatively unscathed" (Rodlauer et al. 2000, p. 1) and observed a period of economic progress in the 1990s due to political stability, a shift towards an export-oriented economy and more foreign direct investments (Rodlauer et al. 2000; Sicat 1999). The country's economic growth is among the highest in Asia, but with little effect on broader human development and poverty eradication.

Despite constant high economic growth over the last years, the gap between a small number of rich people and the majority of the poor is still widening. Whereas the annual GDP more than tripled between 1999 (US$83 billion) and 2014 (US$285 billion), human development improved only marginally, as figures from the Human Development Index (HDI) reveal. The HDI considers not only economic growth, but also aspects such as health, education and gender equality, for the status of development. The HDI for the Philippines increased very slightly from 0.62 in 1999 to 0.668 in 2014. In a global HDI ranking, the Philippines ranks 115 out of 182 countries. According to the Philippine Statistics Authority (Recide 2015), 25.8 percent of the population lived below the national poverty line in 2014, only 0.6 percent fewer than in 2006. Energy poverty represents a major problem, especially in rural areas and remote communities. In 2010, 83 percent of the population had access to electricity, leaving 16 million people without access to modern energy (Navarro et al. 2013). These economic inequalities are closely related to the deficits of the sociopolitical system and the dominance of a very small, but powerful and rich, elite.

Since the end of Marcos' rule in 1986, NGOs have started to play a more active role also in discussing alternative development pathways, demanding social equality and fostering poverty eradication. Acting as a counterpart to businesses and the conglomerates' interests, civil society actors use their freedom to actively advise and guide the government on environmental legislation and criticize the pervasive effects of economic growth. Non-state actors raise awareness of energy-related health impacts as well as effects of climate change. They "play a significant catalyst role in sharpening public awareness of how their situation is affected by such phenomenon as global warming [...] unheard of in their lives a decade ago" (Magallona and Malayang 2001, p. 5). Yet, civil society actors are also susceptible to political influence, corruption and suppression.

Electricity system

Institutional arrangements and competencies in the Philippine electricity system are complex and have changed over time. The Philippine Department of Energy (DOE) regulates the electricity sector. The DOE has been responsible for energy-related issues, plans, laws and programs since 1992 (Government of the Philippines 1992). The DOE should also "be the sole and exclusive authority responsible for the promotion, administration and regulation" (Baculio 2005) of renewables. Since 2002, the Electric Power Industry Management Bureau (EPIMB) under the DOE works on reforms and strategies for the national energy sector. The Energy Regulatory Commission (ERC) – an independent, quasi-judicial regulatory body – monitors compliance with laws and regulations, protects consumer interests, encourages market development and promotes competition. LGUs oversee the implementation of electricity-related projects, although their responsibilities often remain unclear to foreign donors, project developers and even national authorities.

Concerning legislation for renewables, the Global Renewable Energy Policies and Measures Database (IEA and IRENA 2016) listed 16 laws related to renewable energy development in May 2016. Economic instruments and investment incentives are the main focus of policy support – for example, for geothermal (Government of the Philippines 1978) or mini hydro power projects (Government of the Philippines 1991). Two landmark policies have had a major impact on renewable energy development: the 2001 Electric Power Industry Reform Act (EPIRA) and the 2008 Renewable Energy Act (RE Act).

EPIRA (Government of the Philippines 2001) led to a radical reformation, privatization and liberalization of the energy industry and the electricity market – not without criticism.

> It is based largely on perceptions and unfounded beliefs rather than reality and meaningful analysis. This could result in the obfuscation of real challenges confronting the Philippine electricity industry and preclude consideration of meaningful alternatives to improve industry performance.
>
> (Sharma et al. 2004, p. 1497)

EPIRA is considered to be a "landmark law" (Abrenica 2003) in the restructuring of the energy sector (GTZ 2007; Sharma et al. 2004). Passed in 2001, the law's goal was to stimulate private sector participation and competition in the electricity sector to improve energy security. Until then, only a limited number of private power contracts existed – including for rural areas, where renewable energy projects should be most beneficial and competitive compared with fossil fuels. The restructuring led to an unbundling of the electricity sector into the four main elements of electricity generation, transmission, distribution and supply. Private actors have entered all four areas and have acquired a dominant role. Economically unattractive off-grid areas still lack private sector participation (Larona et al. 2013).

EPIRA enforced the privatization of the electricity sector, which was formerly run by the Philippine government. It strengthened the ERC as the primary monitoring body. The assets of the National Power Corporation (NPC) in electricity generation were privatized, except for hydro plants in Mindanao. The government's role in electricity generation was limited to small islands and isolated grids (SIIG) through NPC's Small Power Utilities Group (SPUG). The National Electrification Administration (NEA) is responsible for rural electrification as well as the technical capability and financial viability of the electric cooperatives under its jurisdiction. New entities were established by EPIRA: the Wholesale Electricity Spot Market, the Power Sector Asset and Liabilities and Management Corporation, as well as the National Transmission Corporation. A Joint Congressional Power Commission was introduced as a congressional oversight commission. EPIRA thus led to a liberalized market with a complex institutional structure and partly competitive, partly regulated elements.

The 2008 RE Act (Government of the Philippines 2008) is another important law for the development of renewables. Translating the general aims and ambitions of the national government to promote renewables into concrete action, the RE Act formulates a strong commitment to renewable energy development and provides various fiscal and non-fiscal incentives for its promotion. The RE Act sets a defined proportion of renewables for the electricity suppliers' energy mix and aims to

> accelerate the exploration and development of renewable energy resources [and] increase the utilization of renewable energy by institutionalizing the development of national and local capabilities in the use of renewable energy systems, and promoting its efficient and cost-effective commercial application by providing fiscal and non-fiscal incentives.
>
> (Government of the Philippines 2008)

Fiscal incentives include an income tax holiday of up to 7 years, 10 percent income tax rate after the tax holiday, duty-free importation, a special realty tax rate, tax exemption on carbon credits, 0 percent value-added tax (VAT) on renewable energy sales and purchases, and a cash incentive in missionary off-grid areas. A feed-in tariff (FiT), a renewable portfolio standard (RPS), net metering, a green energy option, and the creation of a renewable energy market are the main non-fiscal incentives. Although the law was passed by parliament in 2008, and despite its ambitious claims, the implementation of these incentives is characterized by failure, political struggles and massive delays – with negative effects on the development and deployment of renewable energy projects.

NGOs play a vital role when it comes to renewable energy development. Organizations such as Greenpeace and the Renewable Energy Coalition advocate supportive legislation, provide information and are involved in law-making processes (Greenpeace and EREC 2008). However, any impact of NGOs on decision-making processes remains hard to define, because legalized political structures and procedures for the participation of non-state actors are generally missing.

Renewable energy projects

Due to the Philippines' geographical conditions, renewable energy projects have the potential to meet the people's energy needs, especially in remote areas, and support decentralized and community-based development at the same time. On the one hand, projects run by private investors and with funding from international facilities such as the Clean Development Mechanism (CDM) or the Global Environmental Facility (GEF) create niche markets and demonstrate the feasibility of renewable energy sources that would otherwise not have been competitive with fossil fuels (Marquardt 2010). The most prominent example is the 33 MW on-grid wind power project in Bangui Bay, Ilocos Norte. On the other hand, donor agencies have implemented numerous small-scale renewable energy projects for various technologies (especially hydro, solar and biomass) to support rural electrification programs or demonstrate their general feasibility and advantages in off-grid areas. These donor-driven renewable energy pilot projects have a long history, dating back to the 1970s (mini hydro) or the late 1980s (solar mini grids). Whereas most hydro projects could be sustained successfully, solar PV projects had only very limited success.

The country's constitutional arrangement, with a relatively weak national government but powerful local leaders and networks, heavily affects renewable energy development. The 1991 Local Government Code strengthened and enhanced decentralization and local autonomy after 14 years of authoritarianism under former president Ferdinand Marcos. The code provides a strong framework for local government discretion and downward accountability, but faces severe barriers to implementation due to a culture of patronage and subservience to hierarchy. Such a framework leads to often unclear responsibilities and competencies for renewable energy projects that need to be implemented at the local level. Project developers have to ensure overall approval for their project and a variety of clearances from the local government at both the *barangay* and the city or municipality level. High levels of uncertainty, together with corruption, increase transaction costs, making investments in small-scale electricity projects highly unattractive.

References

Abinales, P.N. and Amoroaso, D.J., 2005. *State and society in the Philippines*, Oxford: Rowman & Littlefield.

Abrenica, M.J.V, 2003. *Contracting for power: The Philippine case*, Tokyo: Asian Development Bank Institute.

Baculio, A.H., 2005. *The Philippine renewable energy policy and updates*, Bonn: World Council for Renewable Energy.

Bankoff, G., 2007. Profiting from disasters. Corruption, hazard, and society in the Philippines. In N. Stern, ed. *Corruption and good governance in Asia*. Abingdon: Routledge, pp. 165–181.

Bowie, A. and Unger, D., 1997. *The politics of open economies: Indonesia, Malaysia, the Philippines and Thailand*, Cambridge: Cambridge University Press.

Case, W., 2002. *Politics in Southeast Asia. Democracy or less*, Richmond: Curzon.

Croissant, A., 2002. *Von der Transition zur Defekten Demokratie. Demokratische Entwicklung in den Philippinen, Südkorea und Thailand.*, Wiesbaden: Westdeutscher Verlag.

Croissant, A., 2004. From transition to defective democracy: Mapping Asian democratization. *Democratization*, 11(5), pp. 156–178.

Croissant, A., 2015. *Die politischen Systeme Südostasiens*, Wiesbaden: VS Verlag für Sozialwissenschaften.

Croissant, A. and Schächter, T., 2010. Institutional patterns in the new democracies of Asia: Forms, origins and consequences. *Japanese Journal of Political Science*, 11(02), pp. 173–197.

DILG, 1991. The local government code of the Philippines. Available at: www.dilg.gov.ph/PDF_File/resources/DILG-Resources-201162-99c00c33f8.pdf [accessed May 27, 2015].

Gonzales, J.L., III, 2001. Philippines: Continuing people power. In J. Funston, ed. *Government and politics in Southeast Asia*. London: Zed Books, pp. 252–290.

Government of the Philippines, 1978. *An act to promote the exploration and development of geothermal resources. Presidential Decree No. 1442*, Manila.

Government of the Philippines, 1991. *An act granting incentives to mini-hydro-electric power developers and for other purposes. Republic Act No. 7156*, Manila.

Government of the Philippines, 1992. *An act creating the Department of Energy's rationale for the organization and functions of government agencies related to energy and other related purposes. Republic Act No. 9513*, Manila.

Government of the Philippines, 2001. *An act ordaining reforms in the electric power industry, amending for the purpose certain laws and for other purposes. Republic Act No. 9136*, Manila.

Government of the Philippines, 2008. *An act promoting the development, utilization and commercialization of renewable energy resources and for other purposes. Republic Act No. 9513*, Manila.

Greenpeace and EREC, 2008. *Energy [r]evolution. A sustainable Philippine energy outlook*, Quezon City: Greenpeace International, European Renewable Energy Council.

GTZ, 2007. *Energiepolitische Rahmenbedingungen für Strommärkte und erneuerbare Energien. 23 Länderanalysen.*, Eschborn: Deutsche Gesellschaft für Technische Zusammenarbeit GmbH (GTZ).

Hawes, G., 1990. Theories of peasant revolution: A critique and contribution from the Philippines. *World Politics*, 42(2), pp. 261–298.

Hedman, E.-L.E. and Sidel, J.T., 2001. *Philippine politics and society in the twentieth century. Colonial legacies, post-colonial trajectories*, London: Routledge.

Hutchcroft, P., 2003. Paradoxes of decentralization: The political dynamics behind the 1991 local government code of the Philippines. In M. Nelson, ed. *KPI Yearbook 2003*. Bangkok: King Prajadhipok's Institute.

IEA and IRENA, 2016. Global renewable energy. *IEA/IRENA Joint Policies and Measures Database*. Available at: www.iea.org/policiesandmeasures/renewableenergy/ [accessed May 29, 2016].

Kerkvliet, B.J.T., 1995. Toward a more comprehensive analysis of Philippine politics: Beyond the patron-client, factional framework. *Journal of Southeast Asian Studies*, 26(02), p. 401.

Kerkvliet, B.J.T., 2009. Everyday politics in peasant societies (and ours). *Journal of Peasant Studies*, 36(1), pp. 227–243.

Kreuzer, P., 2009. *Philippine governance: Merging politics and crime*, Frankfurt: Peace Research Institute Frankfurt.

Lange, A., 2010. Elites in local development in the Philippines. *Development and Change*, 41(1), pp. 53–76.

Larona, F., Meller, H. and Marquardt, J., 2013. *Renewable energies for off-grid power generation in the Philippines. Avenues and examples for private sector participation in the off-grid power sector*, Manila: Deutsche Gesellschaft für Internationale Zusammenarbeit GmbH.

Magallona, M.M. and Malayang, B.S., III. 2001. Environmental governance in the Philippines. In K. Kato et al., eds. *Environmental governance in Asia*. Tokyo: Institute for Global Environmental Strategies, Sophia University Institute for Global Environmental Studies, pp. 59–100.

Marquardt, J., 2010. *Think Global, Act Local? Environmental Regime Effectiveness: Renewable energy projects under the clean development mechanism in the Philippines, India and China.*, Saarbrücken: VDM Verlag Dr. Müller.

Navarro, A., Sambodo, M.T. and Todoc, J., 2013. *Energy market integration and energy poverty in ASEAN*, Manila: Philippine Institute for Development Studies.

Pilny, K., 2008. *Tiger auf dem Sprung. Politik, Macht und Märkte in Südostasien.*, Frankfurt am Main: Campus.

Quimpo, N.G., 2005. Oligarchic patrimonialism, bossism, electoral clientelism, and contested democracy in the Philippines. *The Journal of Comparative Politics*, 37(2), pp. 229–250.

Quimpo, N.G., 2009. The Philippines: Predatory regime, growing authoritarian features. *The Pacific Review*, 22(3), pp. 335–353.

Recide, R.S., 2015. Poverty incidence among Filipinos registered at 25.8%, as of first semester of 2014. *Philippine Statistics Authority*. Available at: www.nscb.gov.ph/press releases/2015/PSA-20150306-SS2-01_poverty.asp [accessed May 8, 2015].

Reese, N., 2007. Potentaten und widerspenstige Untertanen: Das politische System in Theorie und Praxis. In N. Reese and R. Werning, eds. *Handbuch Philippinen. Gesellschaft, Politik, Wirtschaft, Kultur*. Bad Honnef: Horlemann Verlag, pp. 221–236.

Rodlauer, M., Loungani, P., Arora, V.P., Christofides, C., de la Piedra, E.G., Kongsamut, P., Kostoal, K., Summers, V. and Vamvakidis, A., 2000. *Philippines: Toward sustainable and rapid growth : Recent developments and the agenda ahead*, Washington, DC: International Monetary Fund.

SarDesai, D.R., 1989. *Southeast Asia. Past and present*, Boulder: Westview.

Scott, J.C., 1972. Patron-client politics and political change in Southeast Asia. *The American Political Science Review*, 66(1), pp. 91–113.

Sharma, D., Madamba, S.E. and Chan, M.R.L., 2004. Electricity industry reforms in the Philippines. *Energy Policy*, 32(13), pp. 1487–1497.

Sicat, G., 1999. The Philippine economy in the Asian crisis. In H.W. Arndt and H. Hill, eds. *Southeast Asia's economic crisis. Origins, lessons, and the way forward.* Singapore: Institute of Southeast Asian Studies, pp. 41–50.

Sidel, J.T., 1989. Beyond patron-client relations: Warlordism and local politics in the Philippines. *Kasarinlan: Philippine Journal of Third World Studies,* 4(3), pp. 19–30.

Werning, R. and Reese, N., 2007. Konfrontation und Kooptation: Zivilgesellschaft in den Philippinen. In N. Reese and R. Werning, eds. *Handbuch Philippinen. Gesellschaft, Politik, Wirtschaft, Kultur.* Bad Honnef: Horlemann Verlag, pp. 237–245.

Wurfel, D., 1988. *Filipino politics: Development and decay,* Ithaca: Cornell University Press.

Yilmaz, S. and Venugopal, V., 2013. Local government discretion and accountability in Philippines. *Journal of International Development,* 25(2), pp. 227–250.

13 Renewable energy governance

Introduction

The success of an energy transition in general, and renewable energy development in the electricity sector specifically, depends on different dimensions of power, such as macrosocietal structures, the distribution of resources and the ability to mobilize these resources. Project and policy implementation depends on the power constellation within the electricity system and the interaction between national and subnational jurisdictions. This also affects development activities, which can be national or subnational interventions. To better understand the role of different jurisdictional levels and their stake in the decision-making process, it is necessary to incorporate insights from power theory into the multi-level governance framework.

Mapping the distribution of power in a multi-level governance system of a decentralized country like the Philippines allows us to analyze how complex governance structures and power shape energy transitions in developing countries as well as donor-driven renewable energy projects. What are the effects of a multi-level governance system on decision-making in the electricity regime? How do various jurisdictional levels coordinate with each other? How are resources distributed between the central government and subnational authorities? Weak interjurisdictional coordination and issues of central–local relations lead to constraints on renewable energy development. Concerning power, further questions arise. How is power exercised in the context of renewable energy support? Which actor has access to resources, and how strong is the ability to mobilize these resources? It is shown here how the fragmentation of power prevents changes of the status quo of the electricity system and thus an energy transition towards renewables.

Insights from expert interviews

Despite the strong role of the Department of Energy (DOE) as the major legislator for the electricity sector, the governance framework for renewables is complex and involves a variety of national and subnational actors. To shed light on this complexity, 51 interviews with experts from the Philippine electricity sector and development cooperation were carried out (a complete list with all interview partners can be found in Appendix I). Qualitative semi-structured interviews were conducted with experts from national and local governments (16 interviews), donor agencies (12), the public energy sector (7), the civil society (4), renewable energy businesses (7), and academia (5).

Their expertise provided some initial ideas about complex governance systems, renewable energy development and the role of development cooperation. Figure 13.1 summarizes in detail some initial quantitative insights into key barriers for renewable energy development, actors that are perceived to block or foster an energy transition, the role of local authorities and development cooperation, and the motivation for the Philippines to better support renewable energy development. The results are based on open answers in semi-structured interviews. Mentioning multiple aspects was possible. These insights are not fully representative, but they reflect the main perceptions among major stakeholders in the energy sector.

A lack of leadership and control of the national government in the energy sector is perceived to be the major obstacle to renewable energy development, because it leads to delays or failure in supportive policy implementation. The partly liberalized market structure is considered to be a barrier, especially for geothermal development, in which private companies are reluctant to make significant investments due to the higher risks and up-front costs compared with coal. The DOE with its Renewable Energy Management Bureau (REMB) is seen as the most important driving force for renewable energy development and deployment, followed by foreign donors, local government units (LGUs) and the National Renewable Energy Board (NREB). Interestingly, the DOE and LGUs (more than the private sector or the National Economic Development Authority (NEDA)) are considered to be the main veto players, with the ability to block further policy or project developments for renewables in the country.

Governance framework for renewables

From a constitutional perspective, the Philippines represents a democratic, representative and presidential republic with separate and sovereign legislative, executive and judicial branches (Croissant 2015). The unitary state grants most regulatory power to the national government. At the same time, local autonomy is guaranteed by law (DILG 1991). Provinces are the highest administrative level below the national government, but possess relatively little political power. Rather, they administer and implement national government regulations. Below the provincial level, cities and municipalities possess significantly more autonomy, but most of their budget depends on the internal revenue allotment, which is controlled by the national government. *Barangays* (villages) form the smallest administrative unit.

From a more historical perspective, the political system is characterized by a weak national government, but strong forms of informal policy-making. Under

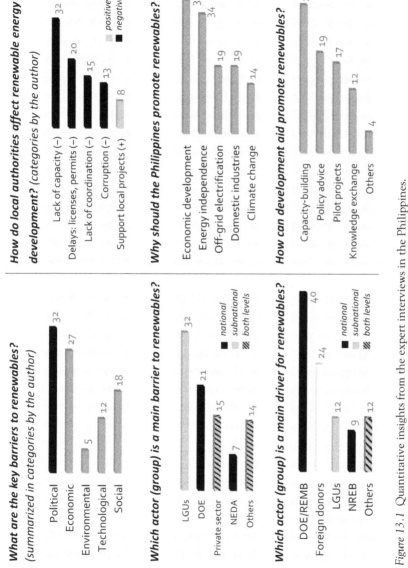

Figure 13.1 Quantitative insights from the expert interviews in the Philippines.

Source: illustration by the author.

Spanish colonial rule (1521–1898), political power was centralized, but the administrative apparatus remained small, with little direct influence at the local level. Local administrative and territorial entities were created under US occupation at the beginning of the twentieth century. Although they remained without substantial power and were not able to make autonomous decisions (Bünte 2008), a system of powerful local elites was established due to a weak central government. These conditions facilitated the development of patronage, clientelism and corruption.

Informal networks and powerful local elites shape the decision-making process in the modern Philippines (Yilmaz and Venugopal 2013). After independence in 1946, the Philippines tried to promote a more decentralized political structure through the Local Autonomy Act (1959) and the Decentralization Law (1967), but the system was recentralized under Ferdinand Marcos' authoritarian leadership (1972–1986). Following the constitutional promise for more local autonomy (Art. X, Section 6), a Local Government Code was passed in 1991, which significantly increased local autonomy (DILG 1991).

These political structures and historical developments also influence the energy sector. Following its constitutional role, the DOE is the dominant regulating authority. The ministry is responsible for energy issues, plans, laws and programs. Within the DOE, different bureaus struggle over their competencies and responsibilities. Among others, conflicts arise between the REMB and the Electric Power Industry Management Bureau (EPIMB). Since 2002, EPIMB has worked on reforms and strategies for the electricity sector, but shows a rather negative and passive attitude towards renewables.

From a more market-oriented perspective, the Philippine electricity sector has gone through substantial reforms, which were initiated in 2001 with the Electric Power Industry Reform Act (EPIRA, Republic Act 9136), leading to the restructuring of the energy sector (Abrenica 2003) and gradual privatization (Sharma et al. 2004). Before EPIRA, the Philippine national government operated the electricity system as an integrated industry. Today, the Energy Regulatory Commission (ERC) – an independent, quasi-judicial regulatory body – monitors compliance with laws and regulations. For renewables, the Philippine parliament passed a comprehensive Renewable Energy Act in December 2008, but its implementation was still challenging in 2013. At this time, only the feed-in tariff scheme was fully operational; other mechanisms, such as the renewable portfolio standard, continued to encounter huge delays. State-owned companies such as the Philippine National Oil Company (PNOC) and the National Power Corporation's Small Power Utilities Group (NPC SPUG) are restricted to certain areas (for electrification) and find themselves in competition with more flexible private actors. The government concentrates its efforts on building up a strong regulatory framework for private companies in order to promote renewables, but the big conglomerates' interest in small-scale renewable energy projects, especially compared with larger coal power investments, is relatively low. They dominate the country's electricity market.

Taking a multi-level governance perspective, the picture becomes even more complex. Electric cooperatives (ECs) mainly cater to the provinces of the country. National intrusion into provincial affairs is limited and mainly coordinated through the Department of the Interior and Local Government (DILG). On the city and municipality levels, LGUs are the political authorities in charge of providing local clearance, licenses and permits, although their responsibilities often remain unclear to practitioners and project developers. Their actual responsibilities vary greatly from municipality to municipality, depending on local resources and capacities. Mayors at the municipal level are highly relevant to project and policy implementation. They even consider themselves "little kings and queens."

The general perception of a relatively weak national government, but powerful local leaders and networks (Yilmaz and Venugopal 2013), is also relevant to the electricity system, which was affected by decentralization and increasing local autonomy following the implementation of the Local Government Code in 1991. Corruption patterns further increase transaction costs, especially for small-scale projects. Coordination between the DOE and local authorities is considered to be weak or non-existent. Projects are delayed, or fail completely, due to a lack of exchange and communication between the national government and local authorities (Marquardt 2015). Summarizing insights from legislative documents and expert interviews, Figure 13.2 portrays the Philippine electricity sector from a multi-level governance perspective and reveals the complexity of the system that affects the development of renewables.

Understanding the complexity of the Philippine electricity system from a multi-level governance perspective provides a useful starting point for analyzing the issues of coordination and power that were raised during the expert interviews.

Power structures, resources and capacities

The role of power in terms of macrosocietal structures, resources and capacities is often explicitly mentioned and discussed in energy transitions research, but often weakly defined, conceptualized and operationalized (Avelino and Rotmans 2009; Smith et al. 2005). Investigating the Philippine case demonstrates how the distribution of power resources and the ability of actors at different jurisdictional levels to mobilize their resources within a multi-level governance framework affect renewable energy development.

The power of local authorities to block renewable energy projects is perceived to be a key reason for delays and problems related to a potential energy transition. Local chiefs claim that they are not involved in the national government's energy planning and are not taken seriously by the DOE in energy-related decisions. Although the DOE has a clear constitutional mandate to implement legislation to promote energy development in the country, and with it renewables (Congress of the Philippines 1992), other

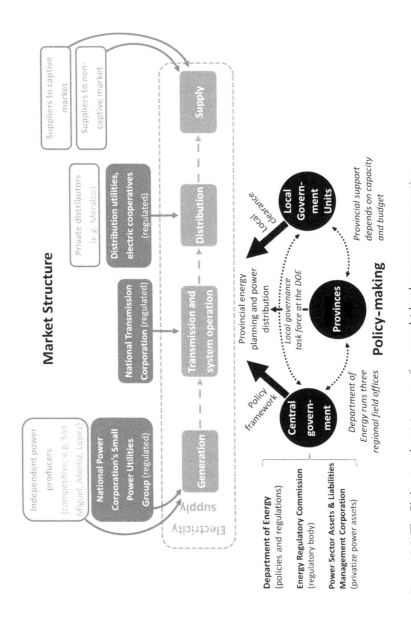

Figure 13.2 The Philippine electricity sector from a multi-level governance perspective.
Source: illustration by the author.

powerful actors seem to hamper its ambitions. Authorities, particularly at different subnational jurisdictional levels, can act as veto players to promoting renewables.

Governance structures (third dimension of power)

As the DOE is responsible for energy policies and regulations in general, it is also the major actor in the specific field of renewable energy development. As illustrated above, the national government has only limited power to implement supportive renewable energy regulations. This can be linked to two fundamental developments in the electricity sector: the liberalization of the electricity market and the empowerment of subnational governments through local autonomy provided by the constitution.

(1) *Liberalization of the energy market.* Since the electricity market structures changed with EPIRA in 2001, the responsibilities of (quasi)-state-owned companies such as PNOC or NPC SPUG are restricted to certain areas (for off-grid electrification), and they find themselves in various forms of market competition. Subnational authorities are not involved in their decisions. The national government concentrates its efforts on the provision of an enabling environment for private investors in order to promote renewables. Implementing these regulations requires consultation and (horizontal) coordination with subnational authorities. Apart from a rather informal ministerial task force for LGU concerns at the DOE that was established in 2013, no formal coordination patterns exist between the DOE and subnational jurisdictions. The national DILG is responsible for coordinating national legislation with provincial governments and LGUs. Its consultation (or vertical coordination) with the DOE often depends on political preferences and interministerial competition.

Since the ECs cater to the provinces, the national government's influence on them is limited. The country's electricity supply market is dominated by the four big conglomerates Aboitiz, San Miguel, Lopez and George Ty, which produce more than 70 percent of the entire power supply. They have relatively little interest in renewables as a decentralized, community-run and independent form of power production. The companies, which frame coal as a more reliable and cheaper form of energy compared with renewables, shape many LGUs' attitudes towards electricity options. Information campaigns, trips to existing power plant sites and various forms of corruption help to "convince" the local officials to approve coal power plants within their jurisdiction. In contrast, learning from local renewable energy projects through bottom-up coordination is limited due to the fact that the DOE runs only three regional field offices across the archipelago. Project developers criticize the lack of a single government authority that coordinates renewable energy project applications and permits for renewable energy activities (a one-stop shop). REMB tries to facilitate the process of establishing such a body, but struggles to implement guidelines at the local level, where necessary permits are often linked to issues of corruption.

(2) Empowerment of Local Government Units. With the implementation of the Local Government Code in 1991, subnational jurisdictions have become increasingly independent levels in the decision-making process. They play an important role when it comes to the implementation of renewable energy policies and projects. The coordination between the DOE and local authorities is considered to be weak, leading to delays or project refusal. LGU representatives criticize the failure of national government to include them in the formulation and implementation of energy-related activities. The interviews revealed that local authorities are not involved at an early stage of project planning. An effort to improve the situation was undertaken in 2013 when the DOE implemented an LGU task force to facilitate the implementation of the 2008 Renewable Energy Act and raise awareness of renewables at the local level with the help of consultations and closer contacts between the DOE and LGUs. Still, institutionalized and formalized forms of consultation are missing. The relation between the DOE and provincial governments is greatly affected by the political positions, party connections and personal relations of the energy minister and the governors.

These insights from expert interviews show a lack of coordination between various jurisdictional levels when it comes to renewable energy development. As a result of radical liberalization, the national government lost control over major parts of the country's electricity market, but failed to establish strong and institutionalized forms of horizontal coordination. Cooperation between national ministries is mainly driven by political factors – and often has to deal with power-related issues.

Distribution of resources (first dimension of power)

Hard power resources. Partly following Rhodes' (1986) differentiation between various forms of "hard" power resources, the following general conclusions can be derived from constitutional documents such as the 1991 Local Government Code as well as from expert interviews. Financial and professional resources are treated as capacities that enable agents to mobilize their constitutional, regulatory and political resources.

From a constitutional resources perspective, the DOE holds a clear mandate over the country's energy system, but EPIRA weakened the national government's role as a regulator due to the privatization of electricity distribution and transmission facilities. Although the DOE oversees the electricity market, subordinated authorities such as PNOC and NPC struggle to foster their own research agenda due to their restricted mandates. The Local Government Code empowers local authorities to handle their own (public policy) affairs more independently of the national government, although they should not affect energy-related policy-making.

Regulatory power resources for renewables are strongest at the national level. The 2008 Renewable Energy Act gives REMB of the DOE its mandate to formulate and implement rules and regulations related to renewables.

REMB collects and administers potential project sites and oversees project applications. At the same time, other DOE bureaus such as the Power Bureau, which are skeptical towards renewables but show a rather positive attitude towards fossil fuels, can act as veto players within the ministry. This leads to conflicts within the DOE and delays in terms of policy formulation. The provincial level sets provincial energy plans and targets, but cannot enforce strong regulations in the field. Enforcing regulations partly depends on local authorities.

As elections are held at every political level and a strong system of representation exists even in the *barangays*, political power resources are significant at all levels of decision-making. Due to the proximity of directly elected local leaders to the electorate, direct public support is highest at the local level, giving mayors substantial political power.

Soft power resources. The distribution of hard resources alone does not say much about the actual potential for introducing renewables. Such an analysis needs to include a discussion about the ability "to argue, to name and to frame" (Arts and van Tatenhove 2004, p. 340) issues. According to the interviewees, this ability is strongest at the national level. Most notably, REMB lobbies for and informs about the potential of renewables as a means of achieving energy security, electricity diversification and security of supply, especially in remote off-grid areas. At the same time, the big electricity providers, other bureaus of the DOE, and members of parliament frame renewables as costly and not competitive compared with fossil fuels.

Despite its weak constitutional and regulatory power, the provincial government can have significant soft power as an agenda-setter when it comes to fundamental decisions concerning renewables. The province of Palawan can be taken as an example. Here, the provincial government announced its ambitious plan to switch to 100 percent renewables, and local resistance prevented the construction of a coal power plant in Narra, Palawan. The municipalities' ability to put renewables on the agenda in general is relatively weak, although some frame them as a beneficial alternative form of energy. Local debates are framed by national arguments such as reliability or costs. Such a situation can be challenging for renewables, because positive local economic and environmental effects are overshadowed by national debates on the high costs of renewables and the need for coal to ensure energy security (as discussions about coal power plants in Mindanao have shown).

Capacity to mobilize resources (second dimension of power)

Mapping the distribution of hard and soft power resources in the electricity sector is still not enough to understand how power affects renewable energy development. It is necessary to understand the actual ability of relevant actors to make use of these resources discussed above to achieve a certain goal or outcome. This largely depends on the availability of information, technical expertise and financial capacities.

Availability of information. Most informational capacity related to renewables is concentrated at the national level – especially with REMB and regulators such as ERC or the National Power Corporation (NPC). The picture looks different at the local level, where a lack of data and knowledge about renewables hinders relevant authorities in dealing with renewable energy projects. Compared with fossil fuels, renewables need stronger forms of awareness-raising at the local level due to their relatively uncommon nature. Relevant information (on electricity supply, planning, land use and so forth) is often collected at the provincial level. Local authorities struggle to provide this kind of information.

Technical expertise and personnel. The lack of local knowledge is closely related to the limited availability of sufficiently trained personnel. Whereas staff with training in energy systems or renewable energy development operate at the national level, local authorities lack manpower and a relevant educational background. Professionalism in the field of renewable energy depends on the economic power of provinces, municipalities and cities. In general, local authorities lack the skills and materials needed to implement and follow up renewable energy policies decided upon by the central government.

Financial capacities. Funding opportunities are limited at the subnational level. Municipalities are able to collect various forms of taxes, but their revenues remain relatively low (DILG 1991). National policy sets the limits for tax rates. The situation is similar for provincial governments, which depend on income and other tax revenues from the national level. Financial constraints, together with a lack of supervision, make the system prone to abuse and corruption. Local officials complain about lack of financial support, but are also accused of being corrupt and introducing taxes that are against national legislation.

Figure 13.3 summarizes the role of power resources and capacities for promoting renewables in the multi-level governance system of the Philippines. It captures the accumulation of resources at the national level, medium capacities at the provincial level, and also substantial power at the municipal level. The figure illustrates how resources and capacities are unequally distributed across different jurisdictional levels in the Philippine multi-level governance system. Note that resources and capacities vary greatly among provinces and municipalities all over the Philippines, reflecting an uneven development across the country.

The following section discusses how donors address these complex multi-level governance structures, challenges in central–local relations, and the fragmented distribution of power resources and capacities at different jurisdictional levels.

Donor-driven interventions

Donor-driven support for modern renewables in the Philippines has a long history, dating back at least to the 1970s. Even official development assistance (ODA) databases such as AidData (2016) do not provide a comprehensive overview of all project activities in this sector, but they give a first impression

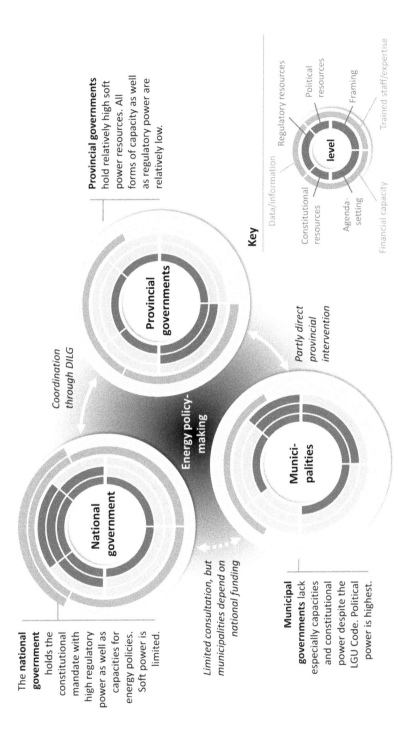

The **national government** holds the constitutional mandate with high regulatory power as well as capacities for energy policies. Soft power is limited.

Provincial governments hold relatively high soft power resources. All forms of capacity as well as regulatory power are relatively low.

Coordination through DILG

Energy policy-making

Partly direct provincial intervention

Limited consultation, but municipalities depend on national funding

Municipal governments lack especially capacities and constitutional power despite the LGU Code. Political power is highest.

Key

Data/information
Regulatory resources
Political resources
Framing
Trained staff/expertise
Constitutional resources
Agenda-setting
Financial capacity

level

National government

Provincial governments

Municipalities

Figure 13.3 Power resources and capacities for renewables in the Philippines.
Source: illustration by the author.

about the field's development. For most projects listed in the database, only limited information is available. For the Philippine energy sector (*energy generation and supply*) alone, AidData lists 715 projects from 31 funding organizations, with US$22.0 billion offered in international funding between 1950 and 2015. Figure 13.4 illustrates how the number of donor organizations and energy project activities in the Philippine energy sector steadily increased between 1970 and 2013.

Donor-driven renewable energy activities have diversified over time – especially after EPIRA in 2001, and again after the RE Act was passed in 2008. Diversification can be observed both at the local and at the national level. Not only the number of implementing agencies, but also the donors, have diversified. For example, the Deutsche Gesellschaft für Internationale Zusammenarbeit (GIZ) implemented renewable energy projects with funding from the Federal Ministry for the Environment, Nature Conservation and Nuclear Safety (BMU) and the Federal Ministry for the Economy and Technology (BMWi), whereas the Federal Ministry for Economic Cooperation and Development (BMZ) has almost completely withdrawn from the Philippines. GIZ managed to keep and broaden its portfolio only with active project acquisition, including from other funding organizations.

Most donor agencies use informal channels to coordinate with each other. However, consultation and information-sharing with other agencies usually start *after* project planning, at a point when the funding organization has already decided on the project design and approved its implementation. Consequently, coordination is limited to the project's own boundaries. As a rare example of an attempt at an institutionalized way of coordination and donor harmonization, the DOE held a donors' forum in 2012 to facilitate exchange among donors and match the DOE's priorities for renewables with the donor agencies' competences (DOE 2012). Long-term continuing cross-donor knowledge management does not exist. Donor organizations have specialized to a certain degree according to their national preferences and technological expertise. For example, GIZ concentrates on solar power activities, whereas the Japan International Cooperation Agency (JICA), the Japanese development cooperation agency, concentrates on mini hydro power. Policy recommendations are also based on the donor countries' experiences. Whereas United States Assistance for International Development (USAID) is in favor of a renewable portfolio standard (RPS) scheme, the German GIZ promotes the feed-in tariff (FiT) for renewables.

How are development projects addressing the complexity of the multi-level governance system during project planning and implementation? Multi-level governance issues and interaction patterns between various jurisdictional levels are high on the donors' agenda during project planning. Project developers highlight crucial factors for diffusion or spill-over effects that should be enforced with the help of renewable energy projects. At the same time, project developers fail to solve the challenge of coordination across multiple jurisdictions during project implementation, despite a high level of awareness on the project developers' side.

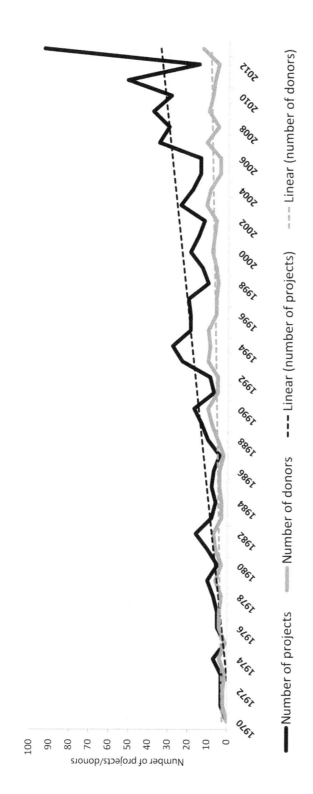

Figure 13.4 Development cooperation over time in the Philippine energy sector.

Source: illustration by the author.

Competing responsibilities and conflicting interests at different levels of decision-making affect development projects in a negative way. Moreover, unsustainable projects are the result of a lack of indicators for project success related to the multi-level governance environment. Learning and diffusion of experiences from one level to another are key factors for the success of development projects – both at the local and at the national level. At the same time, the multi-level governance system represents a major barrier for project developers during project implementation. Often, a dilemma between project planning and the factual reality of the project can be detected.

How do decentralized political structures affect renewable energy projects? The decentralized political system and weakly institutionalized forms of coordination hamper the cooperation between local and national authorities that is essential for the success of donor-driven interventions. Even representatives from the DOE verify a lack of communication with local authorities, which should be improved with the help of a local government task force at the ministry. Local authorities claim that insufficient training and awareness of national electrification programs lead to delays and misconceptions during policy or project implementation. Project developers and donor agencies perceive the problem of uncertainty arising from the decentralized political system, with (often unclear) competencies and responsibilities at different jurisdictional levels as a major barrier to renewable energy projects.

How does the Philippine government coordinate project activities that promote renewables? NEDA develops the Philippines' overarching development plans. The authority is also responsible for coordinating development activities. In theory, it should streamline activities and coordinate efforts. In practice, it plays a rather weak or even chaotic role, because it does not change or even refuse project proposals – even if similar project designs have already failed to deliver sustainable results, as was the case for a number of solar power projects. The DOE is the major partner for projects in the field of renewables. REMB considers itself to be responsible for coordination and streamlining activities to avoid duplication. However, this is a challenging task, because donors also work with other national government departments or divisions within the DOE, such as the Power Bureau.

Renewable energy activities cover various fields. At the national level, numerous donors supported the Philippine government with the formulation and implementation of the RE Act. Passed by parliament in 2008, after more than 20 years of debate, the law aims to boost the deployment and development of renewables. Not until 2013 was the FiT scheme fully implemented as the first of the incentives outlined in the 2008 RE Act. Locally, rural electrification represents a major field of activity. Despite a positive public attitude towards solar power and its use for electrification programs, the technology is considered to be expensive, unreliable and not yet fully developed to provide sufficient power supply or even base load electricity (Meller and Marquardt 2013). Donor agencies have implemented various projects supporting solar power in the context of sustainable rural electrification and for increasing self-sufficiency for almost 30 years. The Philippine government incorporates donor-funded solar power activities in its own expanded rural electrification program, but most of the small-scale activities cannot be sustained due to maintenance and financing issues. These issues can also be linked to the fragmentation of capacities in a complex multi-level governance arrangement.

References

Abrenica, M.J.V, 2003. *Contracting for power: The Philippine case*, Tokyo: Asian Development Bank Institute.

AidData, 2016. AidData 3.0. Open data for international development. Available at: http://aiddata.org/ [accessed March 30, 2016].

Arts, B. and van Tatenhove, J., 2004. Policy and power: A conceptual framework between the "old" and "new" policy idioms. *Policy Sciences*, 37(3–4), pp. 339–356.

Avelino, F. and Rotmans, J., 2009. Power in transition: An interdisciplinary framework to study power in relation to structural change. *European Journal of Social Theory*, 12(4), pp. 543–569.

Bünte, M., 2008. Dezentralisierung und Demokratie in Südostasien. *Zeitschrift für Politikwissenschaft*, 18(1), pp. 25–50.

Congress of the Philippines, 1992. *An act creating the Department of Energy rationalizing the organization and functions of government agencies related to energy and for other purposes*, Manila.

Croissant, A., 2015. *Die politischen Systeme Südostasiens*, Wiesbaden: VS Verlag für Sozialwissenschaften.

DILG, 1991. The local government code of the Philippines. Available at: www.dilg.gov.ph/PDF_File/reports_resources/dilg-reports-resources-2016120_5e0bb28e41.pdf [accessed May 27, 2015].

DOE, 2012. *Renewable energy donor's forum: Documentation report*, Manila: Philippine Department of Energy.

Marquardt, J., 2015. The politics of energy and development: Aid diversification in the Philippines. *Energy Research & Social Science*, 10, pp. 259–272.

Meller, H. and Marquardt, J., 2013. *Renewable energy in the Philippines: Costly or competitive? Facts and explanations on the price of renewable energies for electricity production*, Manila: Deutsche Gesellschaft für Internationale Zusammenarbeit (GIZ) GmbH.

Rhodes, R.A.W., 1986. *Control and power in central-local government relations*, Aldershot: Gower Publishing.

Sharma, D., Madamba, S.E. and Chan, M.R.L., 2004. Electricity industry reforms in the Philippines. *Energy Policy*, 32(13), pp. 1487–1497.

Smith, A., Stirling, A. and Berkhout, F., 2005. The governance of sustainable sociotechnical transitions. *Research Policy*, 34(10), pp. 1491–1510.

Yilmaz, S. and Venugopal, V., 2013. Local government discretion and accountability in Philippines. *Journal of International Development*, 25(2), pp. 227–250.

14 Synthesis

Introduction

To avoid energy scarcity and reduce its dependence on fossil fuels, the Philippines has pushed renewable energy development over decades. Renewables meet a substantial part of the country's electricity demand, but their share in the electricity mix is constantly decreasing due to massive current and future investments in coal.

The Philippine case reveals and illustrates very clearly how power struggles and complex governance structures shape an energy transition towards renewables. Shifting the electricity system towards sustainable energy does not only depend on supportive policies and incentive structures, but also on broader sociopolitical factors such as corruption, clientelism and interpersonal relations. Coordination across different jurisdictional levels and the fragmented distribution of power resources and capacities are additional factors influencing the Philippine energy transition.

Bi- and multilateral donors have successfully implemented renewable energy projects, but they often struggle to sustain their activities for more than a few years, replicate results or institutionalize efforts for renewable energy development.

Complex governance challenges

Although the Philippines provides a highly interesting case for investigating the role of coordination and power relations for renewable energy development in decentralized political structures, not much has been written about how political factors influence the energy transition. The archipelago successfully promoted renewable energy sources in the 1980s and 1990s, but – at the same time – struggles to implement its comprehensive 2008 Renewable Energy Act (RE Act). New institutional arrangements and responsibilities due to the empowerment of the local level and the liberalization of the electricity market led to changing power constellations and coordination gaps that affected, and still affect, the promotion of renewables. Issues of coordination are closely linked to the fragmentation of power resources and capacities across various jurisdictional levels. Understanding these links helps to identify crucial barriers to energy transitions and to formulate more appropriate renewable energy policies and project designs.

Coordination matters. Confirming findings from other studies on energy transitions, especially in industrialized countries (e.g. Ohlhorst and Tews 2013), coordination between various jurisdictional levels is key to renewable energy development. National energy planning at the Department of Energy (DOE) often neglects or misunderstands local conditions, although a successful implementation of policies depends on subnational political structures. In contrast, local authorities are often neither capable nor willing to fully support national renewable energy activities due to a lack of awareness, political conflicts, corruption or a lack of capacities. Institutionalized forms of coordination across levels are missing or not well established, both for top-down policy implementation and for bottom-up learning processes.

The distribution of power matters. Aspects of coordination can and should be linked to an issue that has been investigated less prominently in energy transitions research: the role of power resources, their (fragmented) distribution in a complex multi-level governance system, and the ability of agents to mobilize these resources. This analysis revealed that the empowerment of local authorities, especially with the enactment of the Local Government Code, gave local authorities considerable policy discretion for blocking or overruling project activities – or increasing their price, mainly through corruption. At the same time, subnational authorities fail to act as the initiators of a bottom-up process due to professional and informational constraints and their dependency on national funding.

From a theoretical perspective, the Philippine case strongly confirms scholars such as Smith and Stirling (2005) and Avelino (2011), who appeal urgently to energy transitions researchers to consider the meaning of power relations in sociotechnical transitions more seriously. Research on the distribution of power resources and capacities in central–local relations (Boddy 1983; Hinings et al. 1985; Rhodes 1980, 1986) might be more than 30 years old, but it provides a number of substantial ideas about how to explicitly conceptualize power that can make a significant contribution to current debates about the challenges of promoting and developing renewables in multi-level governance systems.

The Philippine archipelago has reached a crossroads concerning its energy transition. Business-as-usual scenarios predict a massive increase of fossil fuels, but a decline of renewables, in the electricity mix of the future. Issues of coordination and power fragmentation need to be considered more seriously in order to identify the factors of success and failure in renewable energy development. Better understanding the country's governance structures and power constellations should also enable development cooperation to provide more sustainable and effective renewable energy interventions that could eventually become a driving force for an energy transition in the Southeast Asian country.

Development cooperation for renewables

Numerous donors have supported renewable energy projects at various levels – mainly for national policy advice or with the help of technology-specific local demonstration projects. Although national-level interventions tackle diverse issues at the same time and are implemented within more complex political frameworks than local activities, clear and measurable indicators that can be assigned to these projects are harder to identify.

Development cooperation has limited structural effects at the national level. Although institutionalized forms of coordination are weak, informal labor division can be observed when it comes to policy mechanisms such as the feed-in tariff (FiT) or the renewable portfolio standard (RPS). Some donor interventions build on previous activities, as numerous references to the Capacity Building to Remove Barriers to Renewable Energy Development (CBRED) project implemented by the United Nations Development Programme (UNDP) show. Donors also interact with civil society actors and renewable energy business associations. A certain degree of flexibility leaves room for actors to react to policy changes or delays (as happened with the implementation of the FiT) and align the projects' efforts with the specific demands of their Philippine counterparts. At the same time, higher transaction costs are likely, due to increasing competition among donors and incoherent advice concerning policy mechanisms that might not be compatible with the national context. A clear assignment of effects to specific activities remains highly interpretative due to high interdependences (attribution gaps).

Development cooperation struggles to provide structural effects at the local level. A number of lessons can be learnt about local project interventions from investigating donor-driven solar power support. Over the past 30 years, a number of donors (including German Technical Cooperation (GTZ), United States Assistance for International Development (USAID), Australian Agency for International Development (AusAID) and UNDP) have had very similar experiences with solar power applications in remote areas. Activities with similar, but in the end ineffective and poor, project designs were implemented over the years, leading to similar negative outcomes and project failure. Most projects collapsed due to a lack of technical know-how, maintenance capacities and financial resources. Lack of knowledge exchange between donors hindered a process of collective learning from mistakes. None of the donor organizations has ever undertaken an ex-post evaluation for a renewable energy development activity. Learning and monitoring capacities are also insufficient on the Philippine government's side. In the short run, all donor-driven solar power interventions contribute to the Philippine rural electrification program, but most of them fail to provide sustainable long-term power supply. Sustaining activities, or even replicating project designs beyond the protected niche created by the donors, is extraordinarily rare. The Alliance for Mindanao Off-Grid Renewable Energy (AMORE) project is one of the few positive examples.

Taking a multi-level governance perspective shows that most donor-driven interventions for renewables contribute to changes at the local level, but fail to

Figure 14.1 Linking donor-driven support for renewables to power in the Philippines.

Source: illustration by the author.

transfer knowledge to the national level or lead to the replication of projects elsewhere. Institutionalization of results is limited or fails completely. Donors struggle to address the barriers to effects that go beyond the actual project environment in a decentralized political system with unclear and changing responsibilities as well as conflicts between the national government and local authorities. Negative results have also occurred due to a lack of specialization among the active donors, despite international commitments to coordination and harmonization, and a fragmented development cooperation landscape.

Figure 14.1 summarizes the link between donor-driven renewable energy projects and insights from the Philippine multi-level governance system for renewables. Simplifying the relation between donor-driven support and the distribution of power at different jurisdictional levels in the Philippines, the figure describes the challenging implementation process as a result of various power resources and capacities at different jurisdictional levels.

Acknowledging and better understanding this political context, especially in a developing country with powerful local authorities, should not only improve the process of project implementation but, especially, shed light on the potential for and obstacles to more structural and long-term change for an energy transition towards renewables through scaling-up or diffusing experiences from development projects beyond their limited project-level context.

References

Avelino, F., 2011. *Power in transition. Empowering discourses on sustainability transitions.* Rotterdam: Erasmus University Rotterdam.

Boddy, M., 1983. Central-local government relations: Theory and practice. *Political Geography Quarterly*, 2(2), pp. 119–138.

Hinings, B., Leach, S., Ranson, S. and Skelcher, C., 1985. Policy planning and central-local relations. *Long Range Planning*, 18(2), pp. 38–45.

Ohlhorst, D. and Tews, K., 2013. Energiewende als Herausforderung der Koordination im Mehrebenensystem. *Technikfolgenabschätzung – Theorie und Praxis*, 22(2), pp. 48–55.

Rhodes, R.A.W., 1980. Some myths in central-local relations. *The Town Planning Review*, 51(3), pp. 270–285.

Rhodes, R.A.W., 1986. *Control and power in central-local government relations*, Aldershot: Gower.

Smith, A. and Stirling, A., 2005. *Social-ecological resilience and socio-technical transitions: Critical issues for sustainability governance*, Brighton: STEPS Centre.

Part V
Indonesia

15 Energy situation in Indonesia

Introduction

Indonesia is Southeast Asia's biggest country, with a rapidly growing economy and increasing energy demand. The country's size matters for the development of the whole region. Changes in the energy system of a fossil fuel-dependent regional power like Indonesia are likely to affect its neighboring countries. With an estimated population of more than 250 million people, it is the world's fourth most populous nation. Abundant natural resources and a huge domestic market make the world's largest archipelago, with 17,500 islands, an economic "heavy-weight of Southeast Asia" (Case 2002, p. 29) and the "primus inter pares" among Association of Southeast Asian Nations (ASEAN) member countries (Smith 2001, p. 80). With 36 percent of total demand, Indonesia is by far the largest energy consumer in the region, using 66 percent more energy than Thailand as the second largest consumer and over 50 times more than the smallest consumer, Brunei Darussalam (IEA 2013, p. 16).

Despite significant potential for renewables, fossil fuels dominate the archipelago's electricity system. The central government has provided incentives for renewables and moved the electricity market towards a more competitive design (Damuri and Atje 2012), but without effects towards more sustainable energy supply. Bi- and multilateral donors have pushed renewable energy development with a variety of projects.

> Indonesia has both significant renewable resource potential and a government committed to its development, but the country's renewable realization is seriously lacking. As with other fast-developing countries it needs to support its strong economic growth with energy supply, with its abundant coal reserves providing an obvious solution, at least in the medium term. But unlike other fast developing economies, Indonesia has a strong environmental conscience with the government keen to present itself as a regional climate action leader.
>
> (Wilcox 2012)

Not only its economic power and geographical conditions, but also the country's social diversity and the complexity of the heavily decentralized political system, affect the likelihood of an energy transition in Indonesia. With more than 700 languages, a variety of religions and more than 300 ethnic groups, Indonesia's society represents one of the most complex (Pilny 2008, pp. 196–234) and heterogeneous (Smith 2001) in the world.

Energy situation

Although Indonesia was severely hit by the Asian financial crisis in 1997/1998, the country's economy recovered relatively quickly, with stable annual gross domestic product (GDP) growth rates since then. In parallel, energy demand and supply have continuously and significantly increased over the years. The total primary energy consumption more than doubled between 2003 and 2013 (IEA 2015). At the same time, the energy sector remains an important factor for exports. In 2012, 20 percent of all merchandise exports came from oil and gas (EIA 2014), resulting in 24 percent of total state revenues coming from the oil and gas sector. Indonesia became the world's largest exporter of coal in 2012, exporting about 383 million short tons of coal. This makes it "by far the dominant producer" of coal (IEA 2013, p. 15) in Southeast Asia. Indonesia also remains the region's largest oil producer, with 890,000 barrels of oil production per day (IEA 2013, p. 21). Providing only about 3 percent of its GDP in 2011 for energy infrastructure investments, Indonesia clearly lags behind its neighboring countries.

Despite a number of initiatives and efforts for stronger private sector participation, such as land reform legislation in 2011 and the Master Plan for Economic Expansion and Acceleration 2011–2025, "many infrastructure projects continue to be delayed, and regulatory challenges and uncertainties have reduced predictability for foreign investors" (EIA 2014). Increasing hand in hand with the growth in energy consumption, the costs for fuel subsidies used to be a major economic and political concern. Subsidies accounted for 7 to 25 percent of the government's annual public expenditures between 2005 and 2013. In 2012 alone, Indonesia spent US$20 billion in fuel subsidies (EIA 2014). According to the IEA (2013, p. 11), these subsidies are a "significant factor distorting energy markets." Subsidies for petroleum products "reduce incentives to develop alternative sources of energy" (Damuri and Atje 2012, p. 6). Organizations such as the Global Subsidies Initiative and the International Institute for Sustainable Development (Braithwaite et al. 2012) urged the country to reform the fuel subsidies system to reduce the burden on the national budget. In 2015, Indonesian President Joko Widodo decided to abolish the fuel subsidy. Only a minimal subsidy (1,000 rupiah or 8 US cents) per liter will remain on diesel for public transport and impoverished fishermen (Roberts 2015).

Energy supply and demand are not evenly distributed across the archipelago. With more than half of the country's population and a contribution of more than 60 percent to the national GDP (BPS Indonesia 2014), the island of Java dominates Indonesia's economy and energy demand. More than 80 percent of the country's electricity is consumed in Java and Bali (Respati 2013). Especially, provinces on the islands of Java and Sumatra have an average access to electricity of more than 60 percent, whereas in many other areas electricity access is below 60 percent (e.g. Kalimantan, Sulawesi) or even below 30 to 40 percent (e.g. Nusa Tenggara, Papua) (Beranda Inovasi 2013). Indonesia's electrification rate was around 84 percent in 2014, leaving about 10 million people, especially in rural areas, without access to modern energy. The IEA (2013, p. 27) estimates that in 2011, about 66 million Indonesians (or 27 percent of the population) still lived without access to modern energy services.

At the same time, the country's electricity system struggles to meet ever-increasing additional demand. In 2013, on-grid electricity consumption was around 198 TW/h. Coal (48 percent of installed electricity generation capacity), oil (12 percent) and natural gas (22 percent) cover the largest share, leaving 18 percent of installed capacity to renewables, especially hydro (11 percent), waste heat (5 percent) and geothermal (2 percent). For rural and off-grid areas, diesel generators are still the dominant technology, despite the increasing number of widely distributed solar home systems (Differ Group 2012, p. 2). Indonesia's impressive economic growth over the last decades is also reflected in the development of the country's energy sector. Comparing energy-related statistics from 1993 and 2013, Table 15.1 summarizes this development.

As most additional energy demand is going to be met by coal, an energy transition to renewables in the near future is not very likely. At the same time, the Indonesian government has ambitious plans to further develop new and renewable energy sources in the near future.

Table 15.1 Key energy-related statistics for Indonesia

Country statistics	1993	2013	+/−
Population	188.02 million	250 million	+32.0%
Gross domestic product	US$188.01 billion	US$452.34 billion	+140.6%
Energy production	194.22 MTOE	459.99 MTOE	+136.8%
Total primary energy supply	118.44 MTOE	213.64 MTOE	+80.4%
CO_2 emissions	181.23 million tons	424.61 million tons	+134.3%
Electricity-related data			
Total consumption	40.62 TWh	197.92 TWh	+387.2%
Electricity consumption/capita	0.22 MWh	0.79 MWh	+259.1%
Production from			
Coal	10,681 GWh	110,452 GWh	+934.1%
Oil	20,897 GWh	26,751 GWh	+28.0%
Gas	4,844 GWh	51,769 GWh	+968.7%
Biofuels	4 GWh	228 GWh	+ 5600%
Waste	0 GWh	40 GWh	−
Hydro	7,884 GWh	16,930 GWh	+114.7%
Geothermal	1,090 GWh	9,414 GWh	+763.7%
Solar, wind, others	0, 0, 0 GWh	5, 1, 0 GWh	−

Source: data from IEA (2015).

Renewable energy status and future development

Indonesia has high potential for renewables, not only for off-grid electrification through small-scale biomass, hydro or solar power projects, but also for large-scale on-grid applications such as geothermal and hydro power facilities. Renewables account for less than 20 percent of installed electricity capacity (Damuri and Atje 2012, p. 6), but contribute only 5 percent to the country's overall energy mix, due to lower capacity factors compared with fossil fuels and the output's dependency on the location, especially for solar and hydro. According to the Directorate General for New and Renewable Energy and Energy Conservation (EBTKE) under the Ministry of Energy and Mineral Resources, "new and renewable energy sources" should cover between 17 and 25 percent of Indonesia's total energy mix by 2025 (Azahari 2012). Although sources for new energy also include nuclear, hydrogen, coal bed methane, liquefied coal and gasified coal, realizing these plans would still push the development of clean energy technologies. Whereas the share of oil and gas in the electricity mix should be reduced to less than 25 percent and 22 percent accordingly, renewables and coal should account for at least 23 percent and 30 percent, respectively, by 2025 (IEA 2013, p. 32).

The addition of renewable energy capacity is also desperately needed for the future. Energy demand is expected to increase substantially over the next decades due to demographic forecasts, economic development and the government's electrification program. The IEA (2013, p. 30) estimates that the Indonesian economy will grow by 4.9 percent annually on average between 2011 and 2035. At the same time, the population is expected to grow by 0.9 percent annually, reaching 301.5 million by 2035 (IEA 2013, p. 34). *Perusahaan Listrik Negara* (PLN), together with the central government, aims to provide 99 percent of the population with access to modern electricity by 2020 (IEA 2013, p. 28).

Beyond the expansion of renewable energy technologies, the government aims to foster energy efficiency measures. Energy intensity should be reduced by 1 percent per annum to meet energy conservation targets. Greenhouse gas emissions should be decreased by 26 percent (or 41 percent with international support) by 2020 compared with the business-as-usual scenario for Indonesia. Primary energy demand is expected to grow by 2.5 percent annually, leading to the need for 358 million tons of oil equivalent (MTOE) in 2035, compared with 196 MTOE in 2011 (IEA 2013, p. 38). Over that time, the share of renewables in the primary energy mix is actually expected to decrease due to higher overall demand, electrification programs and a decreasing consumption of traditional biomass (IEA 2013, p. 52). Table 15.2 summarizes these future developments in the energy sector by providing a number of relevant energy-related statistics.

The future development of Indonesia's electricity mix is following a general trend in Southeast Asia: the share of oil and gas is decreasing in favor of coal and renewables. Whereas coal is expected to quintuple between 2011 and 2035, additional capacity from hydro, geothermal and other renewables will be much more moderate (IEA 2013, pp. 47–48).

Table 15.2 Energy development outlook for Indonesia (2011–2035)

Country statistics	2011	2035
Population	242.3 million	301.5 million
Average annual GDP growth rate	4.7% (1990–2011)	4.9% (2012–2035)
GDP per capita	ca. US$3,500	ca. US$9,000
Energy-related data		
Primary energy demand	196 MTOE	358 MTOE
Per capita energy consumption	0.8 TOE	1.2 TOE
Access to electricity	73%	99% (by 2020)
Energy-related CO_2 emissions	ca. 426 million tons	ca. 830 million tons

Source: data from IEA (2015).

According to the IEA (2013, p. 44), Indonesia will add about 100 GW of total gross electricity generation capacity between 2011 and 2035. Electricity demand will almost triple between 2011 and 2035 at an average annual growth rate of 4.8 percent. Although the share of renewables in electricity generation is expected to increase from 12 to 18 percent over that period, coal-fired generation and natural gas will still dominate the future electricity mix. Most additional renewable energy capacities are assumed to come from geothermal, hydro and wind power. Solar power should accelerate the electrification of remote areas (IEA 2013, p. 53), but remains rather marginal in the total electricity mix. Other scenarios show similar developments, but also discuss the role of nuclear power, which could meet 19 percent of Indonesia's electricity demand by 2050 (Ibrahim et al. 2009, p. 11). By then, overall energy consumption could be at 900 MTOE, about nine times Indonesia's 2009 level (97 MTOE) and equivalent to the 2005 average level in industrialized countries.

References

Azahari, H.L., 2012. New and renewable energy policies. Available at: http://energy-indonesia.com/03dge/03.pdf [accessed April 1, 2014].

Beranda Inovasi, 2013. Kendala Elektrifikasi Daerah Terpencil dan Solusi PLTMH. Available at: http://berandainovasi.com/kendala-elektrifikasi-daerah-terpencil-dan-solusi-pltmh/ [accessed August 17, 2016].

BPS Indonesia, 2014. *Statistik Indonesia 2014: Statistical yearbook of Indonesia 2014*, Jakarta: Badan Pusat Statistik Republik Indonesia.

Braithwaite, D. et al., 2012. *Indonesia's fuel subsidies: Action plan for reform*, Winnipeg: International Institute for Sustainable Development.

Case, W., 2002. *Politics in Southeast Asia. Democracy or less*, Richmond: Curzon Press.

Damuri, Y.R. and Atje, R., 2012. *Investment incentives for renewable energy: Case study of Indonesia*.

Differ Group, 2012. *The Indonesian electricity system: A brief overview*.

EIA, 2014. Indonesia. *U.S. Energy Information Administration*. Available at: www.eia.gov/countries/analysisbriefs/Indonesia/indonesia.pdf [accessed May 27, 2015].

Ibrahim, H.D., Thaib, N.M. and Wahid, L.M.A., 2009. *Indonesian energy scenario to 2050: Projection of consumption, supply options and primary energy mix scenarios*, Jakarta.

IEA, 2013. *Southeast Asia energy outlook. World energy outlook special report*, Paris.

IEA, 2015. IEA non-member countries: Indonesia. *International Energy Agency Statistics*. Available at: www.iea.org/countries/non-membercountries/indonesia/ [accessed March 12, 2015].

Pilny, K., 2008. *Tiger auf dem Sprung. Politik, Macht und Märkte in Südostasien.*, Frankfurt am Main: Campus Verlag.

Respati, J., 2013. *Indonesia energy transition*, Jakarta: Indonesia Renewable Energy Society.

Roberts, J., 2015. Indonesian president abolishes fuel subsidy. *World Socialist Website*. Available at: www.wsws.org/en/articles/2015/01/15/indo-j15.html [accessed June 2, 2015].

Smith, A.L., 2001. Indonesia: Transforming the leviathan. In J. Funston, ed. *Government and Politics in Southeast Asia*. New York: Zed Books, pp. 74–119.

Wilcox, J., 2012. Indonesia's energy transit: Struggle to realize renewable potential. *RenewableEnergyWorld.com*. Available at: www.renewableenergyworld.com/rea/news/article/2012/09/indonesias-energy-transit?page=all [accessed October 21, 2014].

16 Sociopolitical framework

Political context

Indonesia went through a long history of political struggle, colonialism, ethnic conflicts and nationalism (Cribb and Brown 1995; Vickers 2012). The contested idea of a nation called Indonesia as we know it today has developed over time. The archipelago's ethnic and religious diversity make it challenging to promote a sense of being Indonesian and develop a unifying identity. "Efforts to forge a single nation/state from an extremely heterogeneous society have been based on stressing the anti-colonial struggle against the Dutch" (Smith 2001, p. 82). Before the twentieth century, "localism remained the predominant motif of political and cultural identity" (Elson 2008, p. 1) in the area of today's Indonesia. By bringing most of the archipelago under colonial control in 1870 (Netherlands East Indies), Dutch state-building activities set the basis for an Indonesian nation, but it took decades to bring together the "contending visions" (Bourchier and Hadiz 2003, p. 2) of a nation state called Indonesia. Successive efforts were made "to delineate, define and implant a broadly accepted sense of what 'being Indonesian' might mean" (Elson 2008, p. 316).

With *Pancasila*, the first president Soekarno established the five basic principles of the national ideology and the country's constitution that should facilitate a common identity and the process of homogenization: the belief in one supreme God, just and civilized humanity, national unity, democracy led by wisdom and prudence through consultation and representation, and social justice (Bourchier and Hadiz 2003, p. 24). These principles have since then shaped Indonesian politics and are still relevant – even for the energy sector, where the principle of social justice provides a strong justification for energy subsidies, rural electrification and a state-owned electricity supply. *Pancasila* and political Islam are the most dominant political cultures that are "intrinsic in Indonesian politics" (Suryadinata 1999, p. 29). They helped to create and protect a vibrant civil society "that made the transition to democracy possible" (Abuza 2007).

The conflicting ideas about Indonesia need to be considered when dealing with the country's current political situation. They shape the process of decentralization, lead to political cleavages and foster discussions about provincial independence. Issues of coordination and conflicts between various jurisdictional levels also have a profound historical background. Political struggles have led to a number of regime changes in Indonesia since its independence in 1945 (Case 2002; Tamara 2009). The stable "pseudo-democracy" with "few civil liberties and regular, but rigged elections" (Case 2002, p. 79) under former president Haji Mohamed Suharto's *New Order* stands out in Indonesia's political development (Bourchier and Hadiz 2003, pp. 95–274; Case 2002, pp. 29–80; SarDesai 1989, pp. 239–245; Suryadinata 1999, pp. 117–168). In reaction to Soekarno's *Guided Democracy* (SarDesai 1989, pp. 234–239) and his communist policies, Suharto blamed his predecessor for ruining the economy (Bourchier and Hadiz 2003, p. 10). The political program of New Order brought economic progress, but was also "marked by an increasing concentration of political power and an attenuation of civil and political rights" (Bourchier and Hadiz 2003, p. 13). Political opponents were systematically oppressed. Since then, the army has played an important role in politics (Suryadinata 1999). A further important legacy was the massive state apparatus, which "grew enormously during the New Order period and came closely to reflect the regime's patrimonial culture" (Bourchier and Hadiz 2003, p. 21), resulting in a large, but often ineffective, bureaucracy.

> In a society characterized by networks of close knit groups, and lacking a strong democratic tradition, kinship and family obligations can easily tip over acceptable social practice to become systematic corruption.
>
> (Maidment et al. 1998, p. 238)

The end of the Suharto regime in 1998 marked the beginning of a transition process towards democracy with surprisingly few setbacks. Free, peaceful and direct presidential elections have been held successfully since 2004, together with hundreds of local ballots (Pilny 2008, p. 202). Since the presidential elections in 2014, at the latest, Indonesia can be characterized as a consolidated democracy, although democracy indexes such as the *Bertelsmann Transformation Index* define it as "defective democracy" with a "limited" democratic transition, despite substantial improvements (Bertelsmann Stiftung 2014). FreedomHouse (2014) reduced its rating to "partly free" due to the adoption of a law that is considered to restrict the activities of non-governmental organizations (NGOs). Despite their Western bias towards democracy, these indices at least give a first idea of democratic structures, civil liberties and state–individual relations. They reflect an ongoing process of democratic consolidation towards a stabilized democracy (Croissant and Bünte 2011), although still with considerable limitations. Although the military has become "a much less visible player" (Croissant et al. 2010, p. 114) compared with its influential role under President Suharto's New Order regime, issues such as extensive corruption, the dominance of elites and rising social inequalities remain major challenges to Indonesia's democratic transition (Croissant 2015).

The process of *Reformasi*, or the transition phase towards democracy in post-Suharto Indonesia, needs to be considered as another important factor that has influenced and still affects the complex multi-level governance system. *Reformasi* was implemented in response to Suharto's authoritarian rule and the Asian financial crisis in 1997 (Pilny 2008, p. 213) and led to political consolidation, democratization, decentralization, transparency and accountability. During that time, the rule of law was strengthened in the "fight against corruption, collusion and nepotism" (Tamara 2009, p. 29). Bourchier (2000, p. 15) even describes *Reformasi* as the "transition from a virtual dictatorship [...] to a multi-party democracy."

Reformasi also reinforced the Indonesian constitution (Republic of Indonesia 1945) with its strong emphasis on the division of power. As a bicameral parliament, the People's Representative Council and the People's Consultative Assembly reflect regional representation. At the same time, territorial integrity is still a major political concern, especially in the provinces of Aceh and Papua. Little political power was delegated to the 34 provincial governments due to fears of independence and separatist movements (Smith 2001, p. 86). In contrast, the process of decentralization and the expansion of regional autonomy since 1999 have given regencies and municipalities "real power to run their territory in self-government mode" (Tamara 2009, p. 37), including education, culture and taxation. Although Indonesia remains a unitary political system, decentralization led to powerful subprovincial administrative entities.

> Indonesia's 2001 decentralization is rapidly moving the country from one of the most centralized systems in the world to one of the most decentralized ones. Law 22 of 1999 gives broad autonomy to the regions in all but a few tasks that are explicitly assigned to the center [...]. With the authority come the resources, lots of them.
>
> (Hofman and Kaiser 2002, p. 2)

Shifting power from the national to the local government also deepened the process of democratization (Case 2002, p. 72). Civil society actors are becoming increasingly important in political decision-making and public debates with the emergence and professionalization of NGOs. These new actors campaign for issues such as human rights, environmental protection, democracy or transparency, making them active watchdog organizations for the political system (Frings 2012).

Economic development

Also from an economic perspective, former president Suharto had a massive impact on Indonesia's development. He did not only massively suppress socialist and communist movements, but also liberalized the country's economy, opened markets for foreign investments and decreased poverty rates from 60 to 14 percent just before the Asian economic crisis in 1997 (Smith 2001). At the same time, economic success allowed Suharto to establish a wide system of patronage. Huge conglomerates and a system of crony capitalism developed over the years. Indonesia became an interventionist state "with a predilection for state domination of private-sector economic and political activities" (Bowie and Unger 1997, p. 44).

Its extraordinary richness in natural (and energy-related) resources such as oil, coal, gas, bauxite, copper and iron laid the ground for Indonesia's rapid economic development in the second half of the twentieth century. (Smith 2001, p. 82). The country's rapid economic growth was also fundamentally based on the overexploitation of its vast resources – with negative environmental and social effects. Using the country's resources more sustainably and equitably is a fundamental prerequisite "to keep Indonesia's economy competitive in the long run" (Wingqvist and Dahlberg 2008, p. 1).

"Indonesia has embarked on an impressive growth trajectory" (Geiger 2011, p. vii) since 1998, but the relatively low human development index (HDI) of 0.684, ranking 108th globally (UNDP 2015), reveals a gap between economic progress and human development benefits for broader parts of the population. The McKinsey Global Institute (Oberman et al. 2012) predicts that Indonesia will become the world's seventh largest economy in 2030, surpassing developed countries such as Germany and the United Kingdom. According to Schwab (2013), challenges to doing business in the country remain persistent and are closely related to political developments. The five most problematic factors are corruption, inefficient government bureaucracy, inadequate supply of infrastructure, difficult access to financing, and restrictive labor regulations. These aspects also characterize the situation in the largely state-run electricity system.

Electricity system

Beyond the broader sociopolitical and economic framework, different market conditions, technologies, industrial developments, policy frameworks, research activities and cultural aspects shape the Indonesian electricity system. The substantial effort that would be required to change these regime components leads to a relatively stable fossil fuel-based electricity system (Elzen et al. 2004).

The electricity market is dominated by the state-owned electricity company *Perusahaan Listrik Negara* (PLN). It covers 80 percent of electricity generation and controls the entire transmission and distribution system. The highly regulated market leaves little room for competition among private and independent power producers. In 2004, the Indonesian Supreme Court dismissed the privatization of PLN due to the government's constitutional obligation to provide electricity to the people (Hall 2010, p. 193). Until subsidy reforms in 2014, market conditions were for a long time distorted by substantial subsidies on fossil fuels. From a technological perspective, the electricity market is dominated by oil and coal. For both these energy sources, Indonesia has developed extensive knowledge and technological capacities over decades. The country is also the world's third largest geothermal electricity producer, and has established industries mainly around these three mainstream energy technologies. For modern renewables, domestic manufacturing capacities are relatively weak. Most geothermal facilities have been constructed with foreign knowledge in the 1980s or 1990s. For solar power, companies only assemble parts; they are not able to produce them independently.

Indonesian electricity policies are guided by the four main goals of diversification (including the increase of new and renewable energy sources to 25 percent of the electricity mix by 2025), energy conservation, energy sector reforms (including transparency) and rural electrification (increase of energy access to at least 90 percent by 2020). The Ministry for Energy and Mineral Resources (ESDM) is the key authority for national energy policies. The Directorate General for Electricity and Energy Utilization (EBTKE) is responsible for rural electrification and has implemented an electrification program together with the state-owned electricity utility PLN (community-based rural energy development). In 2012, a feed-in tariff system was issued for biomass, biogas and municipal solid waste. A feed-in tariff for mini hydro and solar was introduced in 2014. Additional incentives are available for some islands with a lack of access to electricity and infrastructure. In May 2016, the Global Renewable Energy Policies and Measures Database (IEA and IRENA 2016) listed 11 policies promoting renewable energy sources. These were passed between 2003 and 2013. They all focus on economic incentives, especially for biomass, geothermal and (most recently) solar power.

Electricity-related scientific activities mainly concentrate on engineering aspects – with the universities in Bandung (Institut Teknologi Bandung) and Yogyakarta (Universitas Gadjah Mada) being the most advanced in this field. Academic research focuses on fossil fuel technologies, but has also slowly opened to research initiatives on renewables. Further social and cultural effects related to electricity demand and supply are diverse. Conventional fuels such as coal and oil, and also geothermal, are perceived to be the most reliable and effective in tackling serious electricity problems and providing base load capacities. Small-scale renewable energy applications are often considered for rural electrification or perceived as bridge technologies, but not as substituting for on-grid fossil fuels. The positive aspects of a decentralized electricity system based on renewable energy sources, such as community ownership, local added-value and the people's direct participation in energy development, are rarely considered.

Renewable energy projects

Except for ambitious plans and a small number of incentives for renewables, there is no robust government support for an energy transition. In the long run, energy experts see a shift towards renewables as an imperative for the development of the biggest economy in Southeast Asia (Respati 2013), because oil reserves are expected to be exhausted by 2020 (Pilny 2008, p. 222), but energy demand will increase rapidly at the same time (Ibrahim et al. 2009).

For the world's largest archipelago, decentralized and independent off-grid energy supply plays an important role in electrifying remote areas. Local energy infrastructure can also be associated with poverty alleviation. The Ministry of People's Welfare is responsible for the development and administration of poverty reduction policies and programs. Within its jurisdiction, communities can opt for local energy infrastructure projects such as hydro-powered mini grids. Although not much political power was delegated to the provincial level due to fears of independence and separatist movements (Smith 2001), decentralization gave regencies and municipalities substantial power for implementing their own legislations, including energy issues. The Ministry of Environment coordinates environmental management, but with wide autonomy for local governments (Susilo and Rhiti 2001, pp. 22–24). The lack of incentive structures and local capacity, as well as high levels of local corruption (Klingshirn 2009; World Bank 2009), prevents effective environmental management despite the existence of relevant laws.

Renewable energy projects are largely small-scale projects for off-grid electrification in remote areas. New on-grid facilities such as large hydro or geothermal plants have not been implemented in recent years due to political disputes between different jurisdictional levels or the availability of cheaper fossil fuel alternatives. Small-scale renewable energy projects that create technology-specific niches cover particularly solar power, biomass and mini-hydro facilities. Most of them run under governmental support schemes or were implemented with support from foreign donors. Independently running systems from private investors are also rare due to the monopolistic market structure, with PLN as the dominant actor. Small-scale renewable energy technologies are often considered as bridge technologies at the local level until an area becomes connected to the main grid. These arguments also play a crucial role in donor-driven interventions that struggle to persist beyond a donor's grant period. Donor organizations such as the Asian Development Bank (ADB 2013) support local capacity building with rural electrification projects for sustainable energy access in remote communities, but most renewable energy projects focus on technology-specific small-scale demonstration activities with very limited impact beyond their local environment (World Bank and NTFPSI 2013).

References

Abuza, Z., 2007. *Political Islam and violence in Indonesia*, New York: Routledge.

ADB, 2013. *Scaling up renewable energy access in eastern Indonesia*, Manila: Asian Development Bank.

Bertelsmann Stiftung, 2014. *BTI 2014: Indonesia country report*, Gütersloh: Bertelsmann Stiftung.

Bourchier, D., 2000. Habibie's interregnum: Reformasi, elections, regionalism and the struggle for power. In C. Manning and P. Van Diermen, eds. *Indonesia in transition: Social aspects of Reformasi and crisis*. London: Zed Books, pp. 15–38.

Bourchier, D. and Hadiz, V.R. eds., 2003. *Indonesian politics and society: A reader*, London: Routledge.

Bowie, A. and Unger, D., 1997. *The politics of open economies: Indonesia, Malaysia, the Philippines and Thailand*, Cambridge: Cambridge University Press.

Case, W., 2002. *Politics in Southeast Asia. Democracy or less*, Richmond: Curzon.

Cribb, R. and Brown, C., 1995. *Modern Indonesia: A history since 1945*, London: Longman.

Croissant, A., 2015. *Die politischen Systeme Südostasiens*, Wiesbaden: VS Verlag für Sozialwissenschaften.

Croissant, A. and Bünte, M., eds., 2011. *The crisis of democratic governance in Southeast Asia*, London: Palgrave Macmillan.

Croissant, A., Kuehn, D., Lorenz, P. and Chambers, P.W., 2010. *Democratization and civilian control in Asia*, London: Palgrave Macmillan.

Elson, R.E., 2008. *The idea of Indonesia: A history*, Cambridge: Cambridge University Press.

Elzen, B., Geels, F.W. and Green, K., 2004. *System innovation and the transition to sustainability: Theory, evidence and policy*, Cheltenham: Edward Elgar.

FreedomHouse, 2014. Freedom in the World: Indonesia. Available at: http://freedomhouse.org/report/freedom-world/2014/indonesia-0#.VEpI6FWUc2Y [accessed May 29, 2015].

Frings, M., 2012. Zivilgesellschaft in Indonesien. *Aus Politik und Zeitgeschichte*, 62(11–12/2012), pp. 43–48.

Geiger, T., 2011. *The Indonesia competitiveness report 2011 sustaining the growth momentum*, Geneva: World Economic Forum.

Hall, D., 2010. Community and worker struggles over ownership and control in a transition to a post-petrol world. In K. Abramsky, ed. *Sparking a worldwide energy revolution: Social struggles in the transition to a post-petrol world*. Oakland: AK.

Hofman, B. and Kaiser, K., 2002. The making of the big bang and its aftermath: A political economy perspective. In *Can decentralization help republic Indonesia?* Atlanta: Georgia State University.

Ibrahim, H.D., Thaib, N.M. and Wahid, L.M.A., 2009. Indonesian energy scenario to 2050: Projection of consumption, supply options and primary energy mix scenarios. *Joint Symposium on Energy Links between Russia and East Asia*. Available at: www.sei.irk.ru/symp2010/en/papers/ENG/P3-04e.pdf [accessed August 20, 2016].

IEA and IRENA, 2016. Global renewable energy. *IEA/IRENA Joint Policies and Measures Database*. Available at: www.iea.org/policiesandmeasures/renewableenergy/ [accessed May 29, 2016].

Klingshirn, U., 2009. *Indonesien in der ökologischen Krise – Ein neues Umweltgesetz soll Abhilfe schaffen*, München: Hanns Seidel Stiftung.

Maidment, R., Goldblatt, D. and Mitchell, J. eds., 1998. *Governance in the Asia-Pacific*, London and New York: The Open University/Routledge.

Oberman, R., Dobbs, R., Budiman, A., Thompson, F. and Rossé, M., 2012. *The archipelago economy: Unleashing Indonesia's potential*, New York: McKinsey Global Institute.

Pilny, K., 2008. *Tiger auf dem Sprung. Politik, Macht und Märkte in Südostasien*, Frankfurt am Main: Campus Verlag.

Republic of Indonesia, 1945. *The 1945 constitution of the Republic of Indonesia*, Jakarta: People Consultative Assembly Republic of Indonesia.

Respati, J., 2013. *Indonesia energy transition*, Jakarta: Indonesia Renewable Energy Society.

SarDesai, D.R., 1989. *Southeast Asia. Past and present*, Boulder: Westview.

Schwab, K., 2013. *The global competitiveness report 2013–2014. Full data edition*, Geneva: World Economic Forum.

Smith, A.L., 2001. Indonesia: Transforming the leviathan. In J. Funston, ed. *Government and Politics in Southeast Asia*. London and New York: Zed Books, pp. 74–119.

Suryadinata, L., 1999. *Interpreting Indonesian politics*, Singapore: Times Academic.

Susilo, F.E. and Rhiti, H., 2001. Environmental governance in Indonesia. In Kato, K., Harashima, Y., Katano, Y., Morita, S., eds. *Environmental governance in Asia*. Tokyo: Institute for Global Environmental Strategies, Sophia University Institute for Global Environmental Studies, pp. 15–30.

Tamara, N., 2009. *Indonesia rising: Islam, democracy and the rise of Indonesia as a major power*, Singapore: Select Books.

UNDP, 2015. *Human development report 2015. Work for human development*, New York: United Nations Development Programme.

Vickers, A., 2012. *A history of modern Indonesia*, Cambridge: Cambridge University Press.

Wingqvist, G.Ö. and Dahlberg, E., 2008. *Indonesia environmental and climate change policy brief*, Gothenburg: University of Gothenburg.

World Bank, 2009. *Investing in a more sustainable Indonesia. Country environmental analysis*, Washington, DC: World Bank.

World Bank and NTFPSI, 2013. Private participation in renewable energy database: Indonesia. Available at: http://ppi-re.worldbank.org/Snapshots/Country/indonesia [accessed May 29, 2015].

17 Renewable energy governance

Introduction

Indonesia went through an even more radical process of decentralization than the Philippines, making it a highly relevant case for analyzing renewable energy development from a multi-level governance perspective with a special focus on the distribution of power among different jurisdictional levels. What are the effects of a multi-level governance system on decision-making in the electricity system? How do various jurisdictional levels coordinate with each other? How are resources distributed between the central government and subnational authorities? How do complex governance arrangements shape support for renewables? The Indonesian case shows how fragmentation of power across jurisdictional levels prevents the electricity system from shifting towards renewables, and how a highly decentralized distribution of power in the electricity system leads to constraints on renewable energy support.

Tackling the status quo of the electricity system, or achieving structural changes and a systemic shift towards renewables, depends on power, defined as the access to hard and soft power resources and the ability to mobilize them. Power relations and the distribution of resources and capacities across jurisdictional levels are fundamental determinants for energy transitions. From a multi-level governance perspective, policy-making related to renewables depends on two central issues: patterns of coordination and consultation between jurisdictional levels, as well as the distribution of resources and capacities across these levels. Understanding the complex governance system for renewables is a prerequisite for discussing how development projects cope with such a system.

Insights from expert interviews

What does the governance framework look like in the Indonesian electricity sector? Insights from qualitative interviews provide some initial ideas for answering that question. In 2014, semi-structured interviews with 55 experts of the Indonesian electricity system were conducted in order to shed light on electricity governance and the role of development cooperation in promoting renewables. Experts from national and local governments (16 interviews), development cooperation (17), public energy (3), civil society (5), renewable energy businesses (7) and academia (7) were conducted. A complete list with all interview partners can be found in Appendix I. Findings from these interviews were underlined with more specific information from field trips to particular development projects that support renewables at the national, provincial or local level.

Figure 17.1 is a detailed summary of some initial general findings from the interviews on renewable energy development in Indonesia and the role of the country's multi-level governance system. The results are based on open answers in semi-structured interviews. Mentioning multiple aspects was possible. These insights are not fully representative, but they reflect the main perceptions among major stakeholders in the energy sector.

The results presented in Figure 17.1 are by no means representative, but they reveal a certain attitude towards renewables among key stakeholders of the Indonesian electricity sector and among development cooperation practitioners. To summarize the results, political factors are at least perceived to have a major influence on renewable energy development. Most interview partners consider national authorities such as the Ministry for Energy and Mineral Resources (ESDM) with its Directorate General for New and Renewable Energy and Energy Conservation (EBTKE) or state-owned companies such as *Perusahaan Listrik Negara* (PLN) as the main drivers for solving current obstacles for renewables. In contrast, the districts (*kabupatens*) are considered to be the main barrier to renewable energy development, because they lack the capacity for and a general understanding of promoting renewables. This perception is also underlined by the fact that the process of decentralization and shifting power to the local level in the field of energy is seen to have had a rather negative impact on renewable energy development and deployment in Indonesia. Only a few interview partners highlighted the potential arising from a decentralized decision-making process that could promote local initiatives.

In general, renewables are considered to be especially helpful for meeting additional demand, but not for substituting for fossil fuels and contributing to base load capacity. Renewable energy technologies are also perceived as an appropriate solution for off-grid electrification of remote areas, but only until a proper grid connection has been established. Environmental concerns such as climate change play only a minor role in promoting renewables. The role of development cooperation is interpreted very differently depending on the interview partner's stakeholder group. Whereas donors highlight their ambitions to promote demonstration projects and provide advice for supportive policies, the recipient country's stakeholders prioritize a stronger need for investment mechanisms (with low interest rates), financial risk reduction and forms of direct technology transfer.

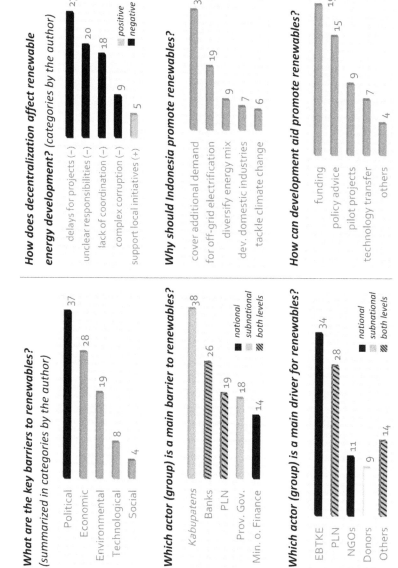

Figure 17.1 Quantitative insights from the expert interviews in Indonesia.
Source: illustration by the author.

Governance framework for renewables

From a rather narrow governance perspective, Indonesia's electricity system seems to be simpler than that in the Philippines or in many other countries of the world, due to PLN's extraordinarily dominating role. As a state-owned company, PLN bundles the entire transmission and distribution system and most (about 80 percent) of the country's power generation. Independent power producers (IPPs) are allowed to sell electricity to the grid, but need to negotiate the price with PLN in order to acquire an official power purchase agreement (PPA) with the state-owned electricity provider. The predominantly state-controlled electricity market has resisted major liberalization efforts due to a constitutional court's decision in 2004 that dismissed the privatization of PLN, because electricity supply should remain the Indonesian government's obligation.

In contrast to the relatively easily understandable electricity market design, respective governance structures and political decision-making processes are complex and often hard to trace. Changes of the political system due to decentralization and recentralization efforts have led to incoherent policies, unclear responsibilities and high degrees of uncertainty.

At the national level, numerous ministries are involved when it comes to electricity-related issues. ESDM is responsible for energy policies and regulations, the Ministry of Finance oversees loans and – most importantly – subsidies in the energy sector, and the Ministry of State-owned Enterprises is a shareholder of PLN. The National Development Planning Body (*Badan Perencanaan Pembangunan Nasional* (BAPPENAS)) functions as an overarching planning authority for development. Depending on the specific source of energy, further ministries can be involved, such as the Ministry of Forestry for geothermal projects or the Ministry of Agriculture for hydro projects. All these ministries influence the electricity system of the country and can act as critical veto players when it comes to steps towards an energy transition. Whereas the Ministry of Finance tends to block renewable energy developments due to cost concerns for the country's national budget, the Ministry of Energy emphasizes oil and coal as the two dominant sources in the electricity mix. Renewables are seen as a good means for rural electrification, but not for constant supply. Supportive policies for renewables are prepared and drafted by interministerial working groups that are pushed by EBTKE, but then cannot be enforced due to a lack of support from the heads of ministries that are involved in the consultation process.

Besides this horizontal power struggle or fragmentation of responsibilities among central government authorities, a vertical differentiation along the policy-making process shapes decisions that promote or obstruct renewable energy development. Due to a process of rapid decentralization between 1999 and 2004 (especially Law No. 22/1999 and Law No. 32/2004), the local regencies (*kabupatens*) and cities (*kotas*) are responsible for the policy field of energy. This includes electricity planning and development, the provision of permits and licenses, project implementation and so forth. Numerous subnational offices (*dinas*) for energy, public works, agriculture and other policy fields can be involved, depending on the district's size and administrative apparatus. These authorities check (often independently of each other) whether a certain renewable energy policy or project is in line with current rules and regulations. Any of these relatively small authorities can significantly delay a project's implementation and increase the costs through corruption or additional "project fees." Project developers cannot implement their renewable energy activities without the local governments' support. This is critical, especially when public land needs to be acquired. Although a process of recentralization was initiated in 2014 (Law No. 23/2014) to reduce local autonomy, direct effects of more central government authority are yet to be seen.

Being administratively located between the national and the municipal governments, the relatively weak provinces (*provinsi*) mainly facilitate the process of coordination, communication and negotiation between national authorities and the local governments. However, if a proposed project crosses the borders of at least two *kabupatens*, the provincial government takes the lead in negotiating this activity between the national government and local authorities. Responsibilities and coordination capacities of provincial authorities vary significantly from province to province, the provinces in Java and Bali being the most advanced.

Summarizing insights from legal documents and interviews, Figure 17.2 presents the complex multi-level governance arrangement of the Indonesian electricity sector.

Such a complex governance arrangement leads to questions of coordination, conflicts and coherence between various jurisdictional levels that all shape the process of an energy transition. Power structures and struggles between national, provincial and municipal governments therefore need to be investigated.

Power structures, resources and capacities

One of the key arguments for delays and problems related to an energy transition towards renewables is the lack of various forms of resources and the inability of responsible actors to mobilize their resources. In a decentralized political system like Indonesia, central–local relations are a crucial political factor that also defines power relations. For renewable energy development, coordination between national policies and planning (e.g. for long-term targets) and local administrations (e.g. for project implementation) is vital.

Governance structures (third dimension of power)

Although rules and regulations for renewable energy in Indonesia vary significantly across technologies, investigating the electricity sector from a multi-level governance perspective reveals a number of obstacles to renewable energy policy-making in general, as well as to project developers, that can be linked to issues of coordination and patterns of interaction between various jurisdictional

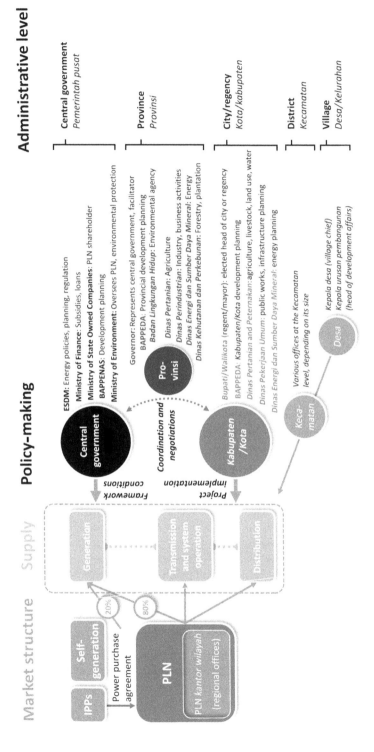

Figure 17.2 The Indonesian electricity sector from a multi-level governance perspective.

Source: illustration by the author.

levels. This section discusses how relevant actors at different jurisdictional levels interact with each other both horizontally and vertically.

(1) Horizontal coordination. At the national level, a number of ministries represent critical veto players for renewable energy development and deployment. For example, the Ministry of Finance is involved in decisions related to support schemes such as feed-in tariffs (FiT); the Ministry of State-owned Enterprises decides on issues that affect the state-owned electricity provider PLN; and the Ministry of Forestry needs to approve geothermal explorations that are carried out in protected forest areas. Interministerial working groups negotiate policies related to renewables in order to prepare for decisions by the appropriate ministers. Although these consultations are considered to be efficient and productive processes for policy formulation by the authorities involved, the outcomes are often rejected by the head of one or more of the ministries. This makes the whole negotiation process prone to delays and uncertainties.

Horizontal coordination at the local level – especially for *kotas* and *kabupatens* – involves various agencies (for energy, agriculture, public works and so forth). Depending on the scope of a renewable energy policy or the project's character as well as the size and responsibilities of municipal authorities, the number of actors involved and potential veto players varies. According to local government officials, the process of coordination for setting up a local renewable energy plan can involve 10 to 12 administrations that need to be considered. Renewable energy activities need to acquire permits related to land use, water resources, pollution, construction and grid connection. As there is no one-stop shop for renewable energy project developers, and the competencies of local bureaucracies are not always clear, permits from these authorities need to be acquired individually, making project planning a time-consuming and costly process. As renewable energy projects are relatively small compared with other energy projects, this lack of coordination and the complex patterns of corruption due to the high number of actors involved significantly increase the projects' transaction costs and the costs per kilowatt/hour electricity output.

(2) Vertical coordination. With Indonesia's decentralization reform program (Holtzappel and Ramstedt 2009), administrative and regulative competencies for the policy field of energy planning and project implementation have shifted significantly to the local level. Yet, the central government remains accountable for providing nationwide regulations and fulfilling the national energy plan. The provincial government is responsible for supporting the central government by implementing projects under state-driven renewable energy programs, such as the solar PV support program *Pembangkit listrik tenaga Surya* (PLTS), or providing provincial energy plans. Except for larger projects that involve more than one *kabupaten* or *kota*, the provincial government has relatively little administrative power to push or block renewable energy activities. However, with its administrative resources and its supervisory function, the provincial level is a crucial source of data and information for potential project developers (concerning promising locations, resources, energy plans and so forth) as well as for the

national government (experiences with local activities, learning from projects and so forth).

Most interjurisdictional conflicts and problems have been raised concerning the relation between the national government and municipalities or cities. Local officials are accused of raising additional taxes in conflict with national legislation, creating additional licenses or permits, and rejecting the central government's policies. This leads to uncoordinated efforts in the field of energy, project delays and high uncertainties due to changing responsibilities – which also affects donor-driven renewable energy support.

Distribution of resources (first dimension of power)

Hard power resources. Taking Rhodes' (1986) differentiation between constitutional, regulatory and political resources, the distribution of hard power resources can be discussed for the field of renewable energy development in Indonesia. Financial and professional resources are considered as capacities.

From a constitutional perspective, the policy field of energy was decentralized in line with the country's Decentralization Act in 1999. As a consequence, the main legislative power for energy projects and planning – including renewables – has shifted to the local (*kabupaten/kota*) level. The national government formulates general guidelines and policies, whereas the provincial government acts as a facilitator between national and local interests. By law, energy projects involve various aspects, such as land use, water supply or grid infrastructure, and therefore need to acquire permits from different national and local stakeholders with constitutional power.

With decentralization, regulatory power should also be strongest at the local level, although the national government provides the major rules and regulations, plans and guidelines for the energy sector. This can lead to uncoordinated rules, competing legislations or conflicting mechanisms. Among central government authorities, regulatory resources for the energy sector are distributed among different ministries (e.g. for energy, finance, state-owned companies). These can act as veto players and block potential renewable energy legislation. Even when central government regulations for renewables exist, their local enforcement remains challenging due to resistance from municipal regents (*Bupatis*), the cities' mayors (*Walikotas*) or other municipal authorities (*dinas*). Regulatory uncertainties remain due to the radical process of decentralization.

> Since 1999, Indonesia has undergone far-reaching political and fiscal decentralization, but it was only with the passing of the 2009 Electricity Law that energy planning was devolved to district governments. The law provides a greater role for district and municipal governments to participate in the provision of electricity services, such as energy planning and setting a regional/local tariff within the bracket established by the central government. However, details remain unclear as implementing regulations have yet to be issued.
>
> (Putri and Ardiansyah 2013)

Due to elections at every administrative level and a strong system of representation even in *Desas* (where the village chief has had to be elected by popular vote since 2004), political power is significantly high at all jurisdictional levels that shape the decision-making process. Due to the direct election of local leaders, the politicians' proximity to the electorate and the people affected by political measures, public support – or resistance – is in general highest at the local level, giving *Bupatis* and *Walikotas* strong political power.

Analyzing power resources reveals how various forms of power are unevenly distributed among different jurisdictional levels and various agents involved in the decision-making process. As a consequence of decentralization, power is not concentrated, but highly fragmented, in the Indonesian energy system, despite a strong state monopoly in the electricity sector.

Soft power resources. The distribution of hard power resources alone does not say much about the actual potential for promoting renewables and substantially changing the electricity system towards clean and sustainable energy sources. Such an analysis needs to include a discussion about the agents' capacity "to argue, to name and to frame" relevant issues (Arts and van Tatenhove 2004, p. 340). Based on the interviews, this ability – or soft power – is strongest at the national level. EBTKE especially is lobbying for and informing about the potential of renewable energy sources to frame them as a means of energy security, electricity diversification and security of supply, above all in remote off-grid areas. The Ministry of Finance and the Ministry of State-owned Enterprises are important veto players that frame renewables as costly and not yet competitive compared with fossil fuels.

Despite its weak constitutional and regulatory power, the provincial government can be a significant agenda-setter when it comes to fundamental decisions related to renewable energy projects. An example is the provincial government of Bali's decision to reject the construction of a geothermal plant in the province – officially for religious reasons. Bali's governor strongly emphasized that position to gain political support from the population, and finally the plans to construct the facility in Bali came to nothing.

The local governments' ability to frame renewables in one or the other way is – in general – relatively weak, although they are most open to modern renewable energy sources as an alternative form of electricity supply that can help to meet basic or additional demand. Various *kabupatens* and *kotas* even actively promote the idea of becoming "renewable energy regions," but complain of a lack of support from the national government.

On the island of Sumba, a range of donors such as the Dutch Humanist Institute for Cooperation (HIVOS), the Asian Development Bank (ADB) and the Norwegian Embassy aim to provide electricity and meet demand entirely by renewable energy sources, to develop a showcase for the feasibility and sustainability of small-scale renewables on a larger scale. The initiative stresses that "co-operation between all parties involved is crucial" (HIVOS 2013, p. 2) for success. In collaboration with the national government and local authorities, it has created a powerful vision, framing electricity with 100 percent renewables as feasible even in remote off-grid areas. Various renewable energy projects have been realized, but it remains to be seen whether and how they can be sustained, maintained and further expanded without external funding.

These examples highlight the meaning of soft power in supporting or rejecting activities for an energy transition towards renewables. The highly decentralized multi-level governance framework provides opportunities for experimentation, creativity and innovation. At the same time, it is challenging for renewables, because potential supporters for environmentally friendly, decentralized and mainly small-scale energy projects have relatively few power resources, whereas agents that are skeptical towards renewables or even oppose them, especially at the national level, are relatively strong concerning their power resources. No significant pressure can be observed across jurisdictional levels for promoting renewables (multi-level reinforcement).

Capacity to mobilize resources (second dimension of power)

The described patterns of coordination and the distribution of hard and soft power resources that are relevant for influencing the electricity sector still do not necessarily answer the question of how power affects the Indonesian energy transition. Such an argument also needs to include the ability of an actor group (or any jurisdictional level) that is involved in the decision-making process to mobilize these resources. Or, in other words, a power-based analysis needs to investigate the actual capacity of actors and actor groups to make use of their resources in order to achieve certain goals and outcomes that reflect their interests and preferences related to renewable energy.

Most technical capacity and expertise related to renewables are concentrated at the national level, and especially with EBTKE and PLN. From a capacity perspective, they have the technical and financial ability to implement renewable energy projects, plans or legislation. The picture looks different at the local level, where a lack of data, trained personnel and general knowledge about renewables hinders relevant authorities in most districts from dealing with initiatives promoting renewable energy technologies. Compared with fossil fuels, renewables are often not yet seen as an established form of energy supply. Such a high degree of skepticism leads to the need for further efforts for any local actor aiming to advocate for renewables.

Coordinating and cooperating with the large number of *dinas* involved in energy-related decisions in *kabupatens* and *kotas* and convincing them about renewables requires a significant amount of professional and financial resources that are often not available at the municipal level, where interests, goals and capacities are highly fragmented. The provincial government could improve this situation by acting as a facilitator and knowledge broker for the local authorities. Provincial administrations could collect and distribute data on energy planning, potential renewable energy sites and so forth, but they lack the ability to raise their own funding for such initiatives. Moreover, the provinces' ability to actually implement plans or programs remains restricted due to their constitutionally weak role compared with the *kabupatens* and *kotas*.

Finally, financial capacity is strongest at the national level, despite the local authorities' ability to raise their own taxes. Indonesia's national state revenues are distributed among provinces. Provinces further distribute financial resources to the local level. This system is open to abuse and prone to corruption due to the number of levels involved. Municipal officials complain about lack of financial support, but are also accused of unilaterally introducing taxes that are illegal and against national legislation.

Professional capacity is unevenly distributed and tends to depend on the economic power of provinces, regencies and cities. In general, municipal authorities lack the skills and material to implement the central government's policies. Information relevant to renewables (on electricity supply, planning, land use and so forth) often exists at the provincial level, whereas municipal (and further subnational) authorities struggle to deliver this information. Most expertise and technical know-how related to renewables are centered at the national level, especially with EBTKE and PLN.

Figure 17.3 summarizes this qualitative analysis of the multi-level governance framework of the Indonesian electricity sector and renewable energy development. Note that resources and capacities, as well as the administrative structure, can vary significantly from province to province as well as from *kabupaten/kota* to *kabupaten/kota*, mainly depending on their size and economic situation. The actual power of subnational authorities across the archipelago can be very different. Therefore, Figure 17.3 should be read as a rough overview of the situation in Indonesia. The differentiation between power resources and capacity is not as selective as it might appear. Capacities such as technical expertise, personnel and money are also incremental resources that are needed for an agent's ability to mobilize other (constitutional, legislative and regulatory) power resources. The figure summarizes power resources and capacities for the three major jurisdictional levels in Indonesia – the central government (focusing on the Ministry of Energy, Ministry of Finance, Ministry of State-owned Enterprises, BAPPENAS, Ministry of Environment, Ministry of Forestry), provinces (governor, provincial *Badan Perencanaan Pembangunan Daerah* (BAPPEDA), Environmental Agency, *dinas* for agriculture, industry, energy and forestry) and municipalities (*Bupati/Walikota*, local BAPPEDA, *dinas* for agriculture, public works and energy).

The following section discusses how development cooperation considers these complex multi-level governance structures, central–local relations, and the distribution of power resources and capacities at different jurisdictional levels.

Donor-driven interventions

Donors have promoted renewables in Indonesia for decades. Although AidDATA (2016) does not provide a comprehensive overview of all project

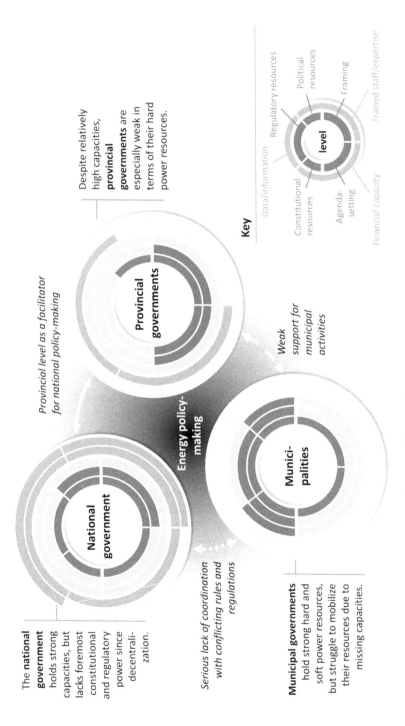

The **national government** holds strong capacities, but lacks foremost constitutional and regulatory power since decentralization.

Serious lack of coordination with conflicting rules and regulations

Provincial level as a facilitator for national policy-making

National government

Provincial governments

Weak support for municipal activities

Energy policy-making

Munici-palities

Despite relatively high capacities, **provincial governments** are especially weak in terms of their hard power resources.

Key

Data/information

Regulatory resources

Political resources

Constitutional resources

level

Framing

Agenda-setting

Trained staff/expertise

Financial capacity

Municipal governments hold strong hard and soft power resources, but struggle to mobilize their resources due to missing capacities.

Figure 17.3 Power resources and capacities for renewables in Indonesia.

Source: illustration by the author.

activities, the database gives a first impression of the field's development. For the Indonesian energy sector (*energy generation and supply*), AidDATA lists 1,146 projects from 25 funding organizations, with US$38.7 billion offered in international funding between 1957 and 2015. Figure 17.4 illustrates how the number of donor organizations and energy project activities in Indonesia developed between 1970 and 2013.

Bi- and multilateral donors are not considered to be a major driver for an Indonesian energy transition, but they are confronted with a substantial demand for funding and policy advice. Thus, their potential contributions to renewable energy development are manifold – for large-scale facilities and industrial development (e.g. geothermal), rural electrification with small-scale applications (e.g. solar) and capacity building (e.g. advisory for political incentives).

Can development activities promote structural change in the electricity sector through learning, diffusion or upscaling? Development cooperation for renewables has a long history in Indonesia. Donors supported and implemented large-scale geothermal facilities as well as smaller solar and mini hydro applications for rural electrification in the 1970s. These mainly technical project activities have not only increased, but also diversified over the last decades – with an additional focus on training, capacity building and political advisory activities. Donors represent external actors outside the Indonesian governance system, but they can provide considerable project-specific funding. This allows them to create protected environments or niches for technology-specific experiments or demonstration projects. Donors do not only implement local renewable energy projects, but also tackle national frameworks such as market conditions, industrial development or policies to scale up results.

Donor-driven renewable energy projects are recognized to be beneficial for the country, but they have had only limited success in terms of structural change or even promoting a transition towards renewables. As an example, the ADB (2012) aimed to scale up clean energy access in Eastern Indonesia by supporting the development of regional energy plans and identifying priority investment programs. The project tackled clear obstacles for renewables, outlined how to build up capacities, and combined specific demonstration projects with policy support. At the same time, the project design remained silent about how to institutionalize or sustain results without external funding, leading to no outcomes beyond the project's official termination.

Donor-driven renewable energy projects failed to influence the energy system, because either they were badly implemented (project delays or failure due to local resistance, additional demands, corruption and/or weak technical capacity) or they failed to institutionalize forms of learning and coordination across various jurisdictional levels. Although donor agencies stress the role of knowledge management in scaling up results, and despite the donor community's decades of experience with renewable energy projects in the country, development cooperation struggles to provide any kind of best practice examples for successful scaling up of results, multijurisdictional learning or project replication. Donor organizations limit their attention to the time when the project is

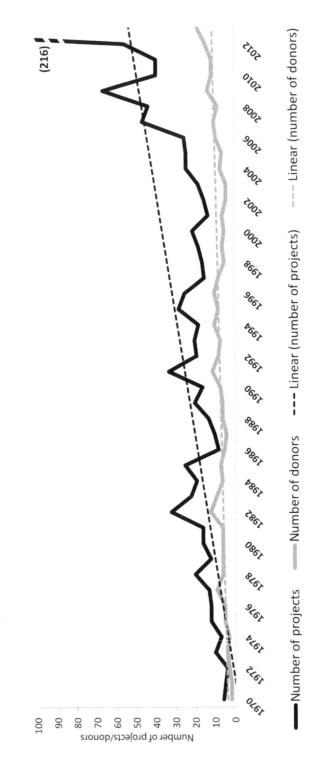

Figure 17.4 Development cooperation over time in the Indonesian energy sector.

Source: illustration by the author.

being implemented and running with donor support; they rarely take action for sustaining and institutionalizing results, or facilitate learning and knowledge management beyond the official duration of the project. Donors struggle to create ownership by including multiple stakeholders from various jurisdictional levels or by promoting structural change through supportive incentives.

Interestingly, donor organizations link most reasons for project problems or failure to the process of (political) decentralization. According to organizations such as United States Assistance for International Development (USAID), Japan International Cooperation Agency (JICA) or Deutsche Gesellschaft für Internationale Zusammenarbeit (GIZ), the ongoing process of radical decentralization and recentralization led to often unclear responsibilities, too powerful local authorities, and delays to implementing projects due to aspects such as increasing corruption.

Finally, donor-driven renewable energy projects are perceived to be a good idea for meeting additional electricity demand or electrifying remote areas, but they are not considered to be capable of substituting for fossil fuels, structurally changing the electricity system and pushing it systematically towards renewables. Except for EBTKE, Indonesian government officials and other actors stress the importance of fossil fuels for energy security even in remote areas, where local authorities perceive renewables as an option only until the area is connected to the grid (bridge technology).

How does development cooperation cope with the complex multi-level governance structures? Donors are greatly concerned with the heavily decentralized political system, which leads to increased transaction costs for implementing any kind of project. This is especially true for technology-driven local experiments that depend on cooperation with local administrations and politicians. Since national authorities such as EBTKE are the common direct counterparts for official development assistance (ODA) activities, they are involved at an early stage of project planning. Local authorities are often only then confronted with the project when its design has already been determined. The more powerful the local administrations are, the more difficult it becomes for the donor agency to implement any project activity without negotiating it beforehand. At the same time, donors complain about the lack of technical capacity, trained personnel and general understanding of renewable energy technologies at subnational jurisdictional levels.

Despite high awareness of these power-related issues, they cannot easily be addressed with the development project designs, which are often short-term interventions and do not fully acknowledge the complexity of the political system. Too often, foreign donors follow a "Western" perception of renewables that would require robust local technical expertise and strong private investments to be successful, but they fail to adapt to the fundamentally different political framework and social context in Indonesia. Donor-driven activities are also unable to address structural issues related to the fragmentation of power resources or capacities that are crucial for the multi-level decision-making process for renewables. Short-term projects, such as Energy and Environment

Partnership's (EEP) intention to establish a regional energy plan in Central Kalimantan, aimed to facilitate coordination and provide capacity building at the local level, but failed to address power relations and conflicts between different authorities, which need to be considered for long-term effects.

Political factors related to the multi-level governance framework, such as lack of coordination, fragmentation of power resources, insufficient capacities and complex corruption patterns, shape renewable energy development in Indonesia, but these are not easy to overcome and cannot be solved by most donor-driven renewable energy projects. Donors implement innovative renewable energy projects at the national, provincial and local levels. Better reflecting the complex political context and coordinating these interventions could substantially increase the donor community's effectiveness and its impact on pushing an Indonesian energy transition towards renewables.

References

ADB, 2012. *Republic of Indonesia: Scaling up renewable energy access in Eastern Indonesia*, Manila: Asian Development Bank.

AidData, 2016. AidData 3.0. Open data for international development. Available at: http://aiddata.org/ [accessed March 30, 2016].

Arts, B. and van Tatenhove, J., 2004. Policy and power: A conceptual framework between the "old" and "new" policy idioms. *Policy Sciences*, 37(3–4), pp. 339–356.

HIVOS, 2013. *Iconic Island Sumba: 100% renewable energy*, Jakarta: HIVOS.

Holtzappel, C.J.G. and Ramstedt, M. eds., 2009. *Decentralization and regional autonomy in Indonesia*, Singapore: Institute of Southeast Asian Studies.

Putri, D.P.A. and Ardiansyah, F., 2013. Hot, clean and complex: Unlocking Indonesia's geothermal power. *Strategic Review*, 3(1), pp. 72–85.

Rhodes, R.A.W., 1986. *Control and power in central-local government relations*, Aldershot: Gower.

18 Synthesis

Introduction

Despite Indonesia's high dependency on fossil fuels, developing renewables is an important consideration for future energy planning and electrification programs. The central government aims to increase the share of renewables in the electricity mix significantly over the coming years. At the same time, coal will still dominate the electricity market for decades (EBTKE 2012).

The Indonesian case reveals how power struggles and complex governance structures affect renewable energy development in a decentralized country with a fossil fuel-based electricity system and rich in energy-related resources. Transforming the electricity system towards clean and renewable energy sources depends not only on supportive policies and incentive structures from the national government, but also on support from local elites and state-owned companies such as *Perusahaan Listrik Negara* (PLN) or Pertamina. Coordination across different jurisdictional levels and the fragmented distribution of power resources and capacities significantly shape the Indonesian energy transition. Complex patterns of corruption in a decentralized political system further hamper the realization of small-scale renewable energy projects.

Bi- and multilateral donors have promoted renewables in Indonesia for decades – but with limited success concerning any structural effects or systemic changes for an energy transition towards renewables. Sustaining development projects for more than a few years, replicating results and institutionalizing efforts remain critical challenges for donor-driven interventions.

Complex governance challenges

Indonesia represents a fascinating case for investigating the role of multi-level governance structures and power in renewable energy development and donor-driven support. The ongoing process of decentralization and recentralization might not allow the formulation of final judgments, but there seems to be no doubt that multi-level governance issues have a significant impact on renewable energy development in Indonesia (Marquardt 2014). There is a strong need for further investigations into that topic to contribute to a debate about renewables in developing countries and emerging economies that often focuses too narrowly on technological or economic arguments.

There are strong links between the political process of decentralization and obstacles to both large-scale on-grid facilities and small-scale applications. Most of the barriers to renewables that were mentioned by the experts interviewed (such as complex corruption, lack of coordination and failure of local inclusion) can be linked to Indonesia's highly decentralized governance structures. A better understanding of these structures helps to analyze the potential of and obstacles to renewables and to provide more demand-driven support that acknowledges the country-specific context.

Investigating all three dimensions of power (structures, resources and capacities) represents a challenging task in a country like Indonesia due to its complex and evolving political system, the gap between written rules and day-to-day practices, lack of awareness of legal processes, high levels of uncertainty, and limited access to resources on different jurisdictional levels.

Multi-level governance structures matter. Indonesian governance structures were identified as a crucial obstacle to renewable energy development. A lack of horizontal coordination between different ministries at the national level that can act as veto players led to delays in policy-making for supportive regulations and incentives. Although the Directorate General for New and Renewable Energy and Energy Conservation (EBTKE) was founded in 2010 to foster the national government's commitment to renewables and to give renewables an institutionalized setting, the directorate needs time to negotiate policy proposals with other ministries that follow different interests. Delays to policy formulation are the result. Going beyond horizontal coordination on the national level and taking a multi-level governance perspective makes the picture of renewable energy governance look even more complex. Despite a relatively homogeneous energy market that is dominated by the state-owned PLN, various subnational authorities need to be considered and coordinated for renewable energy projects. With decentralization in place, the national government cannot implement renewable energy activities without the local governments' approval. This requires patterns of coordination and negotiation, which remain to be established. Such a situation becomes a burden, especially for relatively small-scale renewable energy activities, due to their relatively small size but high administrative expenses.

Hard and soft power resources matter. The structural dimension of renewable energy development is closely connected to the distribution of hard and soft power resources. A dilemma of the political system frames the situation. The national government is the most active jurisdictional level when it comes to the formulation of energy-related policies, programs and so forth. However, most constitutional and regulatory resources can be found at the local level, where authorities and administrative structures are highly fragmented – with often unclear responsibilities when it comes to the topic of renewables. Authorities dealing with public land, development, agriculture, energy and water are all involved to some extent. The provincial level acts as a facilitator, holding in particular soft power resources for framing the topic of renewables (positively or negatively) and bringing it onto the political agenda.

Capacities to mobilize resources matter. Not only power resources, but also financial, professional and technical capacities are distributed unevenly among jurisdictional levels. Unlike the situation of hard power resources, capacities are accumulated at the national level, but massively underdeveloped at the municipal level (depending on the municipality). This leads to a problematic situation for the development of renewable energy sources. Whereas the central government holds the expertise, technical know-how, financial resources and awareness of renewables that are necessary to promote them further, most local government authorities lack these capacities, but hold the actual power resources that are needed to implement, monitor and adjust regulations. Promoting renewables in Indonesia needs a coordinated effort between the jurisdictional level holding most relevant power resources for structural change (municipalities) and the level holding the actual capacities to mobilize these resources for renewable energy development (central government).

Structural elements of the political system, resources and capacities affect renewable energy development in Indonesia in different ways. All three dimensions of power are interdependent. For example, improving coordination between national and subnational authorities requires capacities that are weakly developed in most municipalities. In contrast, local authorities are often unable to mobilize their own resources for promoting renewable energy projects due to inexperienced and weakly developed administrative structures. These issues also affect donor-driven renewable energy interventions. Development cooperation organizations highlight the negative effects of decentralization on their activities and struggle not only to implement, but especially to sustain, renewable energy projects. Scaling up or diffusing experiences beyond a project's jurisdictional level seems to be beyond the donor's control.

Development cooperation for renewables

Taking into account the long history of development cooperation promoting renewables in contrast to the weak role of renewable energy sources in the country's energy mix, donors seem to struggle to achieve any long-term structural effects in favor of renewables. Three critical issues concerning the role of development activities in the fields of renewable energy development and a potential energy transition in the country can be derived from the analysis above.

The governance system strongly affects donor-driven interventions. Taking a multi-level governance perspective reveals potential and actual obstacles to renewable energy projects. Most donor-driven activities concentrate on a specific level of intervention (national, provincial or municipal), but fail to include in their long-term planning other jurisdictional levels that are vital, especially for the sustainability of the project. This fact does not mean that donors are not aware of the multi-level complexity of the political system. On the contrary, most donors even run their own decentralization programs and acknowledge the challenges of the process. Yet, renewable energy projects normally do not take into account the various jurisdictional levels that are necessary for sustainable project outcomes and structural effects through scaling up or diffusing experiences from one level to another.

Donor-driven projects scarcely address relevant issues related to power. Integrating insights from power theory about the distribution of power resources and the ability of decision-makers at various jurisdictional levels to make use of these resources revealed further critical obstacles and challenges for renewable energy project developers. The field is characterized by a high degree of fragmentation concerning power resources and a discrepancy between holding constitutional and/or political power and having the financial and/or technical capacity to mobilize these power resources. Another concern represents the large number of potential veto players that can block or seriously delay renewable energy projects in the Indonesian electricity system. Various national and subnational authorities need to coordinate (both vertically and horizontally) with each other to implement renewable energy policies and projects (approve legislations, exchange information, share technical expertise etc.). Foreign donors cannot easily tackle these structural issues or even accelerate coordination processes between various levels from outside the Indonesian political system.

Donor harmonization falls behind international commitments. For decades, donors have tended to follow a simple project-by-project approach with a lack of overarching long-term programs. More comprehensive activities do exist, but their broad scope and large number of goals, together with relatively little funding, prevent structural effects. Most donor-driven activities are coordinated rather informally with each other. Strong forms of harmonization are missing. This leads to critical issues of fragmentation in the field of renewable energy development, with different donor-driven agendas. A coherent, all-encompassing framework for renewable energy support that connects donor-driven activities at various jurisdictional levels with each other and with the Indonesian long-term development goals is missing.

Figure 18.1 illustrates the complex governance framework with the distribution of resources and capacities to which donor-driven renewable energy activities are exposed. Although a donor's direct counterpart at the national level (such as EBTKE) has the most financial, technical and professional capacities, it does not necessarily represent the most powerful jurisdictional level. As a result of the Indonesian decentralization process, local authorities, especially at the municipal level, combine strong power resources, whereas provincial governments in their role as negotiators and facilitators make use of soft power resources to frame a topic. Donor organizations fail to consider this complex governance framework and struggle to implement on time a project activity that was formulated in consultation with a national counterpart, but not together with the subnational jurisdictions that might also be affected by the project – and need to cooperate for its implementation. The figure simplifies the relation between donor-driven support for renewables and the distribution of power resources and capacities at different jurisdictional levels in Indonesia.

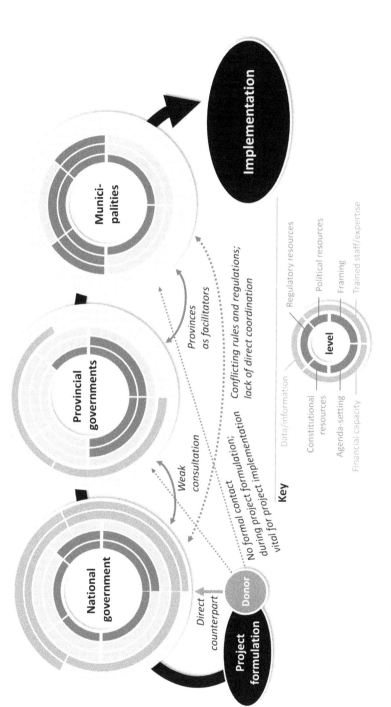

Figure 18.1 Linking donor-driven support for renewables to power in Indonesia.

Source: illustration by the author.

Experiences from Indonesia reveal the complexity of renewable energy governance in emerging economies that are becoming increasingly relevant for global economic development, greenhouse gas emissions and other environmental concerns. Donors need to acknowledge that complexity in order to achieve structural effects – or, at least, to increase their likelihood – for an energy transition towards renewables.

References

EBTKE, 2012. *Development of new and renewable energy and energy conservation in Indonesia*, Jakarta: Ministry of Energy and Mineral Resources Indonesia.

Marquardt, J., 2014. A struggle of multi-level governance: Promoting renewable energy in Indonesia. *Energy Procedia*, 58, pp. 87–94.

Part VI
Conclusions

19 Cross-country comparison

Introduction

Investigating the political dimension of energy transitions in Southeast Asia has been a constant process of learning. Starting with the aim of measuring the impact and effectiveness of donor-driven renewable energy projects and evaluating their sustainability, the focus of this research shifted more and more towards the aid-receiving countries' governance systems. Issues related to coordination and power became the primary concern. How the distribution of power resources and the ability to make use of these resources at different jurisdictional levels shape energy transitions became the focal point of this book. An open multi-level governance framework was applied that incorporates the role of power in central–local government relations.

Discussing how donors aim to foster renewable energy development and how power shapes energy transitions in the Philippines and Indonesia, this chapter provides a cross-country comparison. Insights from both countries are then linked to experiences from Southeast Asia and other developing countries around the world.

How donors foster renewable energy development

Numerous donors have implemented various renewable energy projects in the Philippines and Indonesia over decades. Insights from field trips and expert interviews related to 14 project case studies are summarized here. Project overviews for each of the activities mentioned can be found in Appendix III.

The eight projects in the Philippines either dealt with national advice related to the 2008 Renewable Energy Act or promoted solar electrification in rural areas. The United Nations Development Programme (UNDP) funded the Capacity Building to Remove Barriers to Renewable Energy Development (CBRED) project and a Renewable Energy Based Village Power System in Palawan. The Deutsche Gesellschaft für Internationale Zusammenarbeit (GIZ) and its predecessor organization German Technical Cooperation (GTZ) implemented a photovoltaic (PV) mini grid for village electrification on Verde Island, the Renewables Made in Germany initiative and the Supporting the Philippine

Climate Change Commission (Support CCC) project. The Climate Change and Clean Energy (CEnergy) project and promoting rural electrification under the Alliance for Mindanao Off-Grid Renewable Energy (AMORE) were activities funded by United States Assistance for International Development (USAID). The Australian Agency for International Development (AusAID) provided solar home systems to remote villages under their Municipal Solar Infrastructure Programme (MSIP).

The six project case studies in Indonesia supported renewable energy development at the national, the provincial or the local level. GIZ funded the Promotion of Least Cost Renewable Energy in Indonesia (LCORE) project and implemented Energising Development (EnDev) to monitor micro hydro and solar PV systems under government-run electrification schemes. The Finnish Energy and Environment Partnership (EEP) supported a project for establishing a regional energy plan in Central Kalimantan, and the Humanist Institute for Cooperation (HIVOS) facilitated the implementation and maintenance of small-scale biodigesters for farming in Bali. A Geothermal Power Generation Development project was initiated by the World Bank, and USAID provided support for a regional climate mitigation plan in Sumatera Utara.

All 14 projects were investigated along six broader dimensions:

- Project level (Did the project lead to positive outcomes at the direct level of intervention?)
- Coordination (Did the project facilitate coordination across different jurisdictional levels?)
- Capacity (Did the project help to build up financial, technical or professional capacity?)
- Institutions (Has project output been institutionalized beyond donor support?)
- Decision-making (Did the project positively affect decision-making processes?)
- Power resources (Did the project change the distribution of power resources?)

Whereas almost all projects had positive outcomes at their direct level of intervention, donors struggled to affect decision-making processes and the distribution of power resources. Outcomes are mixed with regard to coordination, capacity building and institutionalization of results.

Addressing coordination

Donors are highly aware of the need for interjurisdictional coordination for promoting renewables, which they aim to facilitate with different methods. But even if issues of coordination are seriously considered, this does not necessarily lead to sustainable outcomes. To give an example, UNDP constructed a solar-diesel hybrid mini grid in the Philippine municipality of El Nido in 2004 under the Palawan New and Renewable Energy and Livelihood Support Project (PNRELSP). The project provided independent power supply to 232 households in the province of Palawan, where 60 percent of the *barangays* are not yet electrified. Funded by UNDP, the mini grid was a joint and coordinated effort by the provincial, municipal and *barangay* governments. Substituting for diesel generation, the project was documented as a success in a final report (DOE 2006). Although the local population were not actively involved in planning or operation, the project led to a high degree of local political commitment to renewables and supported the development of a local utility (New Ibajay Electric Cooperative). In 2013, the solar component needed to be turned off due to technical problems with the batteries and the converter. The local electric cooperative and the municipal government were not able to solve the problems on their own, without financial or technical support from the national government. Neither national nor provincial authorities considered themselves responsible for maintaining or further financing the system.

Addressing issues of coordination is also challenging in Indonesia. The central government requested each province to establish its own regional energy plan (*Rencana Umum Energi Daerah*, RUED) and also to identify renewable energy potential, developments and future needs. EEP supported the province of Kalimantan Tengah with the development of its regional energy plan through capacity building and training between 2013 and 2014. The project concentrated on capacity building at the provincial level, as well as on three *kabupatens* (Palangka Raya, Kapuas and Kotawaringhin Timur), which were considered as pilots to see whether and how they could contribute to the RUED. The Long-range Energy Alternatives Planning (LEAP) system was introduced, and staff were trained to collect data for the model. The activity was finished after 1 year of funding, but missed its target to establish a draft RUED. The project's duration turned out to be much too short to achieve coordinated efforts. Delays occurred due to a lack of coordination between different local authorities. Relevant data needed to be collected from different stakeholders, but only a single *Badan Perencanaan Pembangunan Daerah* (BAPPEDA) official was responsible for retrieving data from at least eight *dinas* as well as from Pertamina and *Perusahaan Listrik Negara* (PLN). Some of these institutions refused to provide information. Even with a supporting letter from the *Bupati*, some *dinas* were reluctant to cooperate. Clearly, EEP underestimated the effort necessary to retrieve information from different authorities.

USAID had similar experiences with the implementation of a regional climate mitigation plan in the province of North Sumatra. All Indonesian provinces are obliged to develop their own regional climate mitigation plans to contribute to the national target for greenhouse gas mitigation. USAID provided expertise related to renewables and trained local staff. The plan was finalized in 2014, but its actual implementation remained challenging in 2014. The project's direct contribution also remains hard to measure.

To improve the very much underdeveloped Indonesian geothermal sector, the World Bank provided policy advice and technical capacity building, mainly to the Ministry for Energy and Mineral Resources (ESDM). Although the Geothermal Law (No. 27 of 2003) made provincial and district governments the owners of geothermal resources in their constituencies, these subnational authorities were not an integral part of the project design. Despite the long project duration (2008–2013), the overall progress was rated as "unsatisfactory" (World Bank 2012) in a final progress report, mainly because of a lack of coordination across jurisdictional levels.

Addressing capacity

Capacity building activities for renewables were undertaken by various donors. In the Philippines, CBRED was one of the first and most prominent examples. Implemented by UNDP between 2003 and 2011, the program acted as an overarching hub for renewable energy support activities related to political, financial and technical aspects. Although the actual results are difficult to measure, and various issues have only been addressed superficially, the Renewable Energy Management Bureau (REMB) greatly acknowledged the support of the project, which helped to coordinate between relevant stakeholders, institutionalized market services, and provided capacity building for national and local government representatives. The project's scope was in line with the country's demands for clean domestic energy supply, and thus addressed capacity issues that were highly relevant to its Philippine counterparts.

As part of its Support CCC project, GIZ also facilitated the implementation of a countrywide feed-in tariff (FiT) in the Philippines. Although the 2008 Renewable Energy Act (RE Act) had already announced an FiT scheme, its enforcement and implementation suffered from huge delays. GIZ aimed to foster the implementation of the FiT through political advice and capacity building for the Department of Energy (DOE). The project raised awareness of renewables in general and provided training for feeding in renewables into the grid. Results like the announcement of the FiT rates in 2013 cannot be directly linked to the project (attribution gap), but REMB recognized the activity for providing substantial resources to support its own efforts. Due to a limited timeframe and financial constraints, the project followed a narrow, but clear, focus on policy advice for an FiT. Efforts were concentrated at the national level, with REMB being the main counterpart. GIZ was perceived as a knowledge broker and an important source of expertise, but could not tackle deeply rooted political factors such as central–local interactions, corruption patterns or powerful vested interests that significantly affect the FiT.

Combining energy security issues with action against climate change, USAID implemented the CEnergy project between 2010 and 2014. Despite its short project period, CEnergy covered a broad range of topics to mitigate climate change through the improved utilization of clean and renewable energy in the electricity and transportation sectors. Aiming to strengthen existing collaboration between government entities, the private sector, civil society, media and academia, USAID focused on policy implementation and institutional strengthening related to climate change and renewable energy. Covering four broad topics (improving policy implementation, regulatory capacity, climate change mitigation, public understanding and support for renewables), the relatively small project was overwhelmed by the field's complexity, and direct outcomes were hard to trace.

Capacity building on a much smaller scale was undertaken by HIVOS and Foundation of Netherlands Volunteers (SNV) in Indonesia. They implemented more than 630 small-scale biodigesters in Bali and other provinces to provide electricity supply for organic farming and substitute for kerosene. The project site in Gianyar represents one example, where a very small-scale biogas digester (capacity of $4 m^3$, sufficient for dung from up to seven cows) was constructed to serve a single household's consumption and organic farming activities. Local banks, in cooperation with the provincial government, provided a financing scheme, and four local organizations were responsible for construction, maintenance and monitoring. The project site is also part of the Indonesian program *Biogas Rumah* (BIRU), which aims to facilitate knowledge transfer and has helped to build up capacities at various levels. By December 2013, the program had built 11,249 biogas reactors in nine Indonesian provinces.

The strong need for capacities to sustain donor-driven interventions, especially at the local level, is underlined by the failure of many solar PV projects in the Philippines. In 1990, GTZ constructed a 3 kW/peak solar power plant and distributed solar home systems to San Agapito on Isla Verde. The facility should have acted as a demonstration project to showcase the feasibility of renewables in remote off-grid areas, but the entire system rapidly collapsed without external support. Solar home systems were also distributed under the MSIP, which was implemented as a joint venture between AusAID and BP solar. Again, efforts at capacity building were minimal. Experiences from *barangays* such as Guiwanon in Guimaras show that the systems could not be maintained. Under the AMORE program, USAID provided solar home systems and solar lanterns to more than 22,000 households in almost 500 remote *barangays* all over Mindanao. Although over 50 percent of all projects stopped running several years after their implementation, some communities managed to self-sustain the facilities. One successful example can be seen in Bantol, where a *Barangay* Renewable Energy and Community Development Association (BRECDA) was founded to run and maintain the systems. Being organized in a cooperative manner, with high involvement of the people as shareholders, the BRECDA managed to build up financial capacity for maintaining the systems and funding further solar home systems without external support. USAID's focus on capacity building with partners and stakeholders was considered to be crucial for success.

Addressing institutions

To sustain project results, efforts towards institutionalization are required. Instead of virtually building small-scale decentralized renewable energy projects,

EnDev built up a monitoring and evaluation system for the Indonesian government to improve the systems' maintenance and long-term operation. Monitoring more than 300 mini grids, GIZ provided technical support, established a knowledge management framework and created ownership for the projects. Since the systems should be self-sustained by Indonesian partners, institutionalization is a key objective for EnDev, but technical problems with solar PV installations cannot be solved without the donor's technical assistance. This happened at a site in Gunung Kidul in the province of Yogyakarta in 2014. Key provincial government authorities, such as the Department of Public Works, were not aware of the project and could not act as facilitators between the district and the national government. Institutionalized forms of capacity building, learning and troubleshooting were yet to be established.

Renewable energy sources are already a cost-competitive alternative to fossil fuels, especially in remote off-grid areas. Implemented by GIZ, LCORE aimed to identify ways to use renewable energy sources in Indonesia in an economically feasible manner. Providing advisory activities, training and workshops, LCORE aligned its efforts with the working areas and targets of EBTKE in order to institutionalize supportive renewable energy frameworks. LCORE also aimed to implement demonstration projects, but struggled to identify appropriate project sites and coordinate activities with subnational authorities.

The German export initiative Renewables Made in Germany was also implemented by GIZ. The project ran between 2011 and 2015 and provided assistance for a robust political framework for renewables and an enabling environment for renewable energy businesses in the Philippines. The initiative's scope shifted from biomass to solar power regulations. GIZ organized training and published guidebooks about technical aspects related to solar PV. Philippine government officials widely acknowledged the support of the project, which succeeded in formulating and institutionalizing rules and regulations for net metering and the interconnection of rooftop PV systems.

Addressing decision-making and power

Decision-making in the Philippines and the Indonesian energy sector is complex and determined by a variety of formal and informal rules of the game. None of the 14 donor-driven renewable energy project case studies described here was successful in facilitating or even changing patterns of decision-making between different actors or across jurisdictional levels. Also, none of the projects significantly tackled issues of power and the distribution of resources.

Insights from 14 donor-driven projects in two countries might not provide a comprehensive picture of development cooperation, but they allow some general remarks concerning their potential and limitations when promoting energy transitions. Representing actors outside the political and economic systems of the recipient countries, donors are relatively flexible concerning their priorities and projects. They can introduce new ideas and technologies and create protected niches for sociotechnical innovations such as solar mini grids on isolated islands, small-scale biomass projects or self-organized cooperatives for electricity supply, which might not have been introduced without foreign investment. Capacity building activities and advisory projects for political incentive schemes have even broadened the donors' portfolios and their ability to foster an energy transition.

Development cooperation has facilitated coordination and built up capacity for renewables in the Philippines and Indonesia, but the ability to address complex decision-making processes, or even change power relations, remains marginal. The projects presented here demonstrate that sustaining and institutionalizing project results largely depends on the political will of central governments and local authorities. Shifting power resources and changing structural elements of the system are often far outside the donors' direct control. Even capacity building has limited effects, since it depends on complex institutional arrangements and personal factors.

How power shapes energy transitions

This book has focused on the Philippines and Indonesia as in-depth case studies in order to ensure a more profound analysis of the recipient countries' governance frameworks. This limitation allowed us to fully reflect on the meaning of strong subnational authorities, the fragmentation of power resources and capacities among different jurisdictional levels, and the donors' commitments to renewables in order to respond to the two central research questions:

> How do complex governance structures in the developing country's electricity sector affect renewable energy development and donor-driven interventions?

> How does development cooperation address the complexity of energy-related governance structures in developing countries?

To answer these questions, three dimensions of power were investigated:

1   Concentrating on the meaning of national, provincial and municipal governments, the role of different jurisdictional levels for promoting renewables was analyzed from a multi-level governance perspective (structural power).
2   Within this governance arrangement, aspects related to the distribution of various forms of hard and soft power resources were discussed.
3   Finally, the capacity or ability of actors at different jurisdictional levels to mobilize these resources was investigated.

From a very general perspective, development activities are recognized for making a useful contribution to developing renewables. Most donor-driven activities also seem to be successful at the direct project level of intervention (households electrified, living conditions improved, jobs created and so forth), but structural effects (scaling up or diffusing experiences beyond the projects' narrow scope) remain controversial due to vague indicators and a lack of ex-post evaluations. Tracing, or even measuring, the outcomes of national-level interventions is harder than it is for projects at the local level.

Renewable energy technologies have been promoted by donor organizations for decades. Even from an economic perspective, renewables are a feasible alternative, especially in remote off-grid areas in archipelagos such as the Philippines or Indonesia, where they could substitute for relatively expensive electricity production from diesel generators. Despite these positive conditions, renewables face major constraints. Their contribution to the electricity mix is either decreasing from a relatively high share (the Philippines) or remaining stable at a marginal level (Indonesia). Analyzing the political dimension of energy transitions and how governance structures affect donor-driven interventions revealed some arguments that explain the tough situation for renewables in developing countries.

Structural effects from donor-driven renewable energy projects can be examined from two major perspectives (levels of analysis). On the one hand, structural effects depend on the specific project design and the donor's general approach in a recipient country (development project design). On the other hand, the recipient country's governance framework, particularly in the electricity sector, determines the limits to and potential for structural effects (governance structure). Based on this general distinction, four main hypotheses were formulated. Table 19.1 links these hypotheses with the respective empirical results from the Philippines and Indonesia.

Argument related to hypothesis 1: Even in unitary states such as the Philippines and Indonesia, various jurisdictional levels influence energy transitions towards renewables. Development cooperation often fails to acknowledge these complex governance frameworks in its project designs. As a consequence, donors struggle to achieve structural effects for renewables, such as learning or institutionalization of results beyond a project's narrow, direct level of intervention.

The more jurisdictional levels actively participate during the implementation of a development project, the more likely it is that there will be structural effects beyond the project's level of intervention. The potential for transferring experiences from the project level to a broader context and moving the recipient country's electricity system towards renewables depends on the involvement of relevant actors at different levels at an early stage of planning. This argument might seem to be obvious, but in practice, donors often struggle to fulfill this aim. Donor organizations are in consultation with counterparts in the national government, but often fail to consider subnational authorities. The role of coordination and consultation with local authorities is rarely conceptualized, although subnational jurisdictional levels and powerful local elites act as powerful veto players in highly decentralized political systems. This situation also hampers the projects' potential for scaling up or diffusing results beyond their limited scope. Despite the declared aim of practitioners to apply a multi-level approach (Neumann-Silkow 2010), surprisingly little effort in terms of

Table 19.1 Linking empirical findings to hypotheses

Hypothesis	Results
H 1 The more jurisdictional levels are involved during the implementation of a donor-driven project, the more likely it is that there will be structural effects beyond the project level of intervention.	Donors cooperate with national counterparts, but fail to include local stakeholders during project planning. As a consequence, conflicts during project implementation cannot be solved, or lead to significant project delays.
H 2 National advisory projects are more likely to achieve structural effects for renewables in the recipient countries' electricity systems than local demonstration projects or technology-specific experiments.	Donor activities have diversified over time. In recent years, not only local demonstration projects, but also national activities, have been implemented. Yet, donors struggle to measure their national advisory projects' (structural) effects with clear indicators. In contrast, local-level experiments can be measured more easily, but are often implemented unsustainably or fail.
H 3 The more centralized governance structures are in the electricity sector, the more likely it is that structural changes will result from donor-driven renewable energy projects.	On the one hand, energy-related decision-making in the Philippines is more centralized than in Indonesia. On the other hand, the state-owned electricity provider PLN dominates the Indonesian electricity sector. In both countries, donors struggle to address the large number of veto players with unclear responsibilities at various jurisdictional levels.
H 4 The more fragmented the necessary power resources and capacities to mobilize these resources for promoting renewable energy across jurisdictional levels, the harder it is for development cooperation to achieve structural effects through scaling up or diffusion.	Power resources and capacities in both countries have been described as heavily fragmented. As a consequence, long-term learning and institutionalizing of results becomes challenging. Conflicts between jurisdictional levels prevent upscaling or diffusion of experiences from one level to another.

Source: compiled by the author.

finance, time or capacity is related to the institutionalization or replication of results. Positive project outcomes can often be observed at the direct level of intervention, but few if any effects can be traced beyond this narrow scope. Two examples underline this dilemma. Despite positive experiences with the solar mini grid implemented by GIZ in Isla Verde, the project failed to scale up or replicate experiences elsewhere in the country, and finally collapsed due to a lack of national support and local capacity. In Indonesia, LCORE aimed to identify potential for renewables as a cost-competitive alternative to fossil fuels, but the project struggled to implement demonstration projects due to limited access to subnational authorities.

Rather than constructing new pilot projects, donors should shift their efforts towards multi-level and multi-stakeholder coordination as well as capacity building, especially at the local level (learning, ex-post evaluations, stakeholder consultations and so forth). Even renewable energy projects within a broader programmatic framework, and with support from both national and local stakeholders, have only limited long-term success without strong support after donor funding ends. Projects that involve multiple levels seem to be more successful in achieving their actual project goals, but do not necessarily influence a recipient country's electricity system (structural change) more effectively or sustainably.

Argument related to hypothesis 2: The second hypothesis argues that national advisory projects are more likely to achieve structural effects for renewables in the recipient countries' electricity systems than local demonstration projects or technology-specific experiments. This argument reflects a general trend in development assistance that can be observed also in Southeast Asia. Whereas earlier projects were often technology-specific and implemented as local demonstration projects, more and more donors foster renewable energy development at various levels and also address broader regime components, including policies, research, industry development and so forth. Although these activities hold a greater potential to achieve structural change, their actual effects are harder to measure due to the large number of intervening variables, such as when a donor supports the implementation of a feed-in tariff system that has already been passed by the national parliament.

Bi- and multilateral donors struggle to define clear and traceable indicators for project success at the national level. UNDP's claim that its activities under the CBRED program led to the passage of the Philippine Renewable Energy Act in 2008 can neither be proven nor completely rejected. Relatively short-term advisory projects are also not capable of influencing complex governance structures and institutional arrangements. Contrary to projects intervening at the national level, subnational activities tend to keep silent about relevant national conditions such as market mechanisms or supportive incentive schemes. Protected local project experiments such as solar PV mini grids generally collapse without long-term donor funding and technical support. Failed attempts to introduce modern renewables can even be used as arguments against an energy transition and broader support schemes for renewables. As a result, local renewable energy projects can affect the national debate in a negative way.

Whereas both the previous hypotheses highlight issues that are, in one way or another, discussed not only among development cooperation scholars (Bossuy and Steenbergen 2013; Noferini 2010; Stockmann 2002), but also in multi-level governance literature (Conzelmann and Smith 2008; Levi-Faur 2012; Sovacool 2011), the third and fourth hypotheses investigate energy transitions and donor-driven support for renewables from another angle, namely the role of power resources and capacities in the multi-level governance arrangement of an aid-receiving country. They shift the focus of this book away from the design of donor-driven projects towards the complex governance structures in emerging economies.

Argument related to hypothesis 3: The more centralized governance structures are in the electricity sector, the more likely it is that structural changes will result from donor-driven renewable energy projects. This argument underlines the lack of central–local coordination in decentralized political systems and the need for a coordinating body that facilitates interactions among various stakeholders in multi-level governance arrangements for renewable energy development. This situation can be confirmed for the status of energy transitions in Indonesia and the Philippines in general, and also for specific donor-driven interventions. Decentralization in Indonesia and local empowerment in the Philippines led to political systems with a large number of veto players at various jurisdictional levels, competing interests and often unclear responsibilities when it comes to energy-related projects or policies. As external actors, and with limited resources and time, donors struggle to promote renewables under these conditions.

Implementing renewable energy projects seems to be more conflictual in Indonesia, which went through a more radical process of decentralization than the Philippines. A number of authorities at different jurisdictional levels act as potential veto players. Since competencies for energy planning have mainly shifted to the subnational level, the central government of Indonesia faces severe obstacles to implementing its own development plans and targets for renewables. Local officials pass rules and regulations that are often in conflict with national legislation. These may be additional taxes for project developers or the need for acquiring local permits. In contrast, more powerful national authorities exist in the Philippines (especially the DOE and the National Economic Development Authority (NEDA)), which hold most constitutional and regulatory power resources together with financial and professional capacities. The national government was able to formulate and implement energy regulations such as the Electric Power Industry Reform Act (EPIRA) in 2001 and the RE Act in 2008, although massive delays in their implementation continue. Also in the Philippines, donors, project developers and other stakeholders of the energy system identified issues of central–local relations, such as the fragmentation of power resources, unclear competencies and the high number of powerful actors that can block renewables, as major causes for policy and project delays and failure.

Argument related to hypothesis 4: The discrepancy between having power resources and having the ability to make use of these resources seems to shape the progress of energy transitions significantly. The more fragmented the necessary power resources and capacities to mobilize these resources for promoting renewable energy across jurisdictional levels, the harder it is for development cooperation to achieve structural effects through scaling up or diffusion of results. Understanding and acknowledging the distribution of power resources and capacities among different jurisdictional levels is one of the central arguments behind this book. The discrepancy between having power and effectively making use of power plays a significant role, not only in the general framework in both countries, but also in the context of every single project case study presented here. National authorities mainly hold the financial, professional and informational capacities that are necessary to formulate renewable energy policies and regulations, but most constitutional, regulatory and political power to implement these initiatives or monitor incentive schemes rests at the subnational levels. These often lack the financial and professional capacities to translate rules and regulations into local contexts. Power resources and capacities have turned out to be heavily fragmented in both countries. Jurisdictional levels with a relatively high amount of power resources often lack the capacity to mobilize these resources. Donors fail to involve all relevant actors at different jurisdictional levels, which would be necessary for knowledge management, learning and the institutionalization of project-based experiences, but often exceeds the limits of a donor-driven intervention.

Because donors mainly plan and formulate their projects in coordination with their national counterparts, the role of local power resources and the lack of local capacity are rarely integrated into the project design. Whereas the general lack of (financial, technical and human) capacity is considered to be the key barrier to upscaling experiences from donor-driven projects in the Philippines, the picture looks more complex in Indonesia, where the distribution of power resources between central and local government authorities seems to be more fragmented – also due to the more recent and still ongoing process of decentralization and recentralization. In the Philippines, REMB plays an important role in bundling experiences and learning from local renewable energy projects. In Indonesia, the establishment of the Directorate General for New and Renewable Energy and Energy Conservation (EBTKE) in 2011 as a hub for new and renewable energy development is challenged and contested by conflicting interests among other national administrations as well as the establishment of competing rules and regulations that have been passed by local authorities.

Links to Southeast Asia

At least on paper, Indonesia and the Philippines provide a positive environment for renewable energy development, such as decentralized political structures, a strong demand for electrifying off-grid areas and the potential for large-scale renewable energy applications. Still, both countries are far from an energy transition, due to complex governance structures, conflicts in central–local relations and the fragmentation of power, which prevent a shift towards renewables. The Philippines and Indonesia teach us how complex issues of coordination and the distribution of power in multi-level governance systems affect societal transformation processes and sustainable development. Understanding these factors is a prerequisite for effective clean energy project interventions in other Southeast Asian countries also.

From a political perspective, Southeast Asia is more diverse than almost any other region in the world. Different forms of monarchy (Thailand, Malaysia, Cambodia, Brunei Darussalam), republics (Myanmar, Singapore, Indonesia, Timor-Leste, the Philippines) and socialist one-party systems (Vietnam, Laos) constitute an extraordinarily heterogeneous region. Transitions from autocratic regimes to democracies and vice versa, and sharp economic contrasts between least developed countries (such as Timor-Leste) and nations with per capita incomes above the Organisation for Economic Co-operation and Development (OECD) level (such as Singapore), represent a region full of contrasts, which allows no general blueprint for the politics of an energy transition. Recognizing the region's diversity, development cooperation activities related to renewables range from basic electrification services and local capacity building to policy advice and support for research and development programs.

Except for Myanmar, Laos, Cambodia, Brunei Darussalam and Timor-Leste, most Southeast Asian countries have announced renewable energy targets and provide both fiscal incentives and regulatory policies for renewables in one way or another (REN21 2015).

- Thailand has enforced an FiT for very small power producers and aims to almost triple its installed renewable energy capacity by 2035. The Alternative Energy Development Plan aims to cover 25 percent of energy consumption with renewables by 2021 (Ministry of Energy Thailand 2016). Political instability and high levels of uncertainty concerning future political developments could jeopardize this development.
- In Vietnam, electricity production is dominated by hydropower, but modern renewables such as wind, biomass and waste-to-energy projects are also being supported to contribute to the overarching goals of energy efficiency and energy security as outlined in the country's power development plan (ADB 2015). Determining main developments in the electricity sector, the plan reflects Vietnam's top-down approach to an energy transition in a highly hierarchical political system and monopolistic electricity sector, which leaves little room for substantial bottom-up activities.
- Malaysia has established numerous regulations for renewables, such as the RE Act (2011) and the Renewable Energy Policy and Action Plan (2010). Electricity generation is still largely dominated by coal and natural gas, but Malaysia is slowly preparing to phase out fossil fuels, despite its vast natural resources. By 2030, renewables should cover 11 percent of total electricity generation.
- Singapore has the region's second highest per capita electricity consumption, but needs to import almost all its energy. The city state's small size, high population density and land scarcity limit its renewable energy potential. By 2030, renewables are projected to contribute up to 8 percent of Singapore's peak electricity demand, and will thus continue to cover only a small share of the country's electricity mix.

Being defined as least developed countries and with very low per capita electricity consumption, Timor-Leste (0.11 MW/h per capita), Myanmar (0.16 MW/h per capita), Cambodia (0.23 MW/h per capita) and Laos (2.31 MW/h per capita) have not yet taken considerable regulatory action towards an energy transition.

Brunei Darussalam's rich supply of oil and natural gas led to an extraordinarily stable energy system that is based almost entirely on fossil fuels. Shifting the system towards renewables would require a clear top-down initiative in this stable absolute monarchy.

Going beyond renewable energy development and dissemination, energy efficiency measures also hold great potential to contribute to low-carbon development pathways in Southeast Asia, but are still underestimated in the region. Countries such as Thailand or Indonesia consider energy efficiency measures in their energy plans, and donors promote various programs, but substantial results are yet to be seen.

The region's different political and societal systems require diverse efforts for energy transitions across Southeast Asia. The provision of energy services is highly political, with fundamental implications for the people. As it deals "with livelihood opportunities, (re)distribution of wealth, and environmental implications," Smits (2015, p. 192) argues that renewable energy policies "need to be appropriate and aligned with the local context and livelihoods rather than imposed by state actors [...], NGOs [...], or private companies [...]." Most renewable energy activities we see in Southeast Asia follow a top-down approach. National governments impose targets and incentives for renewables, not to substitute for fossil fuels, but to meet additional energy demand in a rapidly developing region. Central government ministries are the dominant counterparts for development cooperation. Bottom-up pressure and local activities for clean energy are rare, but are desperately needed to shift the electricity systems towards renewables and strengthen the social and democratic elements of an energy transition.

Taking a global perspective

For decades, energy transitions in developing countries have been framed as a shift away from traditional biomass towards commercially traded fossil fuels (Elias and Victor 2005). More than 30 years ago, the World Bank (1983) outlined its skepticism towards large-scale renewable energy deployment in developing countries due to their high costs and the lack of technical capacities. Since then, not only has the global attitude towards renewables changed, but also debates have broadened beyond technical and economic arguments. Modern renewables could help emerging economies to leapfrog an emissions-intensive development path based on fossil fuels. Renewables provide decentralized clean energy systems and can make a substantial contribution to rural electrification (United Nations 2012), their costs have come down significantly (Huenteler et al. 2014) and discussions about appropriate policies and incentive schemes are manifold (REN21 2015; Weischer et al. 2011). International donors actively foster energy transitions in developing countries, but so far with mixed results (Marquardt et al. 2016).

Structural effects of the political system and issues of power are perceived as major factors influencing the likelihood of an energy transition in developing countries. Issues such as corruption, lack of capacity and the role of elites with their vested interests are excessively mentioned as decisive obstacles to renewable energy development, but their explicit conceptualization often remains vague. Certainly, one needs to be cautious about any kind of generalization that is drawn from the two Southeast Asian countries presented here, but reflections about the role of power should also be helpful for investigating energy transitions in other parts of the world and highlight the broader relevance of the power-based analytical framework.

Renewable energy governance and energy sector reforms in other Asian countries, such as India and China, are linked to the need for strong political will, capacities and regulatory frameworks, but international studies remain silent about how to change power relations and decision-making processes (IEA 2012). Investigating the role of national and local energy governance and power relations for the Clean Development Mechanism, Phillips and Newell (2013) confirm the crucial meaning of power-related aspects for the political economy of India's energy development. Looking at how power is distributed and structured among competing interest groups in India and China, Isoaho et al. (2016, p. 1) describe "how a ruling coalition's ability and willingness to promote a clean energy transition is shaped by societal pressures, vested interests, and its power and cohesiveness."

Governance systems in Latin America are complex and have experienced a "quiet revolution" (Campbell 2003) of decentralization and democratization, but major renewable energy market and policy studies fail to consider these broader political conditions with implications for power and coordination (Flavin et al. 2014; IRENA 2015). African countries also went through significant processes towards decentralization and local empowerment, but missing capacities at the local level and issues of fragile statehood remain critical obstacles to renewable energy development (Batchelor et al. 2014). Political economists are most active in discussing the role of power in energy transitions across Africa. Power et al. (2016) revealed how discourses, institutions and material power shape energy transitions in Mozambique and South Africa; Baker et al. (2014) investigate the role of powerful resource conglomerates.

The political dimension of an energy transition towards renewables has become the focus for researchers and policy-makers alike all around the world, but too often they limit their attention to policy designs and incentive schemes. Although many scholars acknowledge the importance of power-related aspects, we still know very little about their actual impact. More country-specific and comparative studies are needed that elaborate more on these issues.

References

ADB, 2015. *Viet Nam: Energy sector assessment, strategy, and road map*, Manila: Asian Development Bank.

Baker, L., Newell, P. and Phillips, J., 2014. The political economy of energy transitions: The case of South Africa. *New Political Economy*, (November 2014), pp. 1–28.

Batchelor, S., Smith, J. and Fleming, J., 2014. *Decentralisation in Sub-Saharan Africa: Prevalence, scope and challenges*, Durham: Low Carbon Energy for Development Network.

Bossuy, J. and Steenbergen, R., 2013. *Development effectiveness at the local and regional level. Fostering synergies between local and regional governments and the EU in the post-Busan era*, Brussels: PLATFORMA.

Campbell, T., 2003. *The quiet revolution: Decentralization and the rise of political participation in Latin American cities*, Pittsburgh: University of Pittsburgh Press.

Conzelmann, T. and Smith, R., 2008. *Multi-level governance in the European Union: Taking stock and looking ahead*, Baden-Baden: Nomos.

DOE, 2006. *Renewable energy based village power system project: Final report*, Manila: Philippine Department of Energy.

Elias, R.J. and Victor, D.G., 2005. *Energy transitions in developing countries: A review of concepts and literature*, Stanford: Stanford University.

Flavin, C., Gonzalez, M., Majano, A.M., Ochs, A., da Rocha, M. and Tagwerker, P., 2014. *Study on the development of the renewable energy market in Latin America and the Caribbean*, Washington, DC: Inter-American Development Bank.

Huenteler, J., Niebuhr, C. and Schmidt, T.S., 2014. The effect of local and global learning on the cost of renewable energy in developing countries. *Journal of Cleaner Production*, 128, pp. 6–21.

IEA, 2012. *Understanding energy challenges in India. Policies, players and issues*, Paris: International Energy Agency.

IRENA, 2015. *Renewable energy in Latin America 2015: An overview of policies*, Abu Dhabi: International Renewable Energy Agency.

Isoaho, K., Goritz, A. and Schulz, N., 2016. *Governing clean energy transitions in China and India. A comparative political economy analysis*, Helsinki: United Nations University WIDER.

Levi-Faur, D., 2012. *The Oxford handbook of governance*, Oxford: Oxford University Press.

Marquardt, J., Steinbacher, K. and Schreurs, M., 2016. Driving force or forced transition? The role of development cooperation in promoting energy transitions in the Philippines and Morocco. *Journal of Cleaner Production*, 128, pp. 22–33.

Ministry of Energy Thailand, 2016. The 10-year alternative energy development plan. *Department of Alternative Energy Development and Efficiency*. Available at: http://weben.dede.go.th/webmax/content/10-year-alternative-energy-development-plan [accessed June 9, 2016].

Neumann-Silkow, F., 2010. *Scaling up in development cooperation. Practical guidelines*, Eschborn: Gesellschaft für Technische Zusammenarbeit.

Noferini, A., 2010. *Development, decentralised cooperation and multilevel governance: Considerations for the current climate*, Barcelona: Observatorio de Cooperacion Descentralizada.

Phillips, J. and Newell, P., 2013. The governance of clean energy in India: The clean development mechanism (CDM) and domestic energy politics. *Energy Policy*, 59, pp. 654–662.

Power, M., Newell, P., Baker, L., Bulkeley, H., Kirshner, J. and Smith, A., 2016. The political economy of energy transitions in Mozambique and South Africa: The role of the rising powers. *Energy Research and Social Science*, 17, pp. 10–19.

REN21, 2015. *Renewables 2015: Global status report*, Paris: Renewable Energy Policy Network for the 21st Century.

Smits, M., 2015. *Southeast Asian energy transitions. Between modernity and sustainability*, London: Routledge.

Sovacool, B.K., 2011. An international comparison of four polycentric approaches to climate and energy governance. *Energy Policy*, 39(6), pp. 3832–3844.

Stockmann, R., 2002. Herausforderungen und Grenzen, Ansätze und Perspektiven der Evaluation in der Entwicklungszusammenarbeit. *Zeitschrift für Evaluation*, (1), pp. 137–150.

United Nations, 2012. *Sustainable energy for all. A global action agenda. Pathways for concerted action towards sustainable energy for all*, New York: United Nations.

Weischer, L., Wood, D., Ballesteros, A. and Fu-bertaux, X., 2011. *Grounding green power. Bottom-up perspectives on smart renewable energy policy in developing countries*, Washington, DC: The German Marshall Fund of the United States.

World Bank, 1983. *The energy transition in developing countries*, Washington, DC: World Bank.

World Bank, 2012. *Implementation status and results. Geothermal power generation development*, Washington, DC: World Bank.

20 Summary

Overview

Addressing the critical links between political structures and renewable energy development in Southeast Asia, this book has offered novel insights into the complexity of environmental governance in emerging economies. Based on empirical findings from the Philippines and Indonesia, an analytical approach was developed that incorporates power theory into a multi-level governance framework. Applied to donor-driven renewable energy projects, this approach allows the challenges to implementing sustainable energy initiatives within complex multi-level governance systems to be mapped. Issues of coordination between jurisdictional levels and aspects related to unevenly distributed power resources and capacities turned out to explain why low-carbon development projects often fail to achieve structural effects despite positive natural, technical and even economic conditions for clean energy technologies.

The book started with an in-depth background on renewable energy development around the world and presented major trends in development cooperation. It then developed a power-based multi-level governance approach that is rooted in development thinking. Empirically, the complex energy governance systems in the Philippines and Indonesia were presented in order to identify mechanisms of coordination and power fragmentation that affect sustainable energy activities. Fourteen donor-driven renewable energy projects functioned as in-depth case studies to highlight critical obstacles to their sustainability, including central–local conflicts, complex corruption patterns and the power of veto players at different jurisdictional levels. Having examined how power relations in multi-level governance systems shape the development and dissemination of renewable energy technologies, this work has also shown how the political process of decentralization affects low-carbon development in emerging economies.

The politics of energy and development

Going far beyond technical aspects, promoting an energy transition is a highly political issue. The strong nexus between the status of the energy system and a country's economic development shapes the political dimension of renewable energy development. Supporting the development of sustainable and clean energy systems has become one of the major domains in development cooperation. Renewable energy development, policy incentives for renewables, and clean energy technology transfer play an increasingly important role in the developing world. Development cooperation aims to foster energy transitions in emerging economies such as the Philippines and Indonesia, but most donors struggle to address factors that are related to the recipient country's political system.

Renewable energy sources have become technologically viable and economically feasible in many parts of the world. Yet, sociopolitical factors often prevent energy transitions towards renewables due to, among other things, complex, diverse and conflictual governance frameworks with often-changing power constellations. Incentive structures, institutional arrangements and macrostructural elements all shape energy transitions around the world. Actors at different jurisdictional levels influence energy-related activities. Investigating energy transitions and the politics of renewable energy development requires a multi-level governance perspective.

Based on a long history of theoretical debates and the availability of numerous in-depth empirical studies, an extensive body of literature exists for the fields of renewable energy development in emerging economies, trends in development cooperation, and multi-level governance. Bringing together these rather separate fields of research, this book discussed the role of governance structures in promoting renewables in developing countries and elaborated on the potentials and shortcomings of donor-driven assistance. Applying a power-based multi-level governance framework to donor-driven interventions in developing countries contributes to governance research and development cooperation.

With its focus on the multi-level governance arrangement, this work emphasized the role of power-related aspects in multijurisdictional systems, which are often overlooked. Yet, this perspective revealed only a single part of a more complex puzzle. Epistemologically, this research strove to better understand the meaning of political factors that play an important role in determining the effectiveness of renewable energy governance and the sustainability of donor-driven renewable energy projects. This work identified patterns of conflicts and cooperation, rather than offering generalizable solutions for overcoming governance- or power-related issues that hinder the promotion of renewables. Making use of grounded theory, the research process mainly followed an inductive approach. In particular, qualitative methods such as expert interviews, participant observation, field trips to renewable energy projects and document analysis were primarily used.

Development cooperation for sustainable energy

Over recent decades, not only the share of renewable energy sources in the electricity mix, but also political support for renewables in terms of policy mechanisms and incentives, has expanded substantially around the world. At the same time, the contribution of modern renewable energy sources to the total global energy supply remains marginal due to a massive increase in overall demand and an expansion of fossil fuels over recent decades. For developing countries, renewable energy technologies are widely discussed in the context of rural electrification and human development. Renewables are a potential alternative to fossil fuels, especially in remote off-grid areas, where they could substitute for diesel-fueled electricity generation.

Donor-driven interventions promoting renewables are vast and diverse, following some major trends in the field. During recent decades, development cooperation has changed and greened over time. A significant fragmentation of donor-driven interventions (leading to increasing transaction costs and the need for coordination due to more donors and activities, but also smaller projects), the consideration of a multi-level perspective for achieving structural change beyond a project's narrow context, and the overall expansion of development cooperation related to the environment and sustainable energy are important trends in development assistance. These can also be found in Southeast Asia, where donors have promoted renewables for decades. The regional energy mix is still dominated by coal and natural gas despite a variety of large-scale renewable energy facilities, especially for hydro (e.g. in Vietnam) or geothermal (e.g. in the Philippines). Future energy projections even predict a decreasing share of renewables in Southeast Asia's electricity mix due to the region's rapid economic development and increasing energy demand. Most additional capacities are likely to be covered by coal. In the light of relatively stable and fossil fuel-dominated energy systems in Southeast Asia, an energy transition towards renewables has yet to come.

Multi-level governance and power

Based on theoretical debates related to development cooperation, this book developed a power-based multi-level governance framework for investigating governance structures related to renewable energy development and donor-driven interventions. Theory-building in development cooperation is shaped by shifting paradigms in mainstream development thinking and the failure of an all-encompassing grand development theory. As a consequence, a grounded theory approach was used to better and more openly derive from the field what affects renewable energy development in emerging countries such as the Philippines or Indonesia, with their complex governance systems, and to reflect experiences from field research and their implications for theory.

Because the role of coordination between various jurisdictional levels in particular, as well as conflicts between national and subnational governments, turned out to be a decisive factor affecting renewable energy development and the performance of related donor-driven projects, a multi-level governance perspective was taken as the starting point for developing an appropriate theoretical framework. Insights from pluralist power theory related to the distribution of hard and soft power resources and capacities in central–local relations enhanced the multi-level governance perspective. As a result, three dimensions of power (structures, resources and capacities) were identified as the three main levels of analysis that need to be considered when investigating the political dimension of energy transitions in complex multi-level governance systems.

Energy transition in the Philippines and Indonesia

Being two archipelagos with high potential for various renewable energy sources, increasing energy demand and decentralized political systems, the Philippines and Indonesia represent two extremely interesting cases for investigating the challenges to and potential for an energy transition in the developing world.

Whereas local autonomy was strengthened in the Philippines in 1991 with the country's Local Government Code, the process of decentralization in Indonesia started in 1999 with a radical shift of power to local authorities, and is still ongoing. In contrast to the liberalized electricity market in the Philippines, the Indonesian power sector is dominated by the state-owned company PLN and leaves little room for private investments. Further significant differences include market conditions, subsidies and incentive schemes for renewables, industrial development, and scientific research and development. Despite these different settings for an energy transition, the multi-level governance perspective for both countries revealed a number of similar structural aspects. Central–local relations are highly fragmented. A lack of vertical coordination between national and subnational authorities and weak horizontal interministerial coordination negatively affect the implementation of renewable energy projects or policies (structural dimension of power). The distribution of hard and soft power resources is fragmented across different jurisdictional levels. Although the national governments are responsible for energy planning and development, significant power rests with local authorities, which can block the central governments' intention (resource dimension of power). At the same time, most capacities, such as technical expertise, funds and information to mobilize resources for promoting renewables, are concentrated at the national level (capacity dimension of power).

This book has revealed how the complexity of governance structures, central–local relations and the fragmentation of power affect renewable energy development in emerging economies with increasing energy demand. Numerous actors at different jurisdictional levels can and do act as potential veto players. Following these in-depth country-level analyses for the Philippines and Indonesia, it was discussed how development cooperation addresses these complex governance frameworks for renewable energy development. Extensive interviews with experts from both countries and field trips to donor-driven renewable energy projects help to shed light on the links between donor-driven interventions and the broader political context. The projects investigated here were implemented at different jurisdictional levels, namely the national, provincial and municipal levels. They do not provide generalizable insights from the field, but add specific information to the more general aspects that were raised by the interview partners.

Cross-country comparison

Lessons from the Philippines and Indonesia have taught us that political factors and complex governance structures shape energy transitions in developing countries. Taking a multi-level governance perspective helps to identify obstacles to renewable energy projects and policy-making, and underlines the need for local inclusion during project implementation, capacity building at various jurisdictional levels, and patterns of coordination across different administrative levels. Not only during implementation, but also at an early stage of planning, project developers need to consider these aspects as crucial factors that determine a project's potential for upscaling results and achieving structural change beyond the project's narrow scope. Experiences from donor-driven interventions in the Philippines and Indonesia have shown that many projects do not only achieve positive results at their direct level of intervention, but also improve coordination, facilitate capacity building and – to a minor degree – support institutionalization of results. However, donors have almost no influence on decision-making processes and issues related to power that shape the countries' energy sector developments.

The situation in the Philippines and Indonesia was then linked to developments in Southeast Asia and other parts of the developing world. Southeast Asia's different political and societal systems require diverse and country-specific efforts for promoting energy transitions. In practice, most activities follow a top-down approach. National governments impose targets and incentives for renewables not to substitute for fossil fuels, but mainly to meet additional energy demand in a rapidly developing region. Renewable energy policies need to acknowledge different political realities and local contexts. Local activities and bottom-up pressure for an energy transition are rare, but desperately needed to shift the electricity systems towards renewables and more decentralized forms of energy supply. Although the debate about the political dimension of energy transitions is still dominated by reflections about regulatory frameworks and policy designs, more and more studies on Asian, African and Latin American countries discuss the impact of power-related aspects on energy transitions in these countries.

21 Practical implications

Lessons learnt

Energy transitions are complex, long-term societal processes that tackle the status quo, not only of a country's energy system. Further social, economic and political power shifts are required to move from fossil fuels towards clean and sustainable energy sources. Many Southeast Asian countries stand at the crossroads concerning their future energy systems. Expanding coal or doing business as usual to meet additional demand due to rapid economic development would determine the energy systems for decades to come, with severely environmentally harmful technological lock-ins. Promoting energy transitions towards renewables with a focus on decentralized small-scale applications allows a much more environmentally friendly path, with additional benefits for human development and local communities, but without putting economic development at risk.

The reality of Southeast Asia's development stands in sharp contrast to this vision. Fossil fuels dominate the energy systems, incentives for renewables cannot easily be implemented, and powerful interest groups prevent changes of the status quo. Various energy outlooks even predict that the share of renewables in Southeast Asia's energy mix could actually decrease until 2030. The Philippines and Indonesia stand as two examples of the challenge to an energy transition in one of the most vibrant and most rapidly developing regions in the world. Wrapping up the lessons learnt from both countries, especially for practitioners in the field of renewable energy development, insights from a comparative perspective cluster around four major themes: (1) renewable energy development in general, (2) the role of multi-level governance frameworks for renewables, (3) the meaning of power resources and capacities, and (4) the limits to and potential of development cooperation.

Renewable energy development

Numerous contextual factors shape renewable energy development in emerging economies such as the Philippines and Indonesia. Both countries went through a process of decentralization or local empowerment after experiencing decades under authoritarian leadership. The Philippines strengthened local autonomy with its Local Government Code in 1991; Indonesia started an even more radical process of decentralization in 1999, which is still ongoing and has shifted not only administrative, but also political and financial, power to the local level.

Electricity systems in Indonesia and the Philippines also significantly differ from each other. Whereas the 2001 Electric Power Industry Reform Act in the Philippines marked the starting point for radical reforms that fostered the privatization and liberalization of the electricity sector and left little room for state-driven interventions, the Indonesian electricity market (in terms of electricity generation, transmission and distribution) is still largely dominated by the state-owned electricity provider and quasi-monopoly *Perusahaan Listrik Negara* (PLN). Attempts to liberalize the electricity market were rejected by the constitutional court. Heavy fuel subsidies regulated energy prices in Indonesia until the end of 2014, whereas non-subsidized electricity prices in the Philippines are among the highest in Asia.

With regard to incentives and support schemes for renewables, a comprehensive Renewable Energy Act from 2008 embodies a set of policies and mechanisms promoting renewables in the Philippines, although it took years for the national government to implement its rules and regulations. In contrast, only a few, relatively weak supportive policies for renewables (especially for geothermal energy) exist in Indonesia. The Directorate General for New and Renewable Energy and Energy Conservation (EBTKE) aims to further stimulate the development of clean energy technologies, but is often blocked by other national ministries, such as the Ministry of Finance or the Ministry of Forestry, which are reluctant to foster renewable energy development.

Additional fundamental differences include the electricity mix, with a high share of renewables in the Philippines compared with a highly fossil fuel-dominated electricity production in Indonesia due to different historical developments and the availability or lack of energy-related resources. Indonesia is rich in fossil fuels and the world's largest coal-exporting country, whereas the Philippines is highly dependent on fossil fuel imports due to a lack of natural resources. Environmental concerns and issues related to climate change are, at least rhetorically, more prominently articulated in the Philippines, which, as a global climate change hotspot, is expected to be severely affected by global warming.

Various similarities also need to be mentioned. Both archipelagos encounter energy scarcity in remote areas and have high potential for rural electrification with the help of modern small-scale decentralized renewables such as wind, solar or modern biomass in off-grid areas. Clean energy technologies could substitute for more costly diesel generation capacities. At the same time, the potential exists for grid-connected large-scale renewable energy applications such as geothermal or large hydro power projects. Indonesia and the Philippines experienced a period of strong economic growth over the last decade, with substantial increase in energy demand. Both countries have declared their willingness to promote renewables in the future and announced ambitious renewable energy targets for the electricity mix until 2030 (Philippines) or 2025 (Indonesia), although new and renewable energy sources in Indonesia also include nuclear, hydrogen and liquefied coal.

Multi-level governance frameworks for renewables

Indonesia and the Philippines face similar challenges concerning the promotion of renewables within their complex multi-level governance systems. High levels of uncertainty, problems of coordination and non-transparent decision-making processes pose major barriers, especially for specific renewable energy project developments. Factors such as the large number of authorities involved, unclear responsibilities, conflictual competencies and corruption at all jurisdictional levels increase the transaction costs for relatively small-scale and novel modern renewable energy projects, making them non-competitive compared with large-scale coal power plants. Modern renewable energy projects are often small in size compared with coal- or gas-powered installations and require relatively high up-front investments, which are often hard to secure due to the high levels of skepticism in the banking sectors of the Philippines and Indonesia.

Issues related to the multi-level governance framework that hamper the development and deployment of renewables include a lack of local capacity, weak coordination between different jurisdictional levels, complex patterns of corruption due to the involvement of various authorities that act as potential veto players, and unclear responsibilities in the decision-making process concerning licenses and permits that need to be obtained by project developers. The situation for renewable energy projects can vary greatly from municipality to municipality, depending on the jurisdiction's size, economic status and administrative arrangement. Whereas provinces such as Cebu in the Philippines and Yogyakarta in Indonesia have sufficient capacities to provide energy-related data, develop energy plans and support the municipalities, administrations in Palawan and Central Kalimantan are poorly equipped. Although central and provincial governments hold comparatively more constitutional and regulatory power resources in the Philippines, this does not guarantee a smoother implementation of national support mechanisms than in Indonesia. Powerful administrative structures are also required at subnational jurisdictions to facilitate the implementation of top-down renewable energy development programs. Competing ministries at the national level and their need for horizontal coordination make the formulation of laws for supportive renewable energy frameworks difficult, especially in Indonesia.

Although it was passed in 2008, the implementation of the Renewable Energy Act remained an ongoing political struggle for years. The Philippine DOE acknowledged the challenge of coordination across jurisdictional levels arising from the multi-level governance system, and established a task force that is responsible for improving the coordination with local authorities. In Indonesia, renewable energy support is also confronted with a complex governance framework. Despite its relatively simple market structure, the decision-making process in the largest Southeast Asian electricity market is also challenging for renewable energy project developers. Delays in policy-making and project development result from a long and difficult process of reaching a consensus between the Ministry of Energy and Mineral Resources, the Ministry of Finance, the Ministry of State-owned Enterprises and other national government institutions.

Despite the unitary, but heavily decentralized, political systems of both countries, renewable energy development is organized in a heavily centralized way, with mainly top-down programs from the national governments rather than bottom-up initiatives for decentralized and environmentally friendly electricity supply. Municipalities in Indonesia, the Philippines and many other developing countries often lack the technical expertise and general awareness of renewable energy technologies. Local government officials even frame renewables as a means of temporary electricity supply to bridge the gap until an area gets connected to the main grid. Financial capabilities to promote renewables at the subnational level are particularly restricted in the Philippines, where the municipalities' budgets depend to a large extent on the national budget. Although energy planning should be a bottom-up process in Indonesia after more than 15 years of continuous decentralization, national plans still dominate the field.

Despite the differences between the two systems, Indonesia can learn from the Philippines and its longer experience with local autonomy since 1992. Having previously experienced local politics as a mayor, the former Philippine Minister of Energy created a coordinating body for implementing the 2008 Renewable Energy Act in cooperation with local authorities. Establishing and experimenting with these kinds of coordination patterns could help to facilitate renewable energy support in decentralized political systems like the ones presented here, but they need to be institutionalized and sustained to become resistant to changing governments and authorities. This also applies to other developing countries with weak subnational bureaucracies, especially after a history of decentralization.

Power resources and capacities matter

The distribution of hard and soft power resources across different jurisdictional levels within the multi-level governance framework greatly affects renewable energy development and the likelihood of an energy transition towards renewables. In the Philippines and Indonesia, delays concerning the passage of renewable energy support mechanisms or the implementation of specific projects were often framed as power struggles and conflicts between actors at different jurisdictional levels. National institutions accused local authorities of misusing their power to block renewables, whereas local government officials accused national authorities of not providing sufficient funding, information or technical expertise. At the local level, responsibilities and competencies among government authorities were not always clear concerning permits, licenses and so forth – leaving room for uncertainty, enhancing chances for corruption, and increasing transaction costs for renewable energy projects.

Interestingly, a relatively strong discrepancy can be observed between the distribution of power resources and the actual ability to make use of or mobilize these resources. Subnational authorities, especially in Indonesia, hold considerable amounts of constitutional, regulatory and political power due to the process of radical decentralization that was initialized in 1999. Yet, most municipalities, especially outside of Java and Bali, lack the personnel and technical expertise to effectively mobilize these resources for promoting renewables. Local authorities struggle to acquire energy-related data and information about renewable energy potential for project developers, and fail to establish complex local or regional energy plans due to the massive coordination effort required for compiling the required information from numerous administrations. Authorities not willing to share information can hardly be sanctioned.

In the Philippines, local governments also depend on the power resources of the national government, especially because they have no right to generate their own tax revenues. Power in central–local relations is also unevenly distributed. In general, local authorities with substantial constitutional and political power resources can act as veto players for renewable energy projects. Mayors in the Philippines and *Bupatis* in Indonesia were both framed as little kings and queens, who often act independently of national regulations. At the same time, local authorities in both countries lack the financial, technical and informational capacities that would be necessary to implement, monitor or evaluate renewable energy projects or policies.

Taking into account experiences from other developing countries, the cross-country comparison revealed that the situation concerning the distribution of power in terms of structures, resources and capacities should be similar in other developing countries in Southeast Asia and beyond. Understanding the complexity of the governance system and the distribution of power resources and capacities across different jurisdictional levels allows discussion of how donors can cope with such a complex and highly volatile situation to effectively promote renewables. The power-based multi-level governance framework developed here aims to capture this complex environment in which development projects are implemented. The approach thus also provides a useful tool for donor agencies, project developers and development cooperation practitioners.

Effects of development cooperation

Donor-driven renewable energy interventions have developed over time, from mainly technology-specific local experiments that demonstrate the feasibility of a certain renewable energy source for electricity supply towards more and more advisory projects for national policies, market structures or industrial development. The donors' advice focuses on renewable energy policies, especially in terms of financial incentives and support mechanisms; market conditions, such as improved conditions for private investors; or technological developments, through research and development programs, among other things. The empirical findings presented here also underline a general trend in development cooperation. They showcase how donor-driven renewable energy programs in general have changed, from donor gifts, through market creation measures, to more comprehensive sustainable programs, but often with too high expectations (Sovacool 2012). This historical development also underlines how development cooperation has been adapted to complex multi-level governance structures and learnt to consider various levels of intervention for renewable energy support. Not surprisingly, donors such as the Deutsche Gesellschaft für Internationale Zusammenarbeit (GIZ) aim to follow a multi-level perspective for scaling up, replicating and institutionalizing project results (Neumann-Silkow 2010).

At the same time, bi- and multilateral donors need to step up their efforts for learning, coordination and knowledge management. Donors have long agreed on better harmonizing their activities with each other (OECD 2008). Taking action in this field could prevent the replication of failed projects and foster learning from renewable energy project experiments to better adapt them to the recipient countries' contexts. National- and local-level projects follow different aims, but they could significantly benefit from each other when they are seen within a broader framework for an energy transition. Too often, donor-driven interventions are implemented independently of each other or with little consideration of the other donors' priorities. Better coordination of activities at various jurisdictional levels could substantially increase their overall effectiveness and impact on the recipient country's electricity system.

Efforts for streamlining activities with national programs and avoiding duplication with the help of a strong coordinating authority are also poorly developed in developing countries with relatively weak administrative structures. Although the Philippine Department of Energy (DOE) tries to coordinate energy-related donor activities through participative donor conferences, and EBTKE in Indonesia hosts an annual conference on clean energy for the country to connect various stakeholders in the sector, a consistent long-term framework for development cooperation related to the electricity sector and/or renewable energy development is missing. The recipient country's long-term energy planning and commitments for renewables should be the primary point of reference for any donor-driven contribution. Otherwise, learning and experiences from the projects might not affect the country's attitude towards renewables.

Despite relatively little donor fragmentation compared with other sectors and countries (Knack and Smets 2013), support for renewables in the Philippines and Indonesia has seen a significant amount of project duplication and failure. This has been particularly the case for solar power in the Philippines (Marquardt 2014), whereas donors in Indonesia seem to be more specialized in certain renewable energy sources. Here, particularly the Japan International Cooperation Agency (JICA) and New Zealand Aid focus on geothermal projects, GIZ concentrates its efforts primarily on solar power and biomass development, and other donors contribute to hydro power development. Streamlining these forms of lead donorship (Steinwand 2015) could bundle experiences and thus improve knowledge management and aid effectiveness.

Insights from the renewable energy project case studies in the Philippines and Indonesia complemented the analysis and highlighted aspects from the more general discussion about the link between complex governance arrangements and development cooperation. For every project case study, a qualitative assessment was carried out to identify patterns related to general issues of coordination and power that influence the projects' performance. These assessments made it possible to compare the perceived contribution of the project with the perceived barriers in the field of activity.

These categories were coded as "project level" (Does the project lead to positive results at its direct level of intervention?), "decision-making" (Does the project affect the decision-making process?), "coordination" (Does the project facilitate coordination across jurisdictional levels?), "power" (Does the project help to centralize necessary power resources?), "capacity" (Does the project build up financial, technical and/or professional capacity?) and "institutions" (Can project results be institutionalized and sustained without donor support?). Table 21.1 illustrates the meanings behind these categories, which account for the perceived barriers in the field as well as for the perceived project contribution.

Accumulating information from 14 donor-driven renewable energy project case studies (see Appendix III for more details about these projects), Figure 21.1

Table 21.1 Qualitative assessment matrix for project case studies

Category	Meaning for barriers in the field	Meaning for project contributions
Project level	Lack of support by the project partners	The donor-driven activity leads to positive outcomes at its direct level of intervention
Decision-making	Fragmented decision-making process	The project facilitates the process of decision-making among relevant authorities
Coordination	Lack of coordination between various levels of decision-making	The project facilitates coordination across different jurisdictional levels
Power	Fragmentation of power resources	The project helps to centralize necessary power resources
Capacity	Lack of capacity in the field	The project builds up financial, technical and/or professional capacity
Institutions	Lack of institutionalization	Project output is being institutionalized and can be sustained without the donor's support

Source: categories developed by the author.

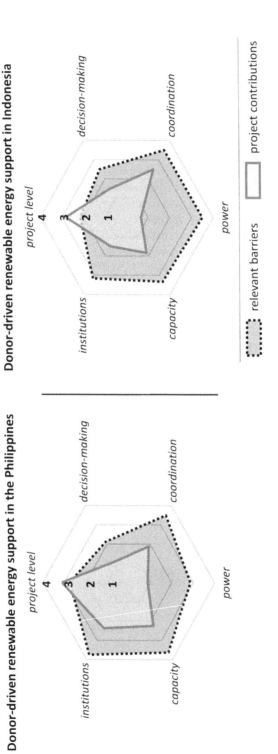

Figure 21.1 Qualitative assessment of donor-driven renewable energy projects.

Source: illustration by the author.

summarizes the results of the qualitative assessment. Based on interviews, document analysis and field trips, every project was assessed for the six categories mentioned above on a scale between 1 ("very low"/"weak") and 4 ("very high"/"strong"). Data from all activities in the Philippines (eight projects) and Indonesia (six projects) were added, and the results were divided by the number of projects. This led to the two graphs in Figure 21.1 that summarize the barriers for different renewable energy contexts and the donor-driven projects' contributions.

The comparative figure reveals a very similar mismatch between the key barriers to renewables and the donor-driven projects' contributions to renewable energy development. Major obstacles to promoting renewables are related to coordination, power resources, capacity and institutions. In the field, most projects fail to tackle these dimensions, although they do achieve positive outcomes at their direct level of intervention. These include improved access to energy, environmental benefits and job creation. National-level interventions and advisory activities aim to trigger systemic change through institutional development, capacity building and other structural elements, but their actual effects remain hard to measure.

These insights from the specific projects as well as the two countries in general do not lead to quantifiable indicators for designing a perfect donor-driven intervention, but they underline that complex governance structures need to be better reflected. Similar results from the Philippines and Indonesia highlight the relevance of political factors such as governance structures, power resources and capacities to development cooperation. Every country has a unique political system; good practices in one country cannot be simply transferred to another. More in-depth empirical studies are required to match the country-specific governance framework for renewables with donor-driven interventions in order to highlight critical obstacles to an energy transition and identify potential fields for contributions from development cooperation.

References

Knack, S. and Smets, L., 2013. Aid tying and donor fragmentation. *World Development*, 44(January), pp. 63–76.

Marquardt, J., 2014. How sustainable are donor-driven solar power projects in remote areas? *Journal of International Development*, 26(6), pp. 915–922.

Neumann-Silkow, F., 2010. *Scaling up in development cooperation. Practical guidelines*, Eschborn: Gesellschaft für Technische Zusammenarbeit.

OECD, 2008. *The Paris declaration on aid effectiveness and the Accra agenda for action*, OECD, ed., Paris: Organisation for Economic Co-operation and Development.

Sovacool, B.K., 2012. Design principles for renewable energy programs in developing countries. *Energy & Environmental Science*, 5(11), p. 9157.

Steinwand, M.C., 2015. Compete or coordinate? Aid fragmentation and lead donorship. *International Organization*, 69(2), pp. 443–472.

22 Theoretical contributions

The politics of renewables, development thinking and multi-level governance

Expanding the field of energy research with more qualitative analyses, as was presented here, is desperately needed to better understand highly country-specific governance structures and energy pathways in the developing world (Sovacool 2014, p. 25). Not only can practical implications, for development cooperation practitioners and policy-makers alike, be derived from this study about energy transitions in Southeast Asia. This work also contributes to theoretical debates, mainly in political science, and underlines the political dimension of an energy transition, which is often underestimated in the field of energy transitions research, dominated by economic perspectives and technocratic concepts. As this book combines a multi-level governance approach with power theory for the context of development cooperation, it contributes to the fields of governance frameworks for renewables, development thinking and multi-level governance.

Contribution to the politics of renewables. The political dimension of renewable energy development goes beyond the mere existence of incentive structures or supportive legislation, which are often taken as important political indicators for the status of an energy transition (REN21 2015). To broaden this narrow perception, debates around governance frameworks for renewables can learn from long-known theoretical reflections about power in central–local relations (Goldsmith 1986; Laffin 2009; Rhodes 1980, 1986). Mapping these country-specific formal and informal patterns of decision-making across jurisdictional levels sheds light on the key obstacles to renewables and potential ways to promote an energy transition. This also means that simply exporting positive supportive mechanisms from one country to another (Dietrich 2011; Hübner 2013) will not necessarily be successful, if it fails to address broader political conditions. Integrating power-related aspects such as the distribution of resources and capacities also allows the investigation and tracing of causal relations.

Contribution to development thinking. This qualitative study confirms the results from numerous quantitative studies about the negative effects of fragmentation in development cooperation (Annen and Moers 2012; Knack and Rahman 2007; McGillivray et al. 2006). Not only has the number of donors increased, but also their levels of intervention have diversified. Identifying power-related aspects that are specific to developing countries (such as corruption, lack of bureaucratic structures, regulatory uncertainties) as key obstacles to renewable energy development in both the Philippines and Indonesia confirms the demand for capacity development, institution-building and good governance (Sagar 2000; Santiso 2001; Weidner et al. 2010). This study also revealed negative side-effects of radical decentralization or market liberalization, which are fostered by development cooperation and reflect mainstream development paradigms, but cannot be taken as a blueprint for successful sustainable development. Donors have fostered free markets and participative governments, but achieved mixed results in terms of economic progress and – above all – human development (Rauch 2009). This is also the case in the field of renewable energy development, where issues of power and coordination are critical for success. Research about multi-level governance and power in central–local relations can thus make a valuable contribution to development theory.

Contribution to multi-level governance. Studies investigating the role of governance and decentralized structures in environmental protection in Southeast Asian countries are rare (e.g. Ardiansyah and Jotzo 2014). This work contributes to this emerging field of research by using the concept of multi-level governance and enhancing its geographical scope. Linking the concept of multi-level governance to development assistance, this book also provides novel insights into a field where multi-level governance has been rarely used. This should help to better understand interactions across jurisdictional levels in complex governance arrangements (Neumann-Silkow 2010). Multi-level governance is often criticized for being an analytical framework that lacks strong theoretical reflections (Eckerberg and Joas 2004; Piattoni 2010). Incorporating aspects of power turned out to be beneficial for understanding relations, interactions and power-related aspects that go beyond the mere structure of the system. Insights from the Philippines and Indonesia also contest the mainstream perception among multi-level environmental governance scholars, who see a highly positive link between decentralization, local empowerment and sustainable development (Benz et al. 2009; Heinelt et al. 2002; Hirschl 2008; Peters and Pierre 2004). Decentralized political structures alone do not automatically enforce the development of mainly small-scale modern renewable energy technologies.

Analyzing structural effects

Taking into account the disillusioning history of development theory (Menzel 1992) and aid effectiveness (Hansen and Tarp 2000; McGillivray et al. 2006), this work started by developing a theoretical approach that covers the complex governance systems of aid-receiving countries, but then goes beyond traditional development thinking. Grounded theory proved to be helpful for developing such a context-specific theoretical framework that acknowledges the unique political context of a country. The relatively loose and open concept of multi-level governance provided an appropriate starting point for such a framework, which aims to understand how a complex governance system affects development cooperation.

Development cooperation benefits from a multi-level governance perspective because it provides a framework for analyzing structural change beyond a project's direct level of intervention (Neumann-Silkow 2010) in line with the sustainable development paradigm that encompasses social, economic and environmental aspects. Such an approach is especially helpful for local demonstration projects that often achieve positive outcomes at their level of intervention, but cannot be sustained or institutionalized due to the complex governance arrangement they are embedded in and the variety of actors that need to be involved. Taking a multi-level governance perspective reveals the relevant political context, which goes beyond the mere constitutional framework or economic development of a country. This allows issues of coordination and diffusion across jurisdictional levels, which are vital not only for implementing development projects, but especially for scaling up or diffusing experiences beyond a project's direct context, to be highlighted.

Multi-level governance turned out to be a useful and informative analytical framework for development cooperation in general, and specifically development activities promoting renewables. In practice, donor-driven projects are implemented at various jurisdictional levels. On the one hand, they function as (technology-specific) pilot projects at the local level that demonstrate the feasibility of a certain technology, such as solar power, or a social innovation, such as a cooperative for power production. On the other hand, they directly tackle national conditions such as the promotion of a feed-in tariff for renewables or the development of an industrial sector. Taking a multi-level governance perspective reflects that complex setting.

As for the multi-level perspective in transitions studies (Marquardt 2015), applying the power-based multi-level governance approach to development cooperation makes it necessary to devote attention to a donor project's planning, implementation and evaluation phases. At an early stage of project planning, development practitioners can make use of the framework as an assessment tool that helps to map the complex governance environment in which a project or program is going to be implemented. Based on such an assessment, the power-based multi-level governance framework can be used as a monitoring tool that helps to track progress and effects at different levels during the phase of project implementation.

If the project has been terminated, indicators of its success or failure can be differentiated between direct project-level effects (jobs created, businesses established, number of households electrified, price for electricity and so forth) and structural effects beyond a project's narrow scope (institutional learning or effects related to upscaling). Eventually, multi-level governance can also contribute to a project's evaluation. In line with the strong demand for more sophisticated impact evaluations in development cooperation that focus on systemic long-term effects rather than simply on the project's direct outputs (Savedoff et al. 2006; Leeuw and Vaessen 2009; Stockmann 2002), the approach developed here reflects structural effects such as learning, replication or institutionalization of results. Such a perspective goes beyond mainstream project evaluations that narrowly focus on the observable results (output) and functional effects (outcome) of a project.

The role of power in its different dimensions needs to be considered in development theory as well as in multi-level governance research. Insights from power theory and the role of power distribution in central–local relations have proven to be a useful contribution to development thinking. Analyzing power structures reveals obstacles and challenges to promoting renewables and fostering an energy transition. Power-related factors help explain why certain decision-makers can act as veto players, and why others struggle to implement supportive regulations or have problems harmonizing their efforts with competing authorities at the same administrative level or across different jurisdictional levels. At the same time, promising channels for promoting renewables, supportive power coalitions or windows of opportunity can be identified.

Distinguishing between (hard and soft) power resources and the capacity to make use of these resources also helps to understand why certain actors or jurisdictional levels fail to promote renewables despite positive natural, technical and economic conditions, the availability of resources, and sufficient capacities. Such a perspective goes beyond analyses that reduce a country's political system to its constitutional setting and formal decision-making procedures, as can often be found in policy guides and studies for renewable energy development in developing countries (Lidula et al. 2007; Long and Hernandez 2012; Ölz and Beerepoot 2010).

Power-related theories enhance our understanding of development projects and their potential for structural change or fundamental socioeconomic "regime shifts" (Loorbach 2007) towards renewables, which form the basis for an energy transition. This can also be seen as a critique of an often too technocratic and positivistic rationale behind development cooperation. Investigating central–local relations sheds light on the effects of decentralization processes in political systems, the distribution of power resources at various jurisdictional levels and the work that goes into coordination between these levels. The fundamental role of power in central–local relations should be acknowledged not only by practitioners, but also by theorists in the field.

Links to transitions studies

Energy transitions are a key issue in sustainability transitions literature (Kemp 2010; Smith and Stirling 2005; Verbong and Loorbach 2012). Achieving structural changes for an energy transition can be linked to a regime shift in the energy system. Although this book has not explicitly applied any of the field's main concepts, such as transition management, strategic niche management, technological innovations systems or the multi-level perspective, two main contributions can be derived in order to contribute to debates in sustainability transitions research.

Dealing with "the role of power and politics" (Geels 2011, p. 29) ranks high on the research agenda in transitions studies. Power determines regime stability and the success of technological niches, but power has rarely been explicitly conceptualized in transitions studies. Integrating power into frameworks such as the multi-level perspective remains a major challenge (Avelino 2011; Smith and Stirling 2005). This book suggests how to explicitly conceptualize power in complex multi-level governance arrangements, which should also be fruitful for the debates around the conceptualization of power in transitions studies. Investigating the distribution – and fragmentation – of resources and capacities among relevant actors within their broader political structures could help to reveal the reasons for regime stability, identify powerful coalitions that prevent a change of the status quo, or identify areas for potentially successful interventions.

Distinguishing between niche-level experiments, the regime-level context and overarching landscape conditions, transitions studies deals with complex societal transformation processes, but is criticized for its narrow focus on OECD countries. Experiences from other regions of the world are needed to enrich theoretical debates (Loorbach 2010, p. 179). The multi-level perspective could be a useful concept for investigating renewable energy development in emerging economies. Covering broader country-wide conditions, the landscape would include formal and informal aspects of the political system, the economic situation, and social cleavages in the recipient country. The electricity system would represent the regime structure, which is – in general – extraordinarily stable. Regime components include policies, market structures, the industrial sector, academic research and development, technologies and cultural aspects. Experimentation with sociotechnical innovations (for renewables) occurs in protected niches. Donor agencies either promote niche experiments through technology-specific demonstration projects or aim to tackle the regime-level context by providing expertise and support for renewable energy policies, market conditions or industrial development. Covering the complexity of niche–regime-level interventions, transitions studies could map the environment in which donor-driven interventions are implemented.

Methodological implications

From a methodological perspective, this exploratory research stressed the need for a qualitative research design in order to enhance both our empirical and our theoretical understanding about renewable energy development and its support in emerging economies and developing countries.

Grounded theory turned out to be an appropriate approach for investigating a field that is dominated by technological and economic reflections (Sovacool 2014) and recommendations derived from OECD-centric theories. Insights from field research broadened the perspective and highlighted the role of the political system, which was further investigated. Using the grounded theory approach in emerging economies such as the Philippines and Indonesia contests mainstream positions in multi-level governance research, but also widens its perspective. As well as a rather positive attitude towards multi-level governance systems as an enabling factor for renewables (Corfee-Morlot et al. 2009; Schreurs and Tiberghien 2007; Verbong and Geels 2007), field research also revealed obstacles arising from decentralized political structures. Multi-level reinforcement as experienced in the European Union (Schreurs and Tiberghien 2007) becomes challenging or impossible in weakly institutionalized settings with unclear responsibilities, high levels of corruption and missing patterns of central–local coordination. Discussing countries outside the OECD confronts multi-level governance scholars with a huge variety of fundamentally different political contexts. Grounded theory helps to identify the crucial factors related to the governance frameworks in developing countries that affect environmental innovations, but have been rarely addressed so far by most scholars.

In the light of decades of donor-driven renewable energy support with only limited success and a series of project failures, this research also underlines the need for more qualitative research designs that capture the complexity of a recipient country's political system. Better acknowledging the multi-level governance arrangement in a developing country turned out to be a key factor that determines a donor-driven project's ability to achieve structural change towards renewables. The qualitative approach helped to develop a context-specific, power-based, multi-level governance framework. Applying it to other developing countries should enhance our understanding of the politics of energy transitions in the developing world, but this requires country-specific in-depth analyses.

Based on qualitative research methods, this book is at risk from biased perceptions, random experiences and singular events. These might not be fully replicable, but they do matter when it comes to complex societal challenges such as an energy transition. These insights are an important part of the picture concerning renewable energy development in emerging economies. Demonstrating how issues related to power and coordination affect donor-driven renewable energy projects contributes to a debate that is dominated by economic calculations about aid effectiveness (McGillivray et al. 2006), technological learning curves (Huenteler et al. 2014) and theoretical potentials of renewables in off-grid areas (Flavin and Aeck 2005; World Bank 2013).

References

Annen, K. and Moers, L., 2012. *Donor competition for aid impact, and aid fragmentation*, Washington, DC: International Monetary Fund.

Ardiansyah, F. and Jotzo, F., 2014. Decentralization and avoiding deforestation. The case of Indonesia. In S. Howes and M.G. Rao, eds. *Decentralization and avoiding deforestation*. Oxford: Oxford University Press.

Avelino, F., 2011. *Power in transition. Empowering discourses on sustainability transitions.* Rotterdam: Erasmus University Rotterdam.

Benz, A., Breitmeier, H., Schimank, U. and Simonis, G., 2009. *Politik in Mehrebenensystemen*, Wiesbaden: VS Verlag für Sozialwissenschaften.

Corfee-Morlot, J., Kamal-Chaoui, L., Donovan, M.G., Cochran, I., Robert, A. and Teasdale, P.-J., 2009. *Cities, climate change and multilevel governance*, Paris: OECD.

Dietrich, M., 2011. *The "Renewables – Made in Germany" initiative in South-East Asia. Business opportunities through renewable energies: Learnings from Germany*, Cebu City: Deutsche Gesellschaft für Internationale Zusammenarbeit (GIZ) GmbH.

Eckerberg, K. and Joas, M., 2004. Multi-level environmental governance: A concept under stress? *Local Environment*, 9(5), pp. 405–412.

Flavin, C. and Aeck, M., 2005. *Energy for development, the potential role of renewable energy in meeting the Millennium Development Goals*, Paris: Renewable Energy Policy Network for the 21st Century.

Geels, F.W., 2011. The multi-level perspective on sustainability transitions: Responses to seven criticisms. *Environmental Innovation and Societal Transitions*, 1(1), pp. 24–40.

Goldsmith, M., 1986. *New research in central-local relations*, Aldershot: Gower.

Hansen, H. and Tarp, F., 2000. Aid effectiveness disputed. *Journal of International Development*, 12(3), pp. 375–398.

Heinelt, H., Getimis, P., Kaflakas, G., Smith, R. and Swyngedouw, E., eds., 2002. *Participatory governance in multi-level context. Concepts and experience*, Opladen: Leske and Budrich.

Hirschl, B., 2008. *Erneuerbare Energien-Politik: Eine Multi-Level Policy-Analyse mit Fokus auf den deutschen Strommarkt*, Wiesbaden: VS Verlag für Sozialwissenschaften.

Hübner, C., 2013. *Wahrnehmung der deutschen Energiewende in Schwellenländern. Ergebnisse einer qualitativen Expertenbefragung in Brasilien, China und Südafrika*, Bonn: Konrad-Adenauer-Stiftung.

Huenteler, J., Niebuhr, C. and Schmidt, T.S., 2014. The effect of local and global learning on the cost of renewable energy in developing countries. *Journal of Cleaner Production*, 128, pp. 6–21.

Kemp, R., 2010. The Dutch energy transition approach. *International Economics and Economic Policy*, 7(2–3), pp. 291–316.

Knack, S. and Rahman, A., 2007. Donor fragmentation and bureaucratic quality in aid recipients. *Journal of Development Economics*, 83(1), pp. 176–197.

Laffin, M., 2009. Central-local relations in an era of governance: Towards a new research agenda. *Local Government Studies*, 35(1), pp. 21–37.

Leeuw, F. and Vaessen, J., 2009. *Impact evaluations and development: NONIE guidance on impact evaluation*, Washington: Network of Networks for Impact Evaluation (NONIE).

Lidula, N.W.A., Mithulananthan, N., Ongsakul, W., Widjaya, C. and Henson, R., 2007. ASEAN towards clean and sustainable energy: Potentials, utilization and barriers. *Renewable Energy*, 32(9), pp. 1441–1452.

Long, W. and Hernandez, J.A., 2012. Transition to renewable energy in developing countries: Promoting energy policy and innovation. *Lecture Notes in Information Technology*, 13, pp. 479–486.

Loorbach, D., 2007. *Transition management: New mode of governance for sustainable development*, Rotterdam: International Books.

Loorbach, D., 2010. Transition management for sustainable development: A prescriptive, complexity-based governance framework. *Governance*, 23(1), pp. 161–183.

Marquardt, J., 2015. How transition management can inform development aid. *Environmental Innovation and Societal Transitions*, 14, pp. 182–185.

McGillivray, M., Feeny, S., Hermes, N. and Lensink, R., 2006. Controversies over the impact of development aid: It works; it doesn't; it can, but that depends.... *Journal of International Development*, 18(7), pp. 1031–1050.

Menzel, U., 1992. *Das Ende der Dritten Welt und das Scheitern der grossen Theorie*, Berlin: Suhrkamp.

Neumann-Silkow, F., 2010. *Scaling up in development cooperation. Practical guidelines*, Eschborn: Gesellschaft für Technische Zusammenarbeit.

Ölz, S. and Beerepoot, M., 2010. *Deploying renewables in Southeast Asia. Trends and potentials*, Paris: International Energy Agency.

Peters, G. and Pierre, J., 2004. Multi-level governance and democracy: A Faustian bargain? In I. Bache and M. Flinders, eds. *Multi-level governance*, Oxford: Oxford University Press.

Piattoni, S., 2010. *The theory of multi-level governance. Conceptual, empirical, and normative challenges*, Oxford: Oxford University Press.

Rauch, T., 2009. *Entwicklungspolitik. Theorien, Strategien, Instrumente*, Braunschweig: Westermann.

REN21, 2015. *Renewables 2015: Global status report*, Paris: Renewable Energy Policy Network for the 21st Century.

Rhodes, R.A.W., 1980. Some myths in central-local relations. *The Town Planning Review*, 51(3), pp. 270–285.

Rhodes, R.A.W., 1986. *Control and power in central-local government relations*, Aldershot: Gower.

Sagar, A.D., 2000. Capacity development for the environment: A view for the south, a view for the north. *Annual Review of Energy and the Environment*, 25(1), pp. 377–439.

Santiso, C., 2001. International co-operation for democracy and good governance: Moving towards a second generation? *The European Journal of Development Research*, 13(1), pp. 154–180.

Savedoff, W.D., Levine, R. and Birdsall, N., 2006. *When will we ever learn? Improving Lives through Impact Evaluation*, Washington D.C.: Center for Global Development.

Schreurs, M.A. and Tiberghien, Y., 2007. Multi-level reinforcement: Explaining European Union leadership in climate change mitigation. *Global Environmental Politics*, 7(4), pp. 19–46.

Smith, A. and Stirling, A., 2005. *Social-ecological resilience and socio-technical transitions: Critical issues for sustainability governance.*, Brighton: STEPS Centre.

Sovacool, B.K., 2014. What are we doing here? Analyzing fifteen years of energy scholarship and proposing a social science research agenda. *Energy Research and Social Science*, 1, pp. 1–29.

Stockmann, R., 2002. Herausforderungen und Grenzen , Ansätze und Perspektiven der Evaluation in der Entwicklungszusammenarbeit. *Zeitschrift für Evaluation*, 1, pp. 137–150.

Verbong, G. and Geels, F.W., 2007. The ongoing energy transition: Lessons from a socio-technical, multi-level analysis of the Dutch electricity system (1960–2004). *Energy Policy*, 35(2), pp. 1025–1037.

Verbong, G. and Loorbach, D., 2012. *Governing the energy transition. Reality, illusion or necessity?* New York: Routledge.

Weidner, H., Jänicke, M. and Jörgens, H., 2010. *Capacity building in national environmental policy: A comparative study of 17 countries*, Berlin Heidelberg: Springer.

World Bank, 2013. Mapping the renewable energy revolution. Available at: www.worldbank.org/en/news/feature/2013/06/17/mapping-the-energy-revolution [accessed June 2, 2015].

23 Outlook

Introduction

Focusing empirically on two emerging economies reveals a wide range of very specific and profound arguments, but also limits the generalizability of results. Nonetheless, such an in-depth qualitative analysis is necessary to better acknowledge the complexity of societal systems and take into account the manifold governance mechanisms that affect renewable energy development. Limiting the number of country and project case studies allowed the investigation of a variety of very fundamental political issues that are relevant not only to renewable energy development, but also to the field of development cooperation as such. It was possible to analyze in great depth how political structures, decision-making processes and power relations in the Philippines and Indonesia affect the development of renewables and their support in its entirety. Further broad matters raised include the effects of decentralization, aid effectiveness, donor harmonization, upscaling of results and structural change through donor-driven interventions. The cross-country comparison helped to put the results presented here into a global context.

Investigating energy transitions means dealing with extraordinarily complex and long-term societal issues. Such a highly contested field of social sciences requires an open, but context-specific, approach that needs to acknowledge the unique features of a country's governance arrangement. Following its essential research philosophy, this book identified patterns and correlations between the complex political system of a developing country and renewable energy development. Linking the governance system to the status of renewables in a country, the framework is intended to reveal critical obstacles to and potential for renewable energy development and identify the actors and processes that determine an energy transition.

Research agenda

This book does not only provide an assessment tool for development practitioners, but also contributes to the existing literature related to governance frameworks for sustainable energy, the promotion of renewables in developing countries, diversification in development assistance, and multi-level governance research. Investigating energy transitions in Southeast Asia prompts new questions and leaves room for further research, especially to specify the role of governance frameworks for renewable energy development in emerging economies and the effects of donor-driven renewable energy support in developing countries. Three main fields for further research are briefly summarized here.

(1) *Identify political obstacles to promoting renewables in developing countries.* This study revealed a number of political obstacles to promoting renewables in developing countries that differ significantly from the industrialized world. Interview partners stressed the lack of a centralized policy push for renewables, or the need for a strong leader to coordinate activities instead of democratizing energy supply and pushing community-driven applications. Other political factors include complex patterns of corruption, regulatory uncertainties and a lack of capable institutions. These aspects have already been mentioned by other scholars in the context of renewable energy development in developing countries (Flavin and Aeck 2005; IPCC 2000; Jaramillo-Nieves and del Río 2010; Martinot and McDoom 2000; Wilkins 2002), but what makes this book unique is that it shows how these political factors are embedded into deeper societal structures, power relations and complex governance arrangements in which actors at different jurisdictional levels cooperate or compete with each other depending on their power resources and capacities. Discussing the role of these political factors in other countries and regions around the world would substantially contribute to the need for more social sciences in renewable energy research (Sovacool 2014).

(2) *Investigate the political dimension of renewables in developing countries.* Numerous country-specific studies have long discussed how renewables are being or could be promoted in developing countries (e.g. Biswas et al. 2001; Boyle et al. 2006; Geller et al. 2004; Gurung et al. 2011; Mallett 2007), but they rarely reflect on the role of power in complex governance structures. Discussing the link between governance arrangements, power relations and renewables in developing countries will enhance our awareness of the political dimension of energy transitions around the world. Despite positive natural and economic conditions for renewables in the Philippines and Indonesia, a variety of political factors prevent their expansion. These factors vary from country to country. Identifying them with the help of additional in-depth country case studies would present a much more nuanced and precise picture of the political dimension of energy transitions in the developing world. Insights from the Philippines and Indonesia should inspire researchers and practitioners working in other developing countries to reflect on the role of political factors in renewable energy development and its support, especially in Asia, Africa and Latin America, and to map obstacles to and potential for renewables that go beyond technology-centered feasibility studies or economic calculations. To reduce global fossil fuel path dependency and technological lock-ins, further research is needed into the role of governance structures and power relations regarding renewables, especially in emerging economies such as Indonesia, China, Brazil

and India, due to their increasing impact on the global environment and climate change. Rapidly developing countries such as the Philippines, Malaysia and Vietnam also need to be considered, because their massively increasing energy demand in the near future will most likely be met using fossil fuels (IEA 2013). Investing in renewables to diversify energy supply today could prevent technological lock-ins and energy dependency for decades to come.

(3) Reflect on the role of power in multi-level governance systems. From a more theoretical perspective, this book has developed an analytical approach for investigating how complex governance arrangements and the distribution of power affect renewable energy development in developing countries. Although the power-based multi-level governance approach is not a general theoretical framework for all possible cases, it does enhance the multi-level governance framework, which is often lacking a theoretical basis or needs to be enriched by other theories with insights from power in central–local relations. Compared with more technical and economic arguments, political factors related to resources or capacities are often not taken seriously enough when it comes to energy transitions in non-OECD countries. The power-based multi-level governance approach in the context of renewables needs to be tested, further developed and critically reviewed with the help of empirical insights from other countries and contexts in order to develop more robust hypotheses about the relation between different dimensions of power and energy transitions. Comparative analyses with other developing nations, and also OECD countries, seem to be promising for confronting multi-level governance research with a variety of different political systems and institutional settings. Specific factors such as complex corruption, interjurisdictional coordination or the fragmentation of power resources should be investigated.

Finally, this book should not only inspire further research in the field of renewable energy development, but also motivate practitioners and policymakers alike to take more seriously into account the complex governance environment in which every development project is embedded. The power-based analytical framework developed here is not only useful to researchers who investigate how renewables are promoted or blocked in multi-level governance systems. The approach should also guide development cooperation practitioners who can apply it as an assessment tool for their renewable energy projects. From an early stage of project planning, the framework helps to map the governance structures and identify barriers to, as well as potential for, useful contributions from development projects, improve their sustainability and foster structural change beyond the direct level of intervention.

Recommendations

This book raised the question of why development cooperation struggles to achieve structural effects in the energy sector with the help of renewable energy interventions in emerging economies such as the Philippines or Indonesia, although these countries provide supportive government policies and ambitious targets for renewables. A number of crucial political factors were identified that affect a donor-driven project's potential for scaling up or diffusing experiences beyond its narrow level of intervention. These factors may be related to the project design of a development activity as well as to the recipient country's governance system. These are often underestimated or neglected in debates about energy transitions in developing countries. For example, donors often fail to incorporate subnational stakeholders during project planning. In decentralized political systems with powerful local authorities like those in the Philippines or Indonesia, this causes significant conflicts of interest and delays during project implementation.

From a comparative perspective, energy-related decision-making in the Philippines can be described as more centralized than in Indonesia. Due to more constitutional and regulatory power resources as well as financial capacities at the national level, the Philippine Department of Energy (DOE) takes a much more prominent and active role in promoting renewables. In contrast, decentralization in Indonesia disrupted political coordination between central and local authorities. For an energy transition, a large number of veto players exist not only at the national but also at the subnational level. Actual responsibilities can be unclear and vary from municipality to municipality. Power resources and capacities in both countries can be described as heavily fragmented across different jurisdictional levels. As a consequence, learning and institutionalizing experiences from (donor-driven) renewable energy project activities becomes a challenging task, not only for the recipient countries themselves, but also for development cooperation. In light of these findings, this book formulates three main recommendations to policy-makers, project developers and researchers who aim to foster energy transitions towards renewables in developing countries.

(1) Project developers should follow a programmatic approach that reflects the complexity of governance structures. Although clean energy projects have been implemented successfully for decades, their sustainable operation remains a challenging task and a highly complex issue that goes far beyond the scope of a single development project. Establishing a wind farm or a solar mini grid might be technologically manageable and economically feasible on paper, but ensuring supportive political conditions for renewables is an ongoing struggle not only at the national level, but also across subnational jurisdictions. Any renewable energy project activity needs to relate to the recipient country's and the donor community's broader programmatic context. What do other donors focus on? How does it affect the national context? Can advisory activities be supported by local demonstration projects from other donors? These and other questions need to be raised before planning a renewable energy project. To achieve structural and system-wide effects for renewables, single donor-driven activities need to be linked to other projects at the national level and at subnational jurisdictions. Mapping their environment requires reflecting on existing governance arrangements, institutions and decision-making processes.

(2) Coordination across different jurisdictional levels and the distribution of power in complex governance arrangements need to be considered more seriously. Although

donors are aware that different jurisdictional levels are important for clean energy development and challenges arise from coordination between decision-makers at various levels, little effort is typically made to improve the situation. This often leads to unsustainable project activities, as experienced in Southeast Asia and other parts of the world. Projects that promote renewables at a specific jurisdictional level need to consider the power resources and capacities at other levels that might go beyond the project's actual scope, but affect its sustainability by improving learning, knowledge management, upscaling and so forth. Project developers should use the power-based multi-level governance approach as an assessment, monitoring and evaluation tool for donor-driven interventions. Multi-level governance can also learn from development cooperation, with its long history of experience in non-OECD countries. An exchange between researchers and practitioners from both fields should be beneficial for energy transitions and their support in developing countries.

(3) Local inclusion and capacity building are vital for project success. Local authorities play an important role in implementing and sustaining or blocking any donor-driven activity, but little effort is made to include local authorities at an early stage of planning and build up the capacities they need for institutionalizing upscaling or learning effects to sustain project results. Donors cannot change the political landscape, but they can act as honest brokers who set their priorities more independently than internal actors, coordinate between national and local governments, and provide capacity building for local staff that goes beyond the minimum level of renewable energy training, which is typically all that is provided by international donors. Instead of implementing new projects, donors should shift their efforts towards sustaining and institutionalizing results from existing activities.

Compared with the technological status of renewables and their economic performance, governance issues might be considered as soft aspects related to energy transitions in developing countries. This book revealed their hard impact on the development of renewables and donor-driven interventions. Taking the role of governance structures and power relations more seriously into account could improve the performance of renewable energy projects and increase their potential to foster energy transitions in aid-receiving countries in Southeast Asia and around the world.

Concluding remarks

Having discussed the political dimension of energy transitions in Southeast Asia, this monograph covered areas of increasing academic and practical interest, such as low-carbon development in emerging economies (Urban 2014), the meaning of social science in energy research (Sovacool 2014) and sustainability transitions (van den Bergh et al. 2011). This qualitative piece of work provided detailed insights into the status of energy transitions in Southeast Asia, outlined the importance of governance frameworks for project failure or success, and discussed development cooperation from a power-based multi-level governance perspective. Having addressed these aspects, this book is intended to speak to development cooperation practitioners, researchers and decision-makers in aid-receiving countries alike. It aims to raise awareness of the role of power and coordination in complex governance systems. These aspects might be hard to trace, to measure or to quantify, but they are critical for the success of an energy transition in general and donor-driven interventions specifically, as experiences from the Philippines and Indonesia revealed.

Promoting renewables is a highly complex policy field that is affected by technical, economic, social, environmental and political factors. Although the political dimension is considered to be highly relevant, its explicit conceptualization remains vague in most cases. A lack of governance- or power-related studies about energy transitions and renewable energy support in developing countries stands in sharp contrast to the variety of comprehensive economic or technological assessments in the field (Sovacool 2014). Due to the lack of clarity and weak awareness of governance-related issues, this book emphasized the role of political factors in developing countries, with a particular focus on the Philippines and Indonesia. It became clear that not only coordination and issues of central–local relations, but also the distribution of power resources and capacities, matter when it comes to renewable energy development.

Strong forms of decentralization and local empowerment can pose significant obstacles to energy transitions in developing countries. Such a statement stands in sharp contrast to the mainstream perception among governance scholars, who emphasize the positive link between sustainable development, participation and multi-level governance structures (Benz et al. 2009; Heinelt et al. 2002; Hirschl 2008; Peters and Pierre 2004). According to the literature, decentralized political structures should have a positive effect on renewable energy development, and bottom-up processes should be facilitated by powerful subnational jurisdictional levels. However, experiences from the two developing countries showed that constitutional or regulatory decentralization alone does not necessarily enable renewable energy development, and can even prevent it. To be successful, local empowerment needs to go hand in hand with capacity development at the local level, patterns of coordination across jurisdictional levels, and the limitation of possible veto players. Issues of corruption, patronage or clientelism also need to be considered.

Power can be very fragmented across jurisdictional levels. Any analysis of power needs not only to reflect hard and soft power resources, but also incorporate the actors' ability to make use of these resources (capacities). Taking into account the role of governance structures and power at different jurisdictional levels stands in contrast to the current practice in development cooperation, which tends to implement projects with a focus either at the national or at any subnational level. Moving beyond the growing awareness of the importance of multi-level interactions for diffusing, upscaling and institutionalizing results (ADB 2013; Neumann-Silkow 2010), donors need to consider the fragmentation of power and conceptualize the role of various jurisdictional levels in their project designs.

Local donor-driven renewable energy projects might be technologically appropriate for electrifying remote areas, but many of them turned out to be highly unsustainable in the Philippines and Indonesia. They often collapsed after a short period of time without funding or support from donor organizations. Such a finding stands in contrast to the very positive attitude towards modern renewables such as solar photovoltaic (PV), which are framed and pushed by international organizations such as the United Nations (2012), the World Bank (2013) or the International Monetary Fund (IMF 2013) as an attractive altern-ative to diesel generation in remote areas and an ideal solution for rural electrification.

Impact assessments are rare in development cooperation, but project-specific ex-post evaluations are desperately needed to confront overoptimistic project reports (e.g. Böhnke 1992) with actual long-term structural effects and to facil-itate learning from previously failed projects. Having presented a power-based multi-level governance approach here, this book aims to encourage a stronger focus on political factors when dealing with renewable energy development to foster energy transitions in Southeast Asia and beyond.

References

ADB, 2013. *Scaling up renewable energy access in eastern Indonesia*, Manila: Asian Devel-opment Bank.

Benz, A., Breitmeier, H., Schimank, U. and Simonis, G., 2009. *Politik in Mehrebenensys-temen*, Wiesbaden: VS Verlag für Sozialwissenschaften.

Biswas, W.K., Bryce, P. and Diesendorf, M., 2001. Model for empowering rural poor through renewable energy technologies in Bangladesh. *Environmental Science and Policy*, 4(6), pp. 333–344.

Böhnke, H.-W., 1992. *Opening the PV market: The development of a rural photovoltaic elec-trification model in the Philippines*, Eschborn: Deutsche Gesellschaft für Technische Zusammenarbeit.

Boyle, G., Deepchand, K., Hua, L. and La Rovere, E.L., 2006. *Renewable energy technolo-gies in developing countries. Lessons from Mauritius, China and Brazil*, Yokohama: United Nations University Institute for Advanced Studies.

Flavin, C. and Aeck, M., 2005. *Energy for development, the potential role of renewable energy in meeting the Millennium Development Goals*, Paris: Renewable Energy Policy Network for the 21st Century.

Geller, H., Schaeffer, R., Szklo, A. and Tolmasquim, M., 2004. Policies for advancing energy efficiency and renewable energy use in Brazil. *Energy Policy*, 32(12), pp. 1437–1450.

Gurung, A., Gurung, O.P. and Oh, S.E., 2011. The potential of a renewable energy tech-nology for rural electrification in Nepal: A case study from Tangting. *Renewable Energy*, 36(11), pp. 3203–3210.

Heinelt, H., Getimis, P., Kaflakas, G., Smith, R. and Swyngedouw, E.. eds., 2002. *Partici-patory governance in multi-level context. Concepts and experience*, Opladen: Leske and Budrich.

Hirschl, B., 2008. *Erneuerbare Energien-Politik: Eine Multi-Level Policy-Analyse mit Fokus auf den deutschen Strommarkt*, Wiesbaden: VS Verlag für Sozialwissenschaften.

IEA, 2013. *2013 Key world energy statistics*, Paris: International Energy Agency.

IMF, 2013. *Energy subsidy reform: Lessons and implications*, Washington, DC: International Monetary Fund.

IPCC, 2000. *Methodological and technological issues in technology transfer*, Cambridge: Intergovernmental Panel on Climate Change.

Jaramillo-Nieves, L. and del Río, P., 2010. Contribution of renewable energy sources to the sustainable development of islands: An overview of the literature and a research agenda. *Sustainability*, 2(3), pp. 783–811.

Mallett, A., 2007. Social acceptance of renewable energy innovations: The role of technology cooperation in urban Mexico. *Energy Policy*, 35(5), pp. 2790–2798.

Martinot, E. and McDoom, O., 2000. *Promoting energy efficiency and renewable energy: GEF climate change projects and impacts*, Washington, DC: Global Environmental Facility.

Neumann-Silkow, F., 2010. *Scaling up in development cooperation. Practical guidelines*, Eschborn: Gesellschaft für Technische Zusammenarbeit.

Peters, G. and Pierre, J., 2004. Multi-level governance and democracy: A Faustian bargain? In I. Bache and M. Flinders, eds. *Multi-level governance*, Oxford: Oxford University Press.

Sovacool, B.K., 2014. What are we doing here? Analyzing fifteen years of energy scholarship and proposing a social science research agenda. *Energy Research and Social Science*, 1, pp. 1–29.

United Nations, 2012. *Sustainable energy for all. A global action agenda. Pathways for concerted action towards sustainable energy for all*, New York: United Nations.

Urban, F., 2014. *Low carbon transitions for developing countries*, London: Routledge.

van den Bergh, J.C.J.M., Truffer, B. and Kallis, G., 2011. Environmental innovation and societal transitions: Introduction and overview. *Environmental Innovation and Societal Transitions*, 1(1), pp. 1–23.

Wilkins, G., 2002. *Technology transfer for renewable energy: Overcoming barriers in developing countries*, New York: Earthscan.

World Bank, 2013. World development indicators database. Available at: http://databank.worldbank.org/ddp/home.do?Step=12&id=4&CNO=2 [accessed May 29, 2015].

Appendix I
List of interviews conducted

Fifty-one interviews were conducted with energy experts in the Philippines. Table AI.1 provides an overview of the interviewees' organizations and positions.

Fifty-five interviews were conducted with energy experts in Indonesia. Table AI.2 provides an overview of the interviewees' organizations and positions.

Table A1.1 Interview partners in the Philippines (partly anonymous)

Organization	Position of the interviewee	Date of interview
National and local Philippine government		
Department of Energy	Director (Renewable Energy Management Bureau)	June 7, 2013
	Office of the Secretary	June 11, 2013
	Wind and Solar Division Chief (Renewable Energy Management Bureau)	June 18, 2013
	Former Undersecretary	June 25, 2013
Department of Energy Mindanao Field Office	Science Research Specialist	July 15, 2013
Department of Science and Technology	Head of Division	June 14, 2013
Congress of the Philippines	Member of Congress	June 4, 2013
Local Government Units	*Barangay* Captain (S. Agapito)	July 6, 2013
	Electronic Engineer (Guiwanon)	June 25, 2013
	BRECDA President (Bantol)	July 16, 2013
	Head of Planning (El Nido)	July 22, 2013
	Assistant City Engineer (Davao)	July 15, 2013
	Head of Planning and Development (Cebu)	July 26, 2013
	Municipal Engineer (Laguna)	July 29, 2013
League of the Municipalities of the Philippines	Executive Director	June 21, 2013
National Renewable Energy Board	Chairperson	June 20, 2013
Development cooperation		
Deutsche Gesellschaft für Internationale Zusammenarbeit	Principal Advisor	June 3, 2013
	Deputy Country Director	July 7, 2013
	Chief Advisor for Renewable Energy	July 7, 2013
	Senior Advisor	May 31, 2013
	Project Consultant	June 19, 2013

continued

Table A1.1 Continued

Organization	Position of the interviewee	Date of interview
United States Agency for International Development	Energy Policy Specialist	July 11, 2013
Japanese International Cooperation Agency	Sector Chief	May 31, 2013
Embassy of the United Kingdom	Climate Change Attaché	July 4, 2013
United Nations Development Programme	Energy and Environment Team Leader	June 6, 2013
United Nations Industrial Development Programme	Industrial Liaison Officer	June 5, 2013
Kreditanstalt für Wiederaufbau	Local Representative	June 6, 2013
European Union Switch Programme	Senior Energy Advisor	July 18, 2013
Public energy sector		
National Electrification Administration	Deputy Administrator	March 21, 2013
Energy Regulation Commission	Executive Director	July 3, 2013
National Transmission Corporation	General Manager	March 21, 2013
Meralco	Senior Engineer	July 19, 2013
Meralco Batangas	Senior Engineer, Technical Support	July 5, 2013
Philippine National Oil Company	Executive Vice President	July 11, 2013
National Power Corporation – Small Power Utilities Group	Project Manager	July 23, 2013
Civil society		
Greenpeace	Climate & Energy Campaigner	June 13, 2013
World Wide Fund for Nature	Climate Change Director	July 4, 2013
Oxfam	Project Manager	July 17, 2013
Renewable Energy Association of the Philippines	President	July 12, 2013

Renewable energy business

Thor Energy	General Manager	July 10, 2013
Philippine Solar Power Association	President and CEO	June 14, 2013
Winrock	Chief of Party	June 17, 2013
European Chamber of Commerce in the Philippines	Co-Chair LGU Committee	April 22, 2013
New Ibajay Electric Cooperative	Lineman in Charge of Operation	July 21, 2013
Cebu I Electric Cooperative	Power Generation Manager	July 25, 2013
Wind Energy Development Association	Vice President	July 4, 2013

Academia

University of the Philippines Diliman	Assistant Professor	June 19, 2013
Center for Asia Pacific Studies	Professor and President	July 2, 2013
Manila Observatory	Program Manager	July 17, 2013
Ateneo School de Manila	Freelance Technical Consultant	July 23, 2013
Development Academy of the Philippines	Teaching Fellow	July 2, 2013

Source: compiled by the author.

Table AI.2 Interview partners in Indonesia (partly anonymous)

Organization	Position of the interviewee	Date of interview
National and local Indonesian government		
Ministry of Energy and Mineral Resource	Energy Expert	March 27, 2014
Desa Serut, Gedang Sari, Gunung Kidul, Yogyakarta	Head of Village	April 1, 2014
Province of Yogyakarta	Chief of Administration	April 2, 2014
Department for Public Works, Province of Yogyakarta	Chief of Energy Section	April 2, 2014
Kantor Pertambangan dan Energi, DINAS Gunung Kidul	Chief of Kantor	April 3, 2014
National Energy Council Indonesia	Board Member	April 16, 2014
Kahayan Kuala, Pulang Pisau	Head of Village	April 21, 2014
Dinas Energi Central Kalimantan	Head of Dinas	April 24, 2014
BAPEDA Kota Sampit	Head of Team RUED	April 24, 2014
Ministry of Finance (Kementerian Keuangan)	Ministry of Finance	April 28, 2014
Dinas Pekerjaan Umum, Denpasar, Bali	Head of Dinas	May 2, 2014
Bidang Energi Dan Sumbar Mineral, Denpasar, Bali	Kepala	May 2, 2014
Environmental Agency (Badan Lingkungan Hidup)	Head of/Kepala	May 5, 2014
Directorate General of New and Renewable Energy and Energy Conservation	Director of Division	May 9, 2014
BAPPEDA Sumatera Utara	Kepala	May 16, 2014
Ministry of National Development Planning	Direktur	May 30, 2014
Development cooperation		
Deutsche Gesellschaft für Internationale Zusammenarbeit	Senior Advisor	March 5, 2014
	Senior Advisor	March 17, 2014
	Head of Programme	March 20, 2014
Embassy of the United States of America	Energy & Natural Resources Officer	March 18, 2014
Energy and Environment Partnership	Chief Technical Advisor	March 20, 2014
Embassy of Finland	Energy/Climate Change Advisor	March 21, 2014
United States Agency for International Development	Deputy Chief of party	March 21, 2014
	Program Manager	May 16, 2014
New Zealand Aid	Development Counsellor	March 24, 2014
Asian Development Bank	Energy Specialist (Climate Change)	March 27, 2014
World Bank	Energy Specialist	March 28, 2014
United Kingdom Climate Change Unit	Senior Energy Advisor	April 9, 2014

Organization	Position	Date
United Nations Development Programme	Programme Manager	April 10, 2014
Programme Biogas Rumah	Sundar Bajgain	April 15, 2014
Japan International Cooperation Agency	JICA Representative	April 29, 2014
Programme Biogas Rumah, HIVOS	Quality Inspector	May 2, 2014
Kreditanstalt für Wiederaufbau	Senior Project Manager	May 6, 2014
Public energy sector		
Perusahaan Listrik Negara (Persero) PT	Director of Planning & Technology	March 24, 2014
	Head of Division	March 25, 2014
Pertamina	Assistant Renewable Energy Project	March 26, 2014
Civil society		
Association of Indonesian Renewable Energy Supporting Industry	Chairman	March 19, 2014
Greenpeace Indonesia	Climate and Energy Campaigner	March 25, 2014
World Wide Fund For Nature – Indonesia	Energy Officer	March 26, 2014
Association of Indonesian Municipalities	Manager of Local Economics	April 30, 2014
Indonesian Renewable Energy Society	Deputy Secretary General	April 30, 2014
Renewable energy business		
Chevron Geothermal & Power Ltd	General Manager	March 14, 2013
Brama International	President Director	March 12, 2014
Alliance of Low Carbon Businesses in Indonesia	Steering Committee Member	April 16, 2014
Dewata Mason Group	Local CPO	May 2, 2014
PT Indonesia Power	Environmental Expert	May 9, 2014
Berkat Karya Sukses	Director	April 30, 2014
Energy Nusantara	CEO	April 30, 2014
Academia		
Australian National University	PhD Fellow	April 30, 2014
Indonesian Institute for Energy Economics	Executive Director	March 14, 2014
Department for Physical Engineering, Fakultas Teknik, UGM	Professor	March 18, 2014
Pustiklat KEBTKE	Bidang Program dan Kerja Sama	April 2, 2014
International Institute for Clean Energy and Climate Change	Director	April 28, 2014
University of Sumatera Utara	Lecturer	May 16, 2014
Academy for Clean Energy and Sustainability	Director	May 28, 2014

Source: compiled by the author.

Appendix II
List of field trips, workshops and events

During field research in Southeast Asia, a number of field trips to project case studies were conducted. In addition, several workshops and other events were attended by the author. Table AII.1 summarizes these field trips, workshops and events.

Table AII.1 List of field trips, workshops and events

Field trips to domor-driven renewable energy projects in the Philippines

Date	Project title (and domor agency)
June 2013 (interviews)	Capacity Building to Remove Barriers to Renewable Energy Development (UNDP)
May–June 2013 (interviews)	Supporting the Philippine Climate Change Commission (GIZ)
June–July 2013 (interviews)	Climate Change and Clean Energy (USAID)
March and June 2013 (interviews)	Renewables Made in Germany (GIZ)
July 2013 (field trip)	Central Village Electrification on Verde Island (GTZ)
July 2013 (field trip)	Renewable Energy Based Village Power System (UNDP)
July 2013 (field trip)	Barangay Solar Electrification Bantol (USAID)
August 2013 (field trip)	Solar Infrastructure in Guiwanon, Guimaras (AusAID)
July 2013 (field trip)	Mini Hydro Power Plant in Badian, Cebu, Visayas (GTZ)
August 2013 (field trip)	Geothermal Power Plant Rehabilitation, Laguna (JICA)

Field trips to donor-driven renewable energy projects in Indonesia

Date	Project title (and domor agency)
March–May 2014 (interviews)	Promotion of Least Cost Renewable Energy in Indonesia (GIZ)
March 2014 (interviews)	Geothermal Power Generation Development (World Bank)
May 2014 (field trip)	Support for Regional RAD-GRK in Sumatera Utara (USAID)
May 2014 (field trip)	Establishing RUED in Central Kalimantan (EEP)
April 2014 (field trip)	Solar PV under PLTS in Gunung Kidul, Yogyakarta (GIZ)
May 2014 (field trip)	Small Scale Biodigesters for Farming in Gianyar, Bali (HIVOS)
May 2014 (field trip)	Communal Biogas Digesters for Cooking (EEP)
May 2014 (field trip)	Production of Biogas from Farming Waste (EEP)
May 2014 (field trip)	Business Development for Integrated Biomass Power Production (EEP)

continued

Table AI.1 Continued

Workshops and events attended during field research in the Philippines

Date	Title	Short description	Personal remarks (memo)
March 18, 2013	Planning Workshop on Elevating the RE Academic & Research Programs at the UP COE	GIZ, together with the DOE, organized a workshop at the University of the Philippines Diliman to discuss the establishment of a Center for Renewable Energy Technologies (CRET)	• Participants share a technical understanding of renewables • Participants discuss general research fields related to renewable energy, but fail to identify more specific research topics that should be investigated under the newly established CRET • DOE and DOST need to bring together their energy plans and R&D agendas
April 18–19, 2013	Review of the National Renewable Energy Plan	NREB, DOE-REMB and GIZ organized a joint-review workshop to discuss the current status and future plans for renewables	• NREP formulates ambitious targets for renewables, but its implementation is challenging • Major obstacles are at the local level, but subnational authorities are not among the participants • The DOE struggles to implement the rules and regulations for the support mechanisms under the 2008 RE Act
April 24, 2013	Administrative Procedures and Challenges for Solar PV Project Development in the Philippines	GIZ (Renewables made in Germany) organized a workshop about solar PV with participants from DOE and MERALCO as well as project developers	• For local clearances, clear procedures exist in law, but the actual practice looks completely different • LGUs are blamed for delays and blocking RE projects (corruption), but also positive examples of collaborative activities are presented (e.g. USAID)
May 21–22, 2013	Training-Seminar: Grid Integration of Variable Renewable Energies in the Philippines	The DOE, together with GIZ, organized an RE Grid Impact Week (May 20–24, 2013). The activity provided inputs from energy experts from the Philippines, Germany and ASEAN Delegation on the considerations of grid integration of solar and wind energy	• Donor-driven interventions focus on new RE sources such as wind and solar rather than promoting traditional ones in the Philippines (especially hydro and geothermal power) • Severe lack of technical understanding of solar power • The FiT system is widely discussed and perceived as an instrument that will increase the price of electricity

Date	Title	Short description	Personal remarks (memo)
June 27, 2013	Supporting the Energy Transition in Asia – Policies and Regulations to Enhance RE Markets	The GIZ Side Event at the 8th ADB Asia Clean Energy Forum brought together GIZ practitioners and partners from different ASEAN countries to shed light on the current status, obstacles and success stories of the energy transition in SEA	• Experiences from the German energy transition cannot be easily transferred to the ASEAN context • The talk among practitioners seemed to be more fruitful than among high-level politicians, because they were able to discuss current issues and concerns related to their work

Workshops and events attended during field research in Indonesia

Date	Title	Short description	Personal remarks (memo)
March 4–8, 2014	Advanced Training for Trainers in Photovoltaics and Bioenergy	GIZ funded a training that was conducted by the renewable academy (RENAC) for Indonesian officials (mainly technical staff)	• Highly technical issues were at the center of the workshop, which provided basic and advanced information about PV and bioenergy • Neither political/social issues nor the country-specific context were discussed
March 21, 2014	De-Briefing Meeting Untuk Draft RUED Kalimantan Tengah	EEP supported the government of Central Kalimantan to establish a Regional Energy Plan (RUED). The workshop marked the final discussion among stakeholders	• Various stakeholders from different jurisdictional levels discussed the RUED. They pointed out the importance of the tool, but also admitted the early draft status of the RUED, which still needed to be finalized
April 25, 2014	Business Development for Integrated Biomass Power Production in Central Kalimantan	EEP funded the development of an extended feasibility study for the construction of a gasification system that uses agricultural waste for power production. The responsible consortium presented their results concerning the feasibility of the planned project	• The consultant stressed the feasibility of using coconut and palm oil waste biomass for power production in the area and constructing a commercial 1 MW gasification system. Nevertheless, uncertainties (negotiations with PLN, lack of funding for up-front costs, price of biomass waste) are too great for the project to be realized

Source: compiled by the author.

Appendix III
Donor-driven project case studies

Fourteen donor-driven renewable energy projects act as case studies from the Philippines (Projects 1–8) and Indonesia (Projects 9–14). They exemplify what has been discussed for the broader context of multi-level governance structures, power and the role of development cooperation. For each project, a figure shows the project's location and illustrates its achievements and shortcomings in terms of project level, coordination, capacity, institutions, decision-making and power resources (see Chapter 21 for details). Figures AIII.1–14 refer to Projects 1–14, respectively.

Project 1: Capacity Building to Remove Barriers to Renewable Energy Development (UNDP)

Undertaken by the United Nations Development Programme (UNDP) between 2003 and 2011, the Capacity Building to Remove Barriers to Renewable Energy Development (CBRED) project was the first major program supporting the general framework for renewables and capacity building at the national level. CBRED acted as an overarching program for renewable energy support activities related to political, financial and technical aspects and became a hub for activities related to policies and institutional capacity building, market services, information and awareness-raising, financing mechanisms, training, and technology support.

Context: The Philippines aims to push renewable energy development and foster domestic energy sources to decrease energy dependency and improve energy security. To foster private investments, the electricity market was liberalized in 2001. Since then, coal has become the dominant source of electricity. Against this background, the long-term advisory project supported the national government in the formulation and implementation of the 2008 Renewable Energy Act. Project components included supportive policies for renewables, market services and training.

Performance: Due to the broad project portfolio, actual results are difficult to measure (lack of impact-oriented indicators). The Renewable Energy Management Bureau (REMB) greatly acknowledged the support of the project, which also helped to coordinate activities between relevant stakeholders such as the

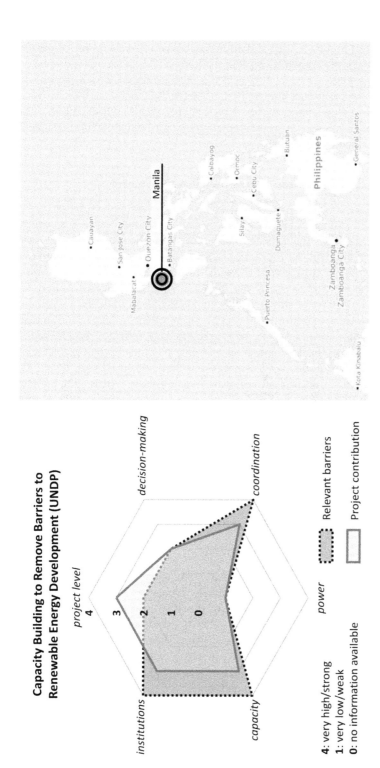

Figure AIII.1 Capacity Building to Remove Barriers to Renewable Energy Development (UNDP).

Source: compiled by the author; map © OpenStreetMap contributors.

Department of Energy (DOE) and other regulators in the field, institutionalized market services, and provided capacity building among national and local government representatives. The project's contributions were in line with the country's strong demands for renewable energy development, but due to the project's broad scope, various issues have only been addressed superficially (lack of focus), and a number of project targets could not be realized until the end of the project phase in 2011.

Project 2: Supporting the Philippine Climate Change Commission (GIZ)

Between 2012 and 2015, Deutsche Gesellschaft für Internationale Zusammenarbeit (GIZ) implemented the Federal Ministry for the Environment, Nature Conservation and Nuclear Safety (BMU)-funded project Support to the Philippine Climate Change Commission with the implementation of the National Climate Change Strategy and the National Climate Change Action Plan (Support CCC). One of the project's components dealt with the implementation of a countrywide feed-in tariff (FiT) for renewables. Support CCC aimed to integrate climate change action plans and strategies into the regular planning system to support the Philippines in adapting to climate change and reduce greenhouse gas emissions. GIZ developed a financing framework for climate-related activities, outlined an innovative monitoring system and promoted climate-friendly planning and project implementation.

Context: The Philippines had already introduced an FiT for renewables in 2008 as part of the Renewable Energy Act, but its enforcement suffered from huge delays in implementation. By supporting REMB at the DOE, the project aimed to foster the formulation of the necessary rules and regulations for the FiT and evaluate their performance. GIZ framed itself as a knowledge broker by raising awareness of renewables and providing training on feeding in renewables into the grid.

Performance: Specific events such as the announcement of the FiT rates cannot be directly linked to the project activity, because numerous other factors also affected the FiT scheme. Despite such a vague connection between project performance and actual outcomes REMB acknowledged Support CCC for providing resources that directly catered to the bureau's activities for renewables. Due to constraints concerning its limited timeframe and financial resources, the project followed a narrow, but clear, focus on policy advice for an FiT. Efforts were concentrated at the national level, with REMB being the main counterpart. GIZ was perceived as an important source of expertise. Other factors that led to delays concerning the implementation of the Renewable Energy Act, such as coordination between the national government and local stakeholders, capacity building at the local level, institutionalization of support, and especially the role of powerful local authorities (*Bupatis*), were not directly addressed by the project.

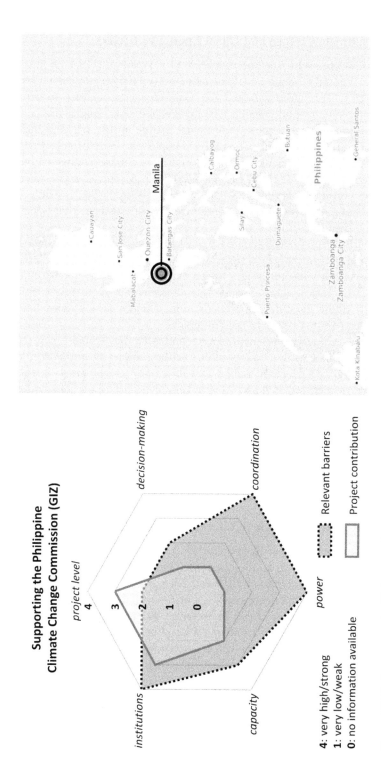

Figure AIII.2 Supporting the Philippine Climate Change Commission (GIZ).
Source: compiled by the author; map © OpenStreetMap contributors.

Project 3: Climate Change and Clean Energy (USAID)

United States Assistance for International Development (USAID) implemented the Climate Change and Clean Energy (CEnergy) project between 2010 and 2014. The activity linked the issue of energy security to action against climate change and covered four interrelated tasks: improving policy implementation, regulatory capacity, climate change mitigation, and public understanding and support for renewables. Despite its short project period, CEnergy covered a broad range of topics to mitigate climate change through the improved utilization of clean and renewable energy sources in the electricity and transportation sectors. USAID also aimed to strengthen existing collaboration between government entities, the private sector, civil society, media and academia.

Context: The Philippine Climate Change Commission is responsible for adaptation and mitigation measures against climate change. The 2008 Renewable Energy Act provides incentives for promoting renewables, but its implementation faced huge delays. The project therefore aimed to foster policy implementation and institutional strengthening, which can be directly linked to the complex political system of the Philippines.

Performance: CEnergy provided reports and scientific studies, but most project results cannot easily be assessed due to the complexity of the field and the large number of relevant variables that affect project outcomes. Issues of coordination between national and local stakeholders, lack of capacity and the role of power conflicts between different levels of decision-making are crucial for implementing renewable energy legislation. Despite its strong focus at the national level, CEnergy actively followed a multi-level approach, with a combination of national advisory activities and experiences from local demonstration projects. Yet, the advisory activities cannot easily be evaluated due to the attribution gap between efforts and actual output.

Project 4: Renewables Made in Germany (GIZ)

The German export initiative Renewables Made in Germany is another project conducted by GIZ, but with funding from the German Federal Ministry of Economics. The project ran between 2011 and 2015 and provided assistance for a robust political framework for renewables and an enabling environment for renewable energy businesses. After its focus on biomass in the first run, the project's scope shifted to regulations for solar photovoltaic (PV). To support German renewable energy businesses in accessing the Philippine electricity market, GIZ organized business trips, matchmaking events and country-specific information for potential project developers.

Context: The Philippine archipelago offers high potential for small-scale renewable energy projects, especially to substitute for diesel generation in off-grid areas. Difficult political and market conditions prevent foreign investors and project developers from entering the market. With a focus on solar PV

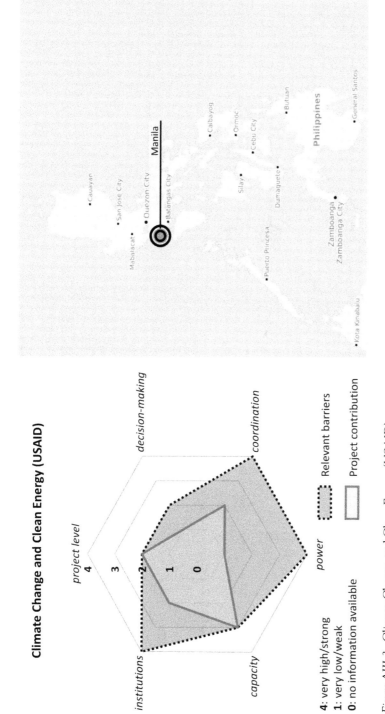

Climate Change and Clean Energy (USAID)

decision-making

coordination

project level

4
3
2
1
0

power

institutions

capacity

Relevant barriers

Project contribution

4: very high/strong
1: very low/weak
0: no information available

Philippines

Cauayan
San Jose City
Mabalacat
Quezon City
Batangas City
Manila
Calbayog
Ormoc
Cebu City
Silay
Dumaguete
Butuan
Puerto Princesa
Zamboanga
Zamboanga City
General Santos
Kota Kinabalu

Figure AIII.3 Climate Change and Clean Energy (USAID).
Source: compiled by the author; map © OpenStreetMap contributors.

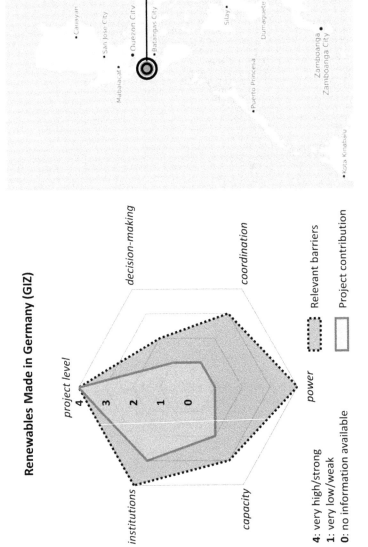

Renewables Made in Germany (GIZ)

decision-making

coordination

project level

power

3
2
1
0

institutions

capacity

┊ Relevant barriers

□ Project contribution

4: very high/strong
1: very low/weak
0: no information available

Philippines

Canayan

San Jose City

Malolos City

Quezon City

Batangas City

Manila

Calbayog

Ormoc

Cebu City

Silay

Puerto Princesa

Dumaguete

Butuan

Zamboanga
Zamboanga City

General Santos

Kota Kinabalu

Figure AIII.4 Renewables Made in Germany (GIZ).

Source: compiled by the author; map © OpenStreetMap contributors.

installations and net metering, the project conducted workshops and studies to improve this situation.

Performance: Government officials confirmed the usefulness of guidebooks and information provided by the project. The project's direct output in terms of capacity building (workshops, studies, guidebooks) was widely acknowledged by Philippine partners and gained support from the national government. Having successfully formulated and institutionalized rules and regulations for net metering and interconnections, GIZ laid the ground for stable market conditions for project developers. Yet, the project barely tackled existing power structures (especially at the local level) or improved patterns of coordination between different jurisdictional levels.

Project 5: Central village electrification on Verde island (GTZ)

In the early 1990s, German Technical Cooperation (GTZ) planned and constructed a 3 kW/peak solar power plant and distributed solar home systems to San Agapito on Isla Verde, Batangas. The facility should have acted as a demonstration project to showcase the feasibility of renewables in remote off-grid areas, but the entire system rapidly collapsed without external support.

Context: The project was part of the German-Philippine Special Energy Program that was implemented between 1987 and 1999. Having identified insufficient electricity supply in rural areas as a major barrier to economic and human development, the program aimed to achieve reliable and affordable rural electrification through small-scale decentralized systems with the help of solar PV and mini hydro power plants.

Performance: The solar project on Isla Verde was implemented in 1990 and framed as a solar mini grid demonstration facility to provide electricity to the community. The project was documented as a success that led to independent electricity supply and substituted for fossil fuels, but a field visit in 2013 revealed another picture. The solar power plant had been completely destroyed and most solar home systems were broken. Diesel generators supplied power to the community for only 4 hours a day. The main reasons for the project's failure were the high costs of exchanging the batteries after 2–3 years and the lack of maintenance capacities, trained technical personnel and ownership. The project was planned as a demonstration facility, but scaling up or replication as a direct result of the project never happened. Capacity building and awareness-raising were restricted to the *barangay* level (and partly successful), but the project design did not mention how the national government could learn from experiences at the local level.

Central Village Electrification on Verde Island (GTZ)

project level

decision-making

coordination

institutions

capacity

power

4
3
2
1
0

[·····] Relevant barriers

[ ] Project contribution

4: very high/strong
1: very low/weak
0: no information available

San Agapito, Batangas

• Cauayan
• San Jose City
Mabalacat •
• Quezon City
• Calbayog
• Ormoc
• Cebu City
Silay •
Dumaguete •
• Butuan

Puerto Princesa •

Philippines

Zamboanga
Zamboanga City
• General Santos

• Kota Kinabalu

Figure AIII.5 Central village electrification on Verde island (GTZ).

Source: compiled by the author; map © OpenStreetMap contributors.

Project 6: Renewable Energy Based Village Power System (UNDP)

In 2004, a solar–diesel hybrid mini grid was constructed in New Ibajay, El Nido, for independent power supply to 232 households. The facility was part of the Palawan New and Renewable Energy and Livelihood Support Project (PNRELSP).

Context: The province of Palawan depends heavily on electricity imports, because it is not connected to the main grid. Sixty percent of the island's *barangays* are not electrified at all. There is a demand for small-scale decentralized and environmentally friendly forms of electricity supply to improve the situation. At the end of 2013, the provincial government announced the target of meeting its future energy demand 100 percent with renewables, but did not specify how this was to be done.

Performance: Providing power to 232 households, the project was a joint effort by the provincial, municipal and *barangay* governments with funding from UNDP. Directly after its implementation, a final report by UNDP and the DOE documented the project as a success that substituted for a considerable amount of diesel during operation. The project led to a high degree of local political commitment to renewables and supported the development of a local utility to operate the system. After 6 years of operation, the solar component has been turned off due to technical problems with the batteries and the converter. The local electric cooperative, as well as the municipal government, felt incapable of solving the problems on their own. Additional financial capacities were needed for changing the batteries, although a relatively high price for electricity was charged (PHP 35 per kilowatt/hour). UNDP coordinated the project's implementation with all relevant jurisdictional levels. The DOE and the provincial (Palawan), municipal (El Nido) and *barangay* administrations were involved. Once the project was operational, only the electric cooperative in New Ibajay remained in charge of the project. It has not been taken as a blueprint for similar projects elsewhere in the Philippines, and learning or spill-over effects cannot be proven.

Project 7: Barangay solar electrification in Bantol, Mindanao (USAID)

Bantol is a small *barangay* north of Davao city, the provincial capital of Mindanao. USAID implemented solar home systems here in 2011, and the site claims to be a best practice example for the Alliance for Mindanao Off-Grid Renewable Energy (AMORE) rural electrification program. AMORE provided decentralized solar and mini hydro electrification schemes to off-grid areas all over Mindanao.

Context: AMORE was implemented in three phases between 2002 and 2013. According to its own records, the program provided solar home systems and solar lanterns to more than 22,000 households in almost 500 remote *barangays*

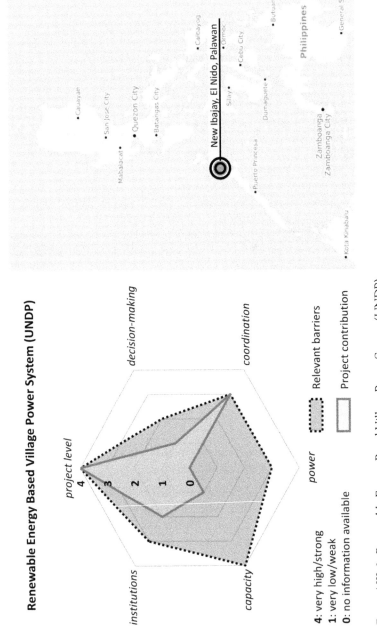

Figure AIII.6 Renewable Energy Based Village Power System (UNDP).

Source: compiled by the author; map © OpenStreetMap contributors.

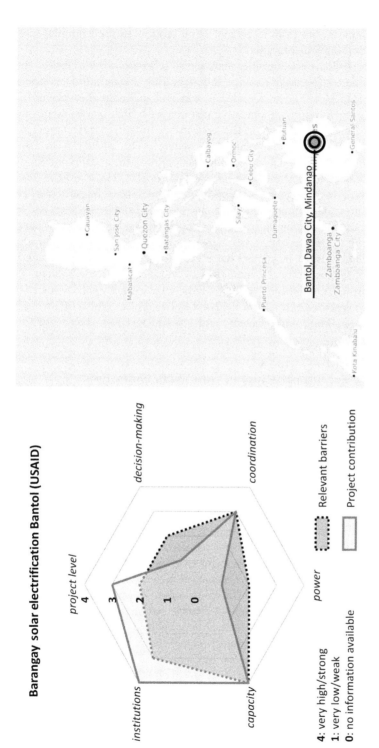

Figure AIII.7 Barangay solar electrification in Bantol, Mindanao (USAID).

Source: compiled by the author; map © OpenStreetMap contributors.

all over Mindanao, but over 50 percent of all projects stopped running several years after their implementation.

Performance: Some communities managed to self-sustain the facilities – such as Bantol, where a *Barangay* Renewable Energy and Community Development Association (BRECDA) was founded to run and maintain the systems. The BRECDA is organized in a cooperative manner, with high involvement of the local people, who have a share in the association. Initially, USAID provided a battery charging station and solar home systems. The BRECDA in Bantol managed to build up financial capacity for maintaining the systems and funding additional solar home systems without external support. However, the overall success of the AMORE program is considered to be mixed. In particular, poor and remote areas with limited access to cities for acquiring spare parts and batteries were not able to maintain or further develop the solar projects. In Bantol, the number of systems installed had increased from the initial 50 to 234 at the time of the field visit. The project has a clear focus at the *barangay* level, but lacks further support from the municipal or the provincial government. Processes of learning and diffusion to the national level cannot easily be traced due to the weak capacities of the DOE field office. The project's focus on ownership and capacity building with partners and stakeholders was considered to be crucial for success.

Project 8: Solar infrastructure in Guiwanon, Guimaras (AusAID)

The Municipal Solar Infrastructure Project (MSIP) was implemented as a joint venture by the Australian Agency for International Development (AusAID) and BP solar. The project distributed solar home systems, solar lanterns and solar pumps for water distribution to remote areas in the late 1990s, and was considered to be the biggest of its kind at that time. Despite extraordinarily positive project reports, documentations and promo material, AusAID refused to provide any comprehensive project-related information about MSIP.

Context: Rural electrification in remote areas is a major concern for the Philippine government, which is promoting renewable energy systems, especially for small and financially weak islands such as Guiwanon. The island is part of Nueva Valencia, a municipality in Guimaras Province, one of the smallest provinces in the Philippines, with 163,000 inhabitants.

Performance: Solar lanterns and solar home systems were installed in Guiwanon, especially for public services such as schools and the *barangay* hall. The *barangay* is situated on a very remote island with no public transportation available to the main island of Guimaras. In Guiwanon, all solar facilities stopped working after 2–3 years due to lack of technical and financial capacity for maintenance. Technical equipment or batteries were not replaced due to long hauls and a lack of technical infrastructure and financial capacity. In 2012, the National Power Corporation Small Power Utilities Group (NPC SPUG) was running a diesel-powered 36 kW mini grid in Guiwanon. AusAID targeted only

Solar infrastructure in Guiwanon, Guimaras (AusAID)

project level

decision-making

coordination

institutions

capacity

power

4
3
2
1
0

┅ Relevant barriers

☐ Project contribution

4: very high/strong
1: very low/weak
0: no information available

Guiwanon,
Nueva Valencia, Guimaras

Figure AIII.8 Solar infrastructure in Guiwanon, Guimaras (AusAID).

Source: compiled by the author; map © OpenStreetMap contributors.

the very local level of the *barangay*, without any further effort at coordinating activities with higher jurisdictional levels or the national government. There is no evidence of project replication, scaling up or spill-over effects. The necessary financial resources and technical capacities for operating and maintaining solar power facilities are particularly limited in extremely remote areas such as Guiwanon. National support is missing, as the DOE was not involved in MSIP.

Project 9: Promotion of Least Cost Renewable Energy in Indonesia (GIZ)

Renewables play only a minor role in the Indonesian electricity mix. Despite the country's high annual growth in energy demand, the market conditions for renewables are challenging. Yet, renewable energy sources can be a competitive alternative to fossil fuels, especially in remote off-grid areas. Promotion of Least Cost Renewables in Indonesia (LCORE) identified ways to use renewable energy sources in the most economically feasible manner.

Context: LCORE was part of a broader GIZ renewable energy portfolio in Indonesia that supported the development of renewables at various levels. In order to reduce greenhouse gas emissions, the Indonesian government is committed to increasing the share of new and renewable energy sources in the energy mix from 4 percent in 2013 to 25 percent by 2025. LCORE supported the national authority Directorate General for New and Renewable Energy and Energy Conservation (EBTKE) with advisory activities, training and pilot projects. EBTKE was established in 2010 to foster renewable energy development.

Performance: LCORE aligned its efforts with the working areas and targets of EBTKE. One important approach was to include the private sector for investments in renewable energy facilities and their operation by conducting studies about solar power, biomass and biogas projects or the design of an appropriate FiT for renewables. LCORE identified three crucial areas for accelerating renewables: the use of waste biomass from agro-industries, the replacement of diesel by on-grid solar power, and innovative business models for off-grid electrification. LCORE conducted and distributed technical guidelines on bioenergy and solar PV. Together with German and Indonesian businesses, a PV pilot project was planned for a diving station to substitute for diesel and bring savings to *Perusahaan Listrik Negara* (PLN). Apart from this, the project struggled to identify appropriate project sites and mainly failed to involve subnational authorities.

Project 10: Geothermal Power Generation Development (World Bank)

Similarly to technical assistance from New Zealand, the Geothermal Clean Energy Investment Project of the World Bank provided US$300 million in loans to support two geothermal fields and strengthen capacity and institutional capabilities at Pertamina. Despite huge potential for its development, electricity production from geothermal energy is confronted with massive obstacles that

Promotion of Least Cost Renewable Energy in Indonesia (GIZ)

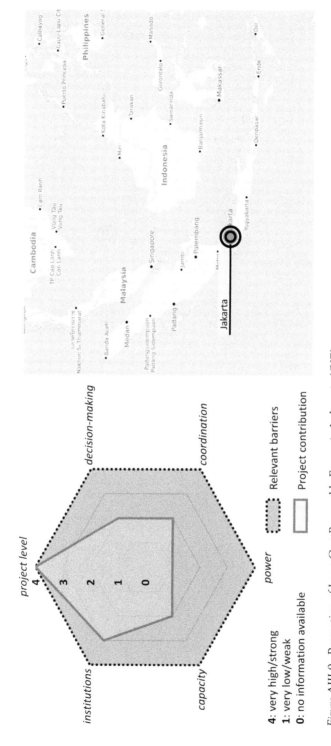

4: very high/strong
1: very low/weak
0: no information available

Relevant barriers

Project contribution

Figure AIII.9 Promotion of Least Cost Renewable Energy in Indonesia (GIZ).
Source: compiled by the author; map © OpenStreetMap contributors.

Geothermal Power Generation Development (World Bank)

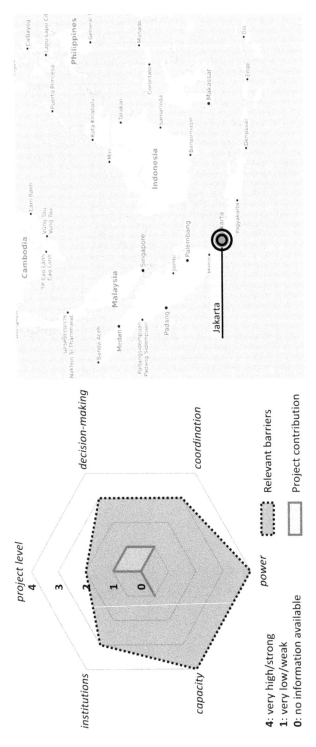

project level

decision-making

coordination

institutions

capacity

power

4: very high/strong
1: very low/weak
0: no information available

[···] Relevant barriers

[ ] Project contribution

Figure AIII.10 Geothermal Power Generation Development (World Bank).

Source: compiled by the author; map © OpenStreetMap contributors.

are closely linked to governance issues and decentralization. As one example, local resistance in Bali prevented the construction of a geothermal power plant. In addition, high up-front investments and risks can scale up costs for geothermal projects significantly.

Context: The World Bank identified a gap between the huge potential for geothermal projects and the lack of actual development and investments. Although the government launched a 10,000 MW fast-track program in late 2008, with geothermal making up 40 percent of the target, no significant geothermal projects have since been implemented. Since 2014, a new geothermal law has allowed geothermal exploration in forest conservation areas.

Performance: Funded by a Global Environment Facility (GEF) grant, the project aimed to reduce CO_2 emissions from the electricity sector by expanding economical and environmentally friendly geothermal power generation. The advisory project tackled the policy framework for scaling up geothermal development, the transactions management for mobilizing investments, technical capacity building for the geothermal sector, and project management assistance. Although the original project duration (2008–2011) was extended for another 2 years, the overall progress was rated as unsatisfactory in a final progress report in 2013.

Project 11: Support for a regional RAD-GRK in Sumatera Utara (USAID)

Indonesia ranks among the top greenhouse gas emitters in the world, mainly due to massive emissions from land use change, deforestation, peat land degradation and forest fires. Although emissions from the energy sector (fuel combustion) are less significant (435 million tons of CO_2 in 2012), they have almost tripled over the last 20 years.

Context: In order to mitigate at least 26 percent of its greenhouse gas emissions compared with the business-as-usual scenario by 2020, the Indonesian government passed its National Action Plan on Greenhouse Gas Emission Reduction (*Rencana Aksi Nasional penurunan emisi Gas Rumah Kaca*, RAN-GRK). All Indonesian provinces are obliged to develop their own regional climate mitigation plans (*Rencana Aksi Daerah penurunan emisi Gas Rumah Kaca* (RAD-GRK)) and outline their commitment and how they propose to contribute to the national target. USAID, together with the Japan International Cooperation Agency (JICA), supported the provincial government of North Sumatra in developing and implementing their RAD-GRK. The plan was finalized in 2012. USAID provided expertise related to renewables and training to local staff.

Performance: The activity in North Sumatra was part of the Indonesian Clean Energy Development (ICED) project, which was implemented by USAID between 2011 and 2014 and aimed to increase access to energy services and reduce energy-related emissions. Although ICED outlined a reduction or avoidance of more than 1 million tons of CO_2 equivalent over the project's lifetime

Support for a regional RAD-GRK in Sumatera Utara (USAID)

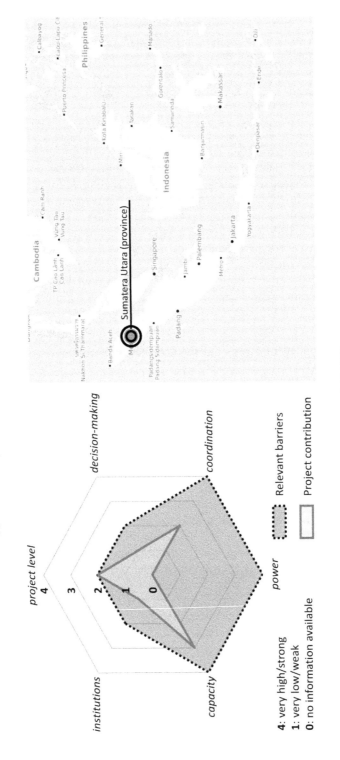

Figure AIII.11 Support for a regional RAD-GRK in Sumatera Utara (USAID).

Source: compiled by the author; map © OpenStreetMap contributors.

as of December 2013, the actual contribution of the project in North Sumatra cannot easily be measured. The RAD-GRK was passed in 2012, but its implementation and the process of monitoring and evaluation were still challenging in 2014.

Project 12: Establishing RUED in Central Kalimantan (EEP)

Between 2013 and 2014, the Energy and Environmental Program (EEP) supported the province of Kalimantan Tengah with the development of its regional energy plan. EEP Indonesia is a joint collaboration between the governments of Indonesia and Finland to promote renewables, energy efficiency and investments in clean energy technology. The program started in 2011 and ended in 2014. EEP aimed to support the wider provision and use of renewable energy with a focus on bioenergy in the two defined target provinces of Central Kalimantan and Riau.

Context: Since 2007, each province has been expected to establish its own regional energy plan (*Rencana Umum Energi Daerah,* RUED). Despite efforts by provincial governments and donor organizations, not a single RUED had been fully implemented in 2014. At the same time, information from the local level is vital to identify energy potential, developments and future needs in line with the national energy plan. For that reason, EEP supported local and provincial capacity building and training for establishing a RUED in Central Kalimantan.

Performance: The project activity concentrated on capacity building at the provincial level as well as in three *kabupatens.* These districts (Palangka Raya, Kapuas and Kotawaringhin Timur) were considered as pilots to see whether and how they could contribute to the RUED. The Long-range Energy Alternatives Planning (LEAP) system was introduced, and staff were trained to collect data and use the model. At the end of March 2014, the activity was closed after 1 year of funding. Its main target, to establish a draft RUED, had not been accomplished. Collecting information and negotiation with different authorities took much longer than expected. EEP supported the project due to a lack of financial capacities at the provincial level. To sustain the activities, funding from the regional budget as well as from the districts is necessary.

Project 13: Solar PV under PLTS in Gunung Kidul, Yogyakarta (GIZ)

Solar power is considered to be a viable solution for off-grid electrification and substituting for diesel generation. The Indonesian government supports various programs to promote decentralized small-scale renewable energy supply. Monitoring the project in Gunung Kidul was part of the Energising Development (EnDev) initiative, a global energy partnership to promote sustainable access to modern energy services. GIZ implemented EnDev in Indonesia with a focus on mini grid installations based on micro hydro power and solar photovoltaic technologies.

Establishing RUED in Central Kalimantan (EEP)

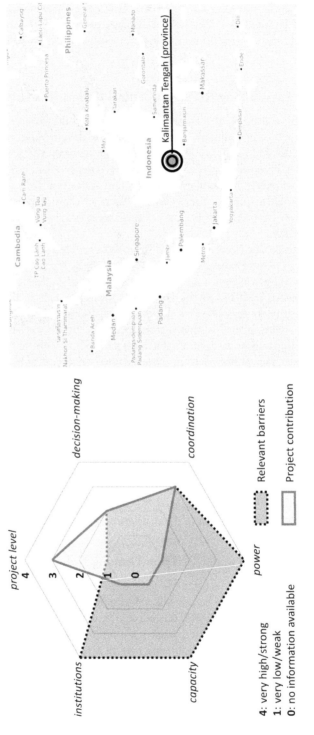

Figure AIII.12 Establishing RUED in Central Kalimantan (EEP).

Source: compiled by the author; map © OpenStreetMap contributors.

Solar PV under PLTS in Gunung Kidul, Yogyakarta (GIZ)

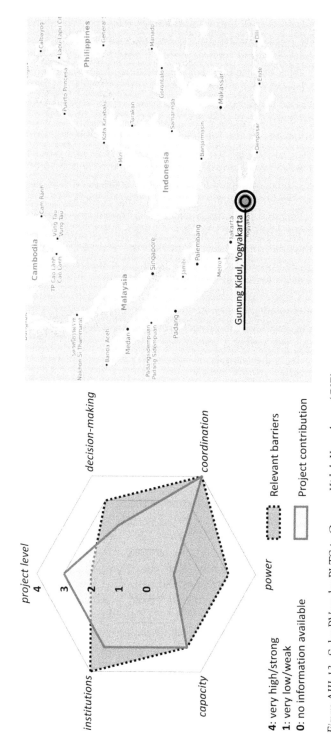

Figure AIII.13 Solar PV under PLTS in Gunung Kidul, Yogyakarta (GIZ).
Source: compiled by the author; map © OpenStreetMap contributors.

Context: Indonesia is rich in natural energy resources, but almost 70 million Indonesians are not connected to the country's electricity grid. Most of these people use diesel, kerosene or traditional biomass as their primary source of energy. Renewables are often not competitive due to high up-front costs, investment risks and government subsidies for fossil fuels. Indonesia has subsidized gasoline, diesel and kerosene since the oil crises in the 1970s. In 2013, US$27.0 billion was spent on energy subsidies, equal to 25 percent of the total government expenditure, before the subsidies system was drastically reformed in 2014 and 2015. Due to a comparatively small FiT for biomass and hydro, lack of incentives for solar power and PLN's dominant role in the electricity sector, renewables are rarely considered for electricity supply in remote off-grid areas.

Performance: EnDev's main activities cluster around technical support, project monitoring and capacity development. Monitoring more than 300 mini grid sites, GIZ established a knowledge management system, but also aimed to create ownership. Self-sustaining the projects by local partners is a key objective for EnDev, but technical problems with solar PV installations cannot be solved without the donor's technical assistance. This happened in 2014 with a site in Gunung Kidul (Yogyakarta) that was built by ESDM in 2012 with a capacity of 15 kW. Key provincial government authorities such as the Department of Public Works were not aware of the project and could not act as facilitators between the district and the national government. Institutionalized forms of capacity building, learning and troubleshooting were yet to be established.

Project 14: Small-scale Biodigesters for farming in Gianyar, Bali (HIVOS)

Together with the Humanist Institute for Cooperation (HIVOS), the Foundation of Netherlands Volunteers (SNV) implemented various small-scale biodigesters in Bali to provide electricity supply for organic farming. The project site in Gianyar is one example.

Context: Although only a small share of Balinese households have no access to the electricity grid, cooking, especially with kerosene, is expensive. The biogas digesters installed by HIVOS and SNV are intended to substitute for kerosene and provide slurry for organic farming. This is indirectly supported by a Balinese government regulation that fosters organic farming and aims to reduce the use of chemical fertilizers and pesticides. The project site is part of the Indonesian program *Biogas Rumah* (BIRU), which aimed at facilitating knowledge transfer. By December 2013, 11,249 biogas reactors had been constructed under the program in nine Indonesian provinces.

Performance: The project at Gelgel, Gianyar uses a simple approach. A very small-scale biogas digester (capacity of $4\,m^3$, sufficient for dung from up to seven cows) can be constructed within about 1 week and serves for a single household's consumption and organic farming activities (using the slurry as a fertilizer). Local banks, in cooperation with the provincial government, provide a financing scheme (*Lembaga Perkrediton Desa*). Since 2010, HIVOS and SNV

Small-scale Biodigesters for farming in Gianyar, Bali (HIVOS)

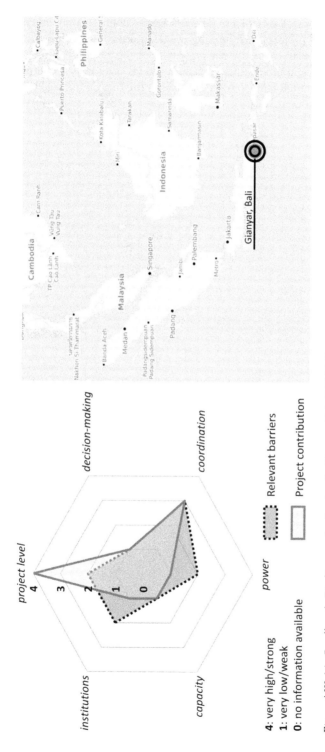

4: very high/strong
1: very low/weak
0: no information available

Relevant barriers

Project contribution

Figure AIII.14 Small-scale Biodigesters for farming in Gianyar, Bali (HIVOS).

Source: compiled by the author; map © OpenStreetMap contributors.

have implemented 631 biogas digesters across Bali. Local financial institutions support these projects with funding at low interest rates for private households. Four local construction partner organizations are responsible for construction, maintenance and monitoring. According to HIVOS, only 13 projects were not operating due to flooding or user mistakes at the time of the field trip in 2014.

Index

Page numbers in **bold** denote figures.

For Product Safety Concerns and Information please contact our EU
representative GPSR@taylorandfrancis.com
Taylor & Francis Verlag GmbH, Kaufingerstraße 24, 80331 München, Germany

www.ingramcontent.com/pod-product-compliance
Ingram Content Group UK Ltd.
Pitfield, Milton Keynes, MK11 3LW, UK
UKHW021618240425
457818UK00018B/630